Year 2

Hospitality and Tourism Management Program

HTMP

Hospitality and Tourism Management Program

Disclaimer

This publication is designed to provide accurate and authoritative information in regard to the subject matter covered. It is sold with the understanding that the publisher is not engaged in rendering legal, accounting, or other professional service. If legal advice or other expert assistance is required, the services of a competent professional person should be sought.

—From the Declaration of Principles jointly adopted by the American Bar Association and a Committee of Publishers and Associations

Acknowledgements

Subject Matter Experts
EI Educational Focus Group

Patricia LeCompte
Marketing/Hotel, Resort, & Tourism Management Instructor
Monroe Career & Technical Institute
Bartonsville, PA

Darron Kirkley
Tourism Director
Kershaw County
Kershaw, SC

Douglas OFlaherty
Director of Operations
South Carolina Hospitality Association
Columbia, SC

Lisa Perras
Business and Hospitality Instructor
Mountain View Academy
White Mountains Regional High School
Whitefield, NH

Subject Matter Experts
Hospitality and Tourism Industry

Frankie F. Miller, Ph.D.
Hospitality, Culinary, Tourism Educational Consultant
Retired Dean, Culinary Institute of Charleston, SC

Jill A. Staples, MS
CHA, CHE, CHS
President
North Star Hospitality, LLC

Dr. Michelle Aldrich
FACS Teacher
Triumph High School, WY

Roberta Allison
Program Director
Roger A. Saunders School for Hotel and Restaurant
Management, MA

Linda Kroll
Adjunct Faculty, Hospitality/Business Division
Central Arizona College, AZ

Peter Ricci, Ed.D., CHA, CHSE, CRME
Director, Hospitality Management Program
Florida Atlantic University, FL

Mariann Tsilis Barnard
Director of Operations
Town & Country Inn and Suites, IL

Alphonse L. Johnson, LEED AP, CHA
COO, DNC Parks and Resorts
Delaware North Company, Inc., NY

Ting Phonsanam, CHA, CHRM
Brand Performance Consultant
Choice Hotels International, MD

Anthony Agbeh
Professor Emeritus
Ferris State University
Southern Illinois University, IL

Britt Mathwich
Assistant Professor of Business
Colorado Mesa University, CO

George R. Conrade
Professor
University of Delaware, DE
Former Executive Vice President AHLEI

James Nickles, CHA, CHSP
Sales Manager
Ramada Maingate West, FL

Steve Shay, CHA, CHRM, CHT
Brand Performance Consultant
Choice Hotels International

Jim Ferguson, CHA
Lecturer, Hospitality and Tourism Division
Hawaii Community College, HI

Brett Hartman, CHA
District Director
Park Inn by Radisson – Country Inns & Suites by Carlson

Technical Assistance

Courtyard by Marriott® Orlando Downtown
Cheryl Seckman, General Manager
David Rodriguez, Chief Engineer

EI Technical Team

Yana Keyzerman, Writer
Kathleen McDermott, Editor
Liz Watkins, Graphic Design

Welcome to the NEW Hospitality and Tourism Management Program

Congratulations on taking the first step in building a career in the hospitality and tourism industry. The U.S. lodging industry currently employs about 1.8 million people, while the American food service industry has about 13 million people working in restaurants. These two segments of the hospitality and tourism industry alone account for more than nine percent of the U.S. workforce. When you consider how vast the industry is, the potential career choices are huge.

The Hospitality and Tourism Management Program has been designed to help you develop and practice performing the knowledge, skills, and tasks required for success as an employee in the hospitality and tourism industry. All you need to do is be willing to learn and put in the effort to achieve. If you are ambitious and want to have a future in this dynamic industry, you have made the right choice to seek career possibilities available to you in hospitality and tourism by enrolling in this exciting career development course of study.

Pineapple Fun Fact

Throughout this textbook, Pineapple Fun Fact boxes will highlight interesting facts about the hospitality and tourism industry, in which you are considering building a career.

Pineapple Fun Fact

Why the Pineapple?

The pineapple originated in South America and was "discovered" by Columbus on his second voyage to the new world. He called it a piña because it resembled a pinecone. In 17th century America, sea captains would place a pineapple outside their front door as a symbol of a safe return. In the 18th and 19th centuries, pineapples became popular as a symbol of welcome. The image of the pineapple began being used to decorate furniture, table linens, and silverware, all for the purpose of making guests feel welcome when stopping for the night at an inn or hotel. Today the pineapple is the hospitality and tourism industry's universal symbol of welcome to guests worldwide.

ADA Box

Throughout this textbook, ADA boxes will highlight how federal requirements determine what the hospitality and tourism industry must do to meet the needs of guests with disabilities.

ADA

What is the purpose of the Americans with Disabilities Act (ADA)?

The ADA is a federal civil rights law that prohibits discrimination against people with disabilities in everyday activities. It was signed into law on July 26, 1990. Businesses that serve the public must modify policies and practices that discriminate against people with disabilities; comply with accessible design standards when constructing or altering facilities; remove barriers in existing facilities where readily achievable; and provide auxiliary aids and services when needed to ensure effective communication with people who have hearing, vision, or speech impairments.

Green Practices Box

Throughout this textbook, Green Practices boxes will highlight the benefits of running a sustainable green hospitality and tourism business.

Green Practices

Why are green practices important?

Today, every organization should participate in environmentally-friendly or "green" practices to ensure that all processes, products, and workplace activities address current environmental concerns. This is known as running a sustainable green business. The hospitality and tourism industry was one of the first to recognize the value of sustainable green practices for protecting the future of its guests, employees, planet, and profits.

Diversity Box

Throughout this textbook, Diversity boxes will highlight the ways in which diversity affects the hospitality and tourism industry.

Diversity

Why is diversity important?

Diversity is a fact of today's hospitality and tourism industry. Global tourism puts industry employees face-to-face with guests from all over the world. The industry's workforce is also diverse, representing people from various races, ages, genders, and ethnic backgrounds. Learning how to manage and interact with diverse guests and employees is an important skill for any hospitality and tourism leader.

Table of Contents

UNIT 4

Year 2

Hospitality and Tourism Management Program

Hospitality and Tourism Management Program

Unit 1
Introduction to Leadership and Management

▶ Chapter 1
Preparing for a Leadership Career

▶ Chapter 2
Hospitality and Tourism Leadership

The hospitality and tourism industry is changing at an ever-increasing pace. New technologies are changing not only the way companies do business but also the structure of those companies. When the structure of a company changes so does the nature of leadership and management in that organization.

There are numerous segments within the hospitality and tourism industry, including lodging, food and beverage, transportation, and attractions. This unit breaks down the types of leadership positions available in each segment. It also covers leadership traits and styles and how they can be adapted to fit different situations.

This unit focuses on the new management skills required to succeed in the 21st century economy. It discusses how embracing diversity as an organization and empowering employees can help meet the needs of global guest audiences.

Chapter 1
Preparing for a Leadership Career

COMPETENCIES

1. List the advantages and disadvantages of a career in hospitality and tourism, and list the benefits of choosing a career in this industry.

2. Describe segments of the hospitality and tourism industry, and explain the process for selecting an industry segment in which to work.

3. Identify the types of leadership positions available in the hospitality and tourism industry.

4. Identify traits of effective leaders.

5. Define traditional management styles.

6. Explain the importance of varying your leadership style in response to organizational needs.

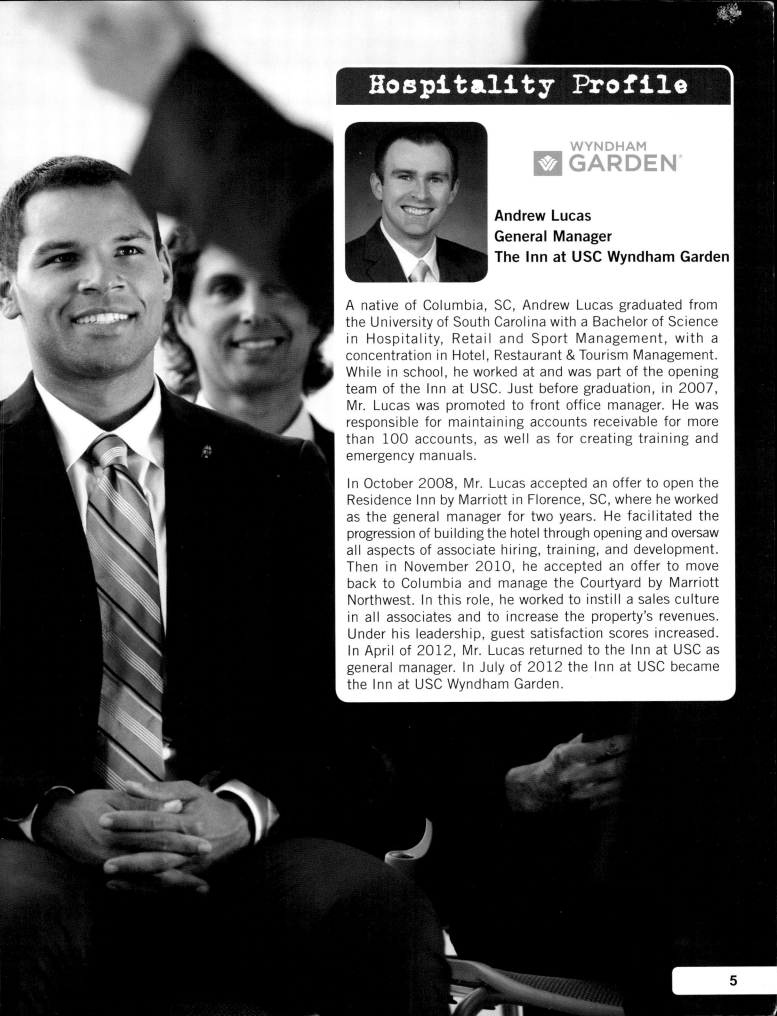

WYNDHAM GARDEN®

Andrew Lucas
General Manager
The Inn at USC Wyndham Garden

A native of Columbia, SC, Andrew Lucas graduated from the University of South Carolina with a Bachelor of Science in Hospitality, Retail and Sport Management, with a concentration in Hotel, Restaurant & Tourism Management. While in school, he worked at and was part of the opening team of the Inn at USC. Just before graduation, in 2007, Mr. Lucas was promoted to front office manager. He was responsible for maintaining accounts receivable for more than 100 accounts, as well as for creating training and emergency manuals.

In October 2008, Mr. Lucas accepted an offer to open the Residence Inn by Marriott in Florence, SC, where he worked as the general manager for two years. He facilitated the progression of building the hotel through opening and oversaw all aspects of associate hiring, training, and development. Then in November 2010, he accepted an offer to move back to Columbia and manage the Courtyard by Marriott Northwest. In this role, he worked to instill a sales culture in all associates and to increase the property's revenues. Under his leadership, guest satisfaction scores increased. In April of 2012, Mr. Lucas returned to the Inn at USC as general manager. In July of 2012 the Inn at USC became the Inn at USC Wyndham Garden.

Introduction

Hospitality and tourism is one of the fastest-growing industries in the world, offering a wide variety of career options. Due to its size, management positions in hospitality and tourism are plentiful. Although hotels and restaurants are the largest sectors of this industry, they are not the only ones. Hospitality managers are needed in clubs, casinos, hospitals, nursing homes, universities and schools, cafeterias, prisons, corporate dining rooms, snack bars, cruise ships, museums, bus companies, airlines, management companies, and many other organizations. Within these organizations, you can go into marketing and sales, event planning, rooms management, housekeeping, food and beverage, engineering, security, accounting, forecasting and planning, human resources, management information systems, recreation, entertainment, and so on.

Moreover, you have a wide choice of places to live and work. You can choose any region of the country or the world—warm or cold climates, cities, suburbs, or undeveloped natural areas. There simply is no other industry that offers more diverse career opportunities.

Pineapple Fun Fact

Hospitality is the world's fastest growing industry, with one new job added every 2.5 seconds. In fact, over the next ten years, the hospitality and tourism industry's total contribution to the world gross domestic product (GDP) is expected to rise by 4% per year, which translates to approximately 69 million new jobs in ten years. The World Tourism Organization (UNWTO) estimates that by 2020, international tourism will reach 1.6 billion tourists, spending $5 billion per day.

Why a Career in Hospitality and Tourism?

Why do people choose the hospitality industry? If you were to ask people who have spent their careers in this business what they like most about it, you would get a variety of answers. Some of the most popular are:

- **The industry offers more career options than most.** No matter what kind of work you enjoy, and wherever your aptitudes lie, there is a segment of the industry that can use your talents.

- **The work is varied.** Because hotels and restaurants are complete production, distribution, and service units, managers are involved in a broad array of activities.

- **There are many opportunities to be creative.** Hospitality managers might design new products to meet the needs of their guests; produce new training programs for employees; or implement challenging advertising, sales promotion, and marketing plans.

- **Hospitality and tourism is a "people" business.** Managers and supervisors spend their workdays satisfying guests, motivating employees, and negotiating with vendors and contractors.

- **Hospitality jobs are not "9 to 5" jobs.** The hours are highly flexible in many positions.

- **There are opportunities for long-term career growth.** If you are ambitious and hard-working, you can move up quickly. The industry is full of stories of people who started as bellpersons or cooks and rose to high management positions or opened their own businesses.

- **There are perks associated with many hospitality jobs.** Many hotels offer staff members deeply discounted rates at their properties worldwide. Airline and cruise employees often get free or reduced-fare travel.

Despite these advantages, there are some aspects of the business that people do not like:

- **Long hours.** In most hospitality businesses, 50- to 60-hour workweeks for managers are not unusual.

- **Nontraditional schedules.** Hospitality managers do not work a Monday-Friday schedule. Weekends and holidays are often the busiest days in many segments since this is when most people are off work.

- **Pressure.** There are busy periods when hospitality managers and employees are under intense pressure to perform.

- **Low beginning salaries.** Entry-level management jobs tend to be lower paying than some other industries.

Before choosing to work in hospitality and tourism, you must decide whether the benefits outweigh the drawbacks. Once you are ready to get into this fast-paced and diverse industry, you must decide which segment of hospitality and tourism best fits your interests and skills.

1.3

Selecting an Industry Segment

Industry Segment—a grouping of similar types of businesses or products under one heading.

O ne of the best ways to select an **industry segment** in hospitality and tourism is to start by listing your own skills. What are the tasks you do best? Most skills fall into one of three areas: skills dealing with data, skills dealing with people, or skills dealing with things. You will probably find that the majority of your skills will fall into one or two of these areas.

Data Skills	Possible Career Paths
• Good in math and science	• Positions in forecasting, such as in a corporate planning department of large chains
• Enjoy working with computers	
• Like analyzing information, working with graphs, comparing figures, and solving abstract problems	• Auditors
	• Accountants
	• Revenue managers

People Skills	**Possible Career Paths**
<ul><li>Enjoy helping people and taking care of their needs</li><li>Can take and give advice and instructions</li><li>Enjoy supervising and motivating other people and find that they respond to your leadership</li></ul>	<ul><li>Positions that require negotiating, selling, and making decisions</li><li>General managers</li><li>Marketing and sales managers</li><li>Independent restaurant owners</li><li>Catering managers</li><li>Club managers</li></ul>

Things Skills	**Possible Career Paths**
<ul><li>Good at building or fixing things</li><li>Like to work with your hands and use tools and gadgets</li><li>Enjoy setting things up, such as for a party</li></ul>	<ul><li>Chefs</li><li>Banquet managers</li><li>Bakers</li><li>Engineers</li><li>Facilities managers</li></ul>

Most of us have skills in more than one area. It is important to identify your skills and rank them according to how much you enjoy using them. This process will help you find an industry segment that suits you.

The type of business you choose for your first hospitality and tourism job puts you into a definite career slot. While skills and experience are usually transferrable within a particular industry segment, it is much more difficult to jump from one kind of industry segment to another. For example, it is unlikely that you would progress from managing a quick service restaurant to being the general manager of a Holiday Inn. Your food and beverage skill set may not necessarily transfer to a lodging property manager as easily as they would transfer to another food and beverage organization. However, you might be able to go from being a rooms division manager of a full service hotel to a rooms division manager of a large cruise ship such as the *Grand Princess* using your lodging skill set. At the same time, it is not unheard of for a person to initially begin pursuing one hospitality segment, realize that a better fit might lie elsewhere, and then make a change.

Types of Available Positions

The types of management positions available in hospitality and tourism depend on the industry segment. Most hospitality and tourism businesses have a variety of departments, which might include human resources/training, finance/accounting, sales and marketing, IT, operations, customer service, facilities management/engineering, logistics, legal, security, planning, and quality assurance. Each department has its own management structure, or career ladder, with smaller companies having fewer rungs and larger companies having many levels of management positions. The position titles vary but can include: shift supervisor, assistant manager, manager, director, vice president, president, or general manager. The largest hospitality and tourism segments are lodging and food and beverage. This chapter provides a closer look at some of the management job titles in each of these segments.

Lodging

There are many types of lodging properties to choose from. There are luxury hotels, full service hotels, resorts, casino hotels, economy hotels, and other types of properties. Some are independently owned and others are chain affiliated. There are advantages and disadvantages to working at each type of property. Would you rather be part of a large chain or work for an independent operation?

Larger properties have more employees and thus require more supervisors and managers. Smaller properties may only have an owner or general manager. The advantages of working for a chain-affiliated property might include better training, better benefits, more opportunities for advancement, and the ability to easily move to another location. One disadvantage might be that it is harder to get recognized for doing an excellent job with so many other employees. A career with an independent property may offer more chances to be creative, more control, and better learning opportunities for entrepreneurs. Some disadvantages of an independent operation may be lower pay and less staff support. However, in a smaller environment, it is easier to get noticed for the job you are doing.

Within a lodging operation, management positions are available in the following areas:

- **General manager**—chief operating officer of a hotel. Responsible for financial performance, hiring and firing, supervising staff and administering policies, attracting guests and making sure they are safe, and many other duties.

- **Catering managers**—promote and sell the hotel's banquet facilities; plan, organize, and manage banquets. Knowledge of food and beverage costs, preparation techniques, pricing, social customs, and etiquette are essential.

- **Engineering/Maintenance**—chief engineers are responsible for the physical operation of the hotel, such as plumbing, heating, air conditioning, electrical, ventilation, and refrigeration systems. They may need various licenses.

- **Food and beverage managers**—direct the production and service of food and beverage. They are responsible for training kitchen staff, planning menus and selecting wines, pricing and cost control, and ensuring quality control.

- **Finance and accounting**—the controller is in charge of the accounting department and all its functions, such as the management of payroll, guest accounts, credit, and all cashiering activities. The controller also prepares the budgets and monthly reports showing revenues and expenses.
- **Human resources managers**—responsible for recruiting, training, employee relations, and ensuring compliance with affirmative action and equal employment opportunity policies.
- **Marketing and sales**—marketing managers develop and implement a marketing plan and budget. Sales managers develop sales promotions and make sales calls on prospects for group and individual business.
- **Rooms management**—responsible for the front office, reservations, housekeeping, gift shops, and recreational facilities. In small hotels, rooms managers are also in charge of security.
- **Management information systems (MIS)**—responsible for managing all the computers used on the property, the company's corporate portals, and central reservation systems; writing simple computer programs and instructions for use; and troubleshooting and problem-solving.

Food and Beverage

Just as there are different types of lodging properties, there is a wide variety of food and beverage operations. Chain restaurants include fast food, or quick service, restaurants like McDonald's and Burger King. Fast casual restaurants, such as Chipotle and Lettuce Entertain You, are the fastest growing segment of the restaurant industry today. Casual dining chain restaurants, such as Chili's, Olive Garden, and Outback Steakhouse, are also popular.

Sample Career Ladders—Lodging

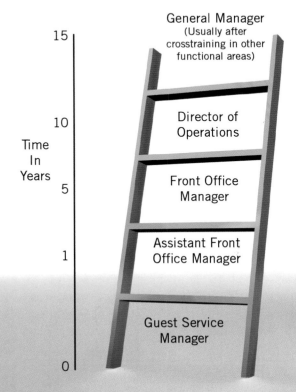

Large Chain Hotels

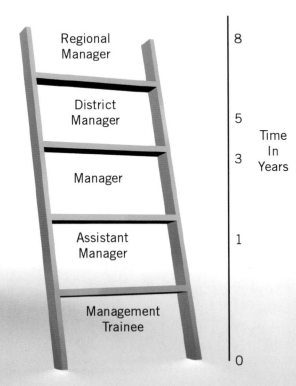

Mid-Scale/Budget Hotels

Independent restaurants are owned and operated by independent entrepreneurs. At the top of this group are luxury restaurants. Many independent restaurants are locally-owned and focus on a specific market niche, such as ethnic cuisine, locally-sourced food, **gastropubs**, and craft breweries. Other types of food service opportunities are social catering, contract food companies, and institutional food service.

A restaurant is usually a small business, with average sales of $535,000 annually. That means that most of the management opportunities in this field, even with large chains, are typically operational or "hands-on" management, as opposed to corporate jobs behind a desk. The duties of a food service manager are generally similar across different food service operations, from independent restaurants to cruise ships to retirement homes.

Chain restaurants recruit the majority of their managers from hospitality schools. Entry-level jobs for college graduates with hospitality degrees are often on the assistant manager level, with progression to manager, then district manager responsible for a group of restaurants, and then to regional manager. Although there is little opportunity for individuality or creativity, these companies offer many prospects for advancement and good benefits. For example, Burger King multi-unit managers can earn between $55,000 and $100,000 a year, plus bonuses and benefits. In addition, if you dream of owning a franchise, the franchise company may help you if you have worked hard in one of its franchises. Most other restaurants have a similar management structure, with a general manager at the top and assistant managers managing the dining room, kitchen, or beverage service. Other typical food service management positions include head chef, maître d', and banquet manager.

Sample Career Ladders—Food Service

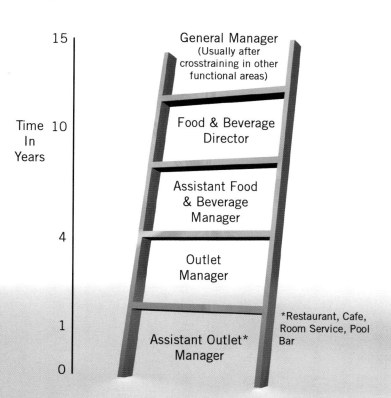

Full-Service Hotel Food & Beverage Operations

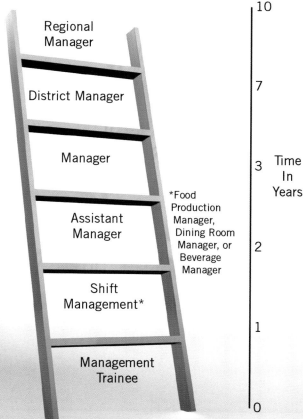

Chain Restaurants

Traits of Leaders

Most employees want their managers to be great leaders, but few feel their managers actually have leadership traits. Listed below are some traits that effective leaders share. Think about leaders you admire. Which of these traits do they have? Which do you think you have?

Strong Desire to Succeed—As a manager, you must have the energy and endurance to complete difficult tasks. You will probably work longer hours than you did before. You must have high expectations for yourself and work hard to meet those goals. You must also show your employees that you want them to succeed. Help employees gain the skills they need to meet standards and expectations.

Job Knowledge—Your ideas will be given more respect if you understand what you are talking about and have the ability to perform in all areas of your job. If you want to be a good leader, read trade magazines, attend training seminars, take online courses, or sign up for classes toward a degree in hospitality.

Good Judgment—Having good judgment means looking at all possible courses of action and choosing the right one. It is important to look at what is good for the company long term, not just what you think is appropriate at that moment.

Value People—Leaders must be able to manage people effectively in order to be innovative and to capitalize on the advantages a varied workforce brings to the organization.

Empathy—A leader who has empathy, or the ability to understand how others might feel, cares about his or her employees and helps them get along with one another. Empathy means following the Golden Rule—treat others the way you want to be treated.

Alexander the Great, born in Pella in 356 B.C., was tutored by Aristotle until the age of 16. By the time he was 30, he had created one of the largest empires of the ancient world, stretching from the Ionian Sea to the Himalayas. He was undefeated in battle and is considered one of history's most successful leaders.

Self-confidence—You must have self-confidence and stand up for your beliefs. However, be careful not to become so confident that you forget to take others' viewpoints into account.

Creativity—Use creativity to improve processes, motivate employees, and enhance guest experiences. Encourage your employees to share their ideas with you, and give them proper credit when their ideas are implemented.

Enthusiasm and Optimism—When you are eager and cheerful, you are better able to motivate yourself and others. Smile often and sit and stand up straight. The way you feel on the inside shows on the outside.

Responsibility—Employees will not like or respect a leader who takes credit for everything that goes right and blames others for things that go wrong. By the same token, employees will not respect a leader who does not hold them accountable for their actions, or lets them "get away with things." Responsible leaders admit and learn from their mistakes.

Analytical Skills—Effective leaders are always looking for ways to do things better. They analyze the information they have and draw conclusions from it. This helps them plan for future challenges.

Section 1.6

Traditional Management Styles

Four traditional styles are those of the autocratic, bureaucratic, democratic, and laissez-faire managers. Management styles are patterns of behavior that managers use to interact with other managers and with their staff.

Autocratic Manager— stresses immediate, short-term results over concerns about people; expects to be obeyed without question and makes decisions without staff input.

Bureaucratic Manager— makes decisions by enforcing rules, regulations, policies, and procedures that are already in place; resists change.

Democratic Manager— focuses more on participative process than on short-term results; shares decision-making and problem-solving responsibilities with staff and is open to new ideas.

Laissez-faire Manager— provides little or no direction and gives employees as much freedom as possible.

Autocratic managers stress immediate, short-term results over concerns about people. They often give orders without explanations and expect employees to obey them without question. They make decisions without staff input and don't usually delegate work. Employees often become extremely dependent on autocratic managers. Work gets done when the manager is present, but things fall apart when the manager isn't there. Since employees are given little input about how to perform their jobs, they learn to simply follow orders.

Bureaucratic managers make decisions by enforcing rules, regulations, policies, and procedures that are already in place. Concerns for results and for people take a back seat to doing things the way they have always been done. Bureaucratic managers resist change. They rely on higher levels of management to make decisions about issues that are not covered "by the book." Employees of bureaucratic managers suppress their initiative and simply follow the rules. When no rule seems to apply to a situation, they cease to act and call the manager.

Democratic managers are almost the reverse of autocratic managers. They tend to focus more on the participative process than on short-term, immediate results. They keep employees informed about matters that directly affect their work and often delegate so employees can gain more experience and job satisfaction. Democratic managers share decision-making and problem-solving responsibilities with their staff. They are open to new ideas and often champion change within their organizations. These managers want employees to be less dependent on them and to take the initiative to get things done themselves.

Laissez-faire managers provide little or no direction and give employees as much freedom as possible. With this style, managers make themselves available for meeting with employees, but they give them the power to develop their own goals, make decisions, and solve problems without direct supervision. Managers are more likely to use this style with a few experienced employees rather than their entire staff. Workers look to a laissez-faire manager not as a boss, but rather as someone who is standing by to help them only if they are needed. Under this management style, workers may produce high-quality work for long periods.

Varying Your Leadership Style

Which management style is the most effective? There are positive and negative aspects to each style. For example, while many find the democratic style the most appealing, even this style—when taken to extremes—can stifle an organization. Democratic managers may overanalyze situations, waste time in unproductive meetings, and give up responsibility through excessive delegation.

Most people think that the autocratic manager has no place in today's work world. However, there are situations in which a manager may need to play this role. This is often the case in times of great stress, because in such situations there may not be time to do things by the book or to consult with employees. For example, consider what happens when twice the expected number of guests need to be served at lunch. The manager must make quick, autocratic decisions to coordinate the staff's actions and deal with the crisis.

While there are some negatives to being a bureaucratic manager, every management position has some bureaucratic functions. For example, legal issues related to hiring and firing require managers to strictly adhere to established policies and procedures. Reckless autocratic or democratic decisions could result in expensive lawsuits.

Many employees probably wish they had a laissez-faire manager who allowed them to do whatever they wanted. However, inexperienced employees would be lost without some level of leadership. They might find themselves behind on work and not sure which projects should be prioritized.

The most effective managers don't restrict themselves to one management style for every situation. Just as a chameleon changes color to help it survive in different environments, recent trends suggest that today's managers need the flexibility to adopt different styles for specific circumstances.

Hurdles to Effective Leadership

Flexibility, however, is not entirely within a manager's control. Three of the most important factors limiting a manager's flexibility in adopting different management styles are the manager's personal background, the characteristics of the organization's employees, and the culture of the organization.

The manager's personal background includes personality, knowledge, attitudes, feelings, and experiences. Some managers feel comfortable delegating work and recognize the need to involve employees in a team approach to resolving problems. Other managers prefer to do almost everything themselves. A manager who has been successful with a particular management style may not be willing to adopt a different one. After all, if it works, why change it?

Employee characteristics often limit which management styles a manager can effectively adopt. Departments with a large number of new and inexperienced employees might benefit from autocratic and bureaucratic styles. An experienced team of employees might benefit from a more democratic approach. The ability of employees to work well in teams might also affect which styles a manager can choose.

The greatest limiting factor in a manager's choice of management styles may be the structure and culture of the organization. Managers invite disaster when they adopt styles that don't fit the traditions or values of their organizations. For example, the democratic style fits well in corporate cultures with relatively few levels of management. Being an autocratic or bureaucratic manager in such an environment would most likely lead to failure.

Apply Your Learning

Section 1.1
1. Why does the hospitality and tourism industry offer such a wide variety of career options?
2. Name three organizations where hospitality managers might work.

Section 1.2
1. What are some advantages and disadvantages of a career in hospitality?
2. How can hospitality managers be creative?
3. Why is a job in hospitality good for long-term career growth?
4. Why might some people like the nontraditional schedules in the hospitality industry while others do not?

Section 1.3
1. What is an industry segment?
2. How can a skills inventory help you decide on a career path?
3. If you like building and fixing things, which career paths might you be suited for?
4. Why is it important to choose wisely when deciding on an industry segment?

Section 1.4
1. What are the advantages of working for a large hotel chain? For an independent hotel?
2. What are some management positions in the lodging industry?
3. Should a hospitality student bypass quick-service restaurant management opportunities? Why or why not?
4. What are some management positions in the food service industry?

Section 1.5
1. Why is a strong desire to succeed an important trait of an effective leader?
2. What does it mean to follow the Golden Rule?
3. How can having too much self-confidence become detrimental to good leadership?
4. Why is responsibility an important leadership trait?
5. How can you show enthusiasm and optimism as a leader?

Section 1.6

1. Which type of manager emphasizes immediate, short-term results over concerns about people in the organization?
2. List some characteristics of a bureaucratic manager.
3. In what kind of a situation would a laissez-faire management style work best?
4. What type of manager is most likely to share decision-making and problem-solving responsibilities with staff?
5. Which type of management style is most appropriate when new, untrained employees who do not know which tasks to perform or which procedures to follow join the team?

Section 1.7

1. Why is a flexible management style considered the best?
2. What is the greatest factor limiting a manager's choice of management style and why?
3. What bureaucratic functions do most management positions have?
4. How might a manager's personal background limit the choice of management style?

Chapter 2
Hospitality and Tourism Leadership

COMPETENCIES

1. Identify 21st century leadership styles.

2. Identify why leaders must create leadership development goals and a path for meeting those goals.

3. Define power and empowerment, and describe how these concepts tend to play out in centralized and decentralized organizations.

4. Explain the need for respect and value for diversity in the hospitality and tourism industry.

5. Describe how managers can lead employees to meet the needs of global guest audiences.

6. Analyze the challenges and opportunities in welcoming diverse cultures to your property.

Gerald A. Fernandez
Founder & President
The Multicultural Foodservice
& Hospitality Alliance

Gerry Fernandez is founder and president of The Multicultural Foodservice & Hospitality Alliance (MFHA). He founded MFHA in 1996, while employed at General Mills, with the original purpose and mission to advance the opportunities for people of all cultural backgrounds in the lodging, restaurant and foodservice industry. Before joining General Mills, Mr. Fernandez spent more than 15 years as a manager in hotels and restaurants, including companies such as The Waldorf Astoria Hotel, owned by Hilton, and The Capital Grille, owned by Darden.

Since MFHA's inception, Mr. Fernandez has advanced the organization to become the leading multicultural organization in the industry. His new endeavor to bring Cultural Intelligence and competency building to the hospitality industry has been widely supported by companies like Hyatt Hotels, Kimpton Hotels & Restaurants, and Choice Hotels. The Cultural Intelligence Initiative is designed to teach skills and deliver solutions to operators that will help them increase sales and profits by leveraging cultural understanding.

Mr. Fernandez holds a Bachelor of Science degree in Foodservice Management and an honorary doctorate in Business Administration from Johnson & Wales University. He has received numerous awards and recognitions. He was recognized by *Lodging Magazine* as one of the "75 Profiles in Leadership" and was named one of *Nation's Restaurant News* "50 Power Players." He also received the National Job Corps Association's Alpha Award.

Introduction

Imagine that you were a restaurant manager just 20 years ago. Your restaurant was located near an airport in a major U.S. city. Because of your restaurant's location, the customer base was predictable—you could depend on a steady stream of business travelers and vacationing families. The mediocre food and service at your restaurant had little impact on your bottom line because you had few repeat customers.

In that same scenario today, you would face a much different market. Today's global economy and the ease of international travel have resulted in an increasingly multicultural audience. As a manager, you have to take the needs of your global audience into account. For example, when planning the menu with the executive chef, you might suggest adding more ethnic dining choices. You might conduct special training to help employees understand different cultural dietary needs or how to deal with language barriers. In addition, tech-savvy customers now have the option of checking out your restaurant ahead of time by reading online reviews. If they encounter too many negative customer reviews, you may lose their business. In this dynamic environment, it is essential that you have the leadership and management skills to help your restaurant stay ahead of the curve.

Pineapple Fun Fact

Hartsfield Jackson Atlanta International Airport is the busiest airport in the world in terms of how many aircraft take off and land, as well as the number of passengers. More than 90 million people travel through the airport every year. London's Heathrow Airport is the busiest airport in terms of international passengers. Heathrow celebrated its busiest day to date on August 13, 2012, with 137,000 people departing following the Summer Olympic Games.

21ˢᵗ Century Leadership Styles

Approaches to **management** and **leadership** change constantly. So do prevailing views of which approach is best. Although the terms are used interchangeably, management and leadership actually mean different things. A management role usually emphasizes control and production, whereas a leadership role focuses on creating a vision and inspiring others to follow. All managers should strive to be leaders because effective leadership will always produce better results than effective management. Leaders get people to perform by inspiring them to do their best. The fast-paced, global 21ˢᵗ century economy demands a new style of leadership.

TERMS YOU SHOULD KNOW

Management—the organization and coordination of the activities of a business in order to achieve objectives.

Leadership—the ability to lead a group of people by creating a vision and inspiring others to follow.

The Focus of Management		The Vision of Leadership
Do things right	vs.	Do the right things
Enforce policies and rules	vs.	Communicate vision and values
Control results	vs.	Support people
Create stability	vs.	Engage in continuous improvement
Direct operations	vs.	Manage guest expectations

Travel Promotion Act of 2009

President Barack Obama signed into law the first-ever national travel promotion and communications program to attract more international travelers to the United States. The program was designed in response to evidence that the U.S. was losing ground in the global travel market. The Travel Promotion Act counteracts this trend by establishing a national tourism board to develop advertising and educational campaigns to help potential travelers navigate U.S. visa requirements and security procedures. The Travel Promotion Act benefits the hospitality and tourism industry and the U.S. economy as a whole. It is estimated that it will bring in $4 billion in new spending annually, create 40,000 new jobs, and generate $321 million in new tax revenue each year. To help achieve this goal, in 2012, the president signed an executive order establishing the Task Force on Travel & Competitiveness to develop a "National Travel & Tourism Strategy." Its goal is to increase American jobs by attracting and welcoming 100 million international visitors, who will spend $250 billion, by the end of 2020.

Up and Down Flow

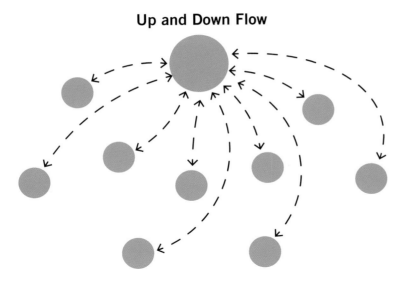

Circular Flow

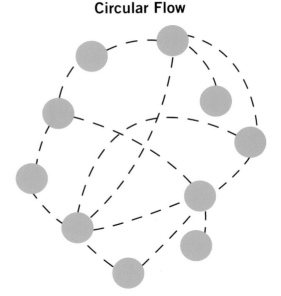

Technology has changed the way information is distributed in an organization. In the past, information flowed up to the corporate offices and was then redistributed back down the chain. This process could take so long that the information was outdated by the time it reached its intended target. Today, information can be distributed throughout an organization in a circular pattern from any point to any other point. These kinds of changes have led many companies to flatten their organizational structures and redistribute decision-making power to lower levels. Working in management today requires being open to change and having a willingness to continue learning. Successful managers have the motivation and flexibility to respond to the changing needs of their organizations.

One of the greatest differences between leadership in the past and leadership in the 21st century is an increased focus on the role of management in meeting and exceeding guest expectations. There is no one-size-fits-all theory of leadership—managers can exercise their talents in a variety of ways, and leadership takes on different forms at different times. The key for managers is to decide which approach works best for their skills and abilities, and which best fits their employees and organization. The four main theories of leadership today are:

Personality-Based Leadership

This theory promotes the idea that charismatic people make good leaders by inspiring strong feelings in their followers. Steve Jobs of Apple was a charismatic leader who inspired loyalty and respect, as well as a sense of power and excitement. However, not all good leaders are necessarily charismatic. Bill Gates of Microsoft has been very successful as a leader despite his subdued personality.

Situational Leadership

Situational leaders recognize that the best leadership style will vary depending on the situation. For example, when an employee is learning a new skill, a manager might lead by directing the employee what to do. However, as the employee becomes more skilled, the leadership style may evolve to coaching or supporting. When the employee has become proficient, it may be time to delegate certain tasks to that person because he or she has reached a level of independence.

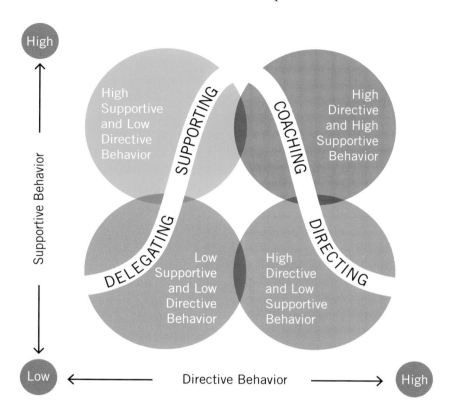

Transactional Leadership

In this style of leadership, employees exchange a certain level of performance for rewards, such as salary, bonuses, and time off. Leaders give out awards for good performance and punishments for bad performance.

Transformational Leadership

Transformational leaders communicate a vision that inspires and motivates people to achieve something extraordinary. They are generally found in organizations where people at different organizational levels participate in decision making. They collaborate with their staff on goal setting and share leadership with others by delegating power.

Leadership Development Goals

Professional Development—the process of continuing education by which an employee becomes proficient in his or her job.

All workers, whether they are in line-level or management positions, should engage in **professional development**. Professional development ensures that you continue to have the knowledge and skills necessary for success. It is a career-long process—there will never be a point at which you can say that you have learned everything there is to learn and are as skilled as it is possible to be. Professional development is particularly important for leaders because they influence other workers' behavior, thus the work they do reflects throughout the entire organization.

The success or failure of your professional development lies primarily in your hands. No one knows your skills, interests, and values as well as you do. Nor can anyone else know the development activities that will be most effective for you. Taking control of your professional development is part of taking control of your career. Professional development:

Maintains your current position. Even if you continue doing the same job, what you are doing will evolve and change, so you have to constantly update your skill set.

Enhances mobility options. Even if you are not formally promoted, professional development may give you the ability to move to a different area of the organization due to gaining new skills.

Makes promotion more likely. If you want to advance in your organization, you must start developing the skills for the position you want.

Create a Plan

The first step in your professional development plan is to create goals for yourself. In order to create goals for the future, you need to conduct a self-assessment to determine where your development needs are. Some tools you can use include:

- Past performance reviews
- Conversations with your peers, managers, and employees
- Lists of strengths, weaknesses, values, and interests

In the early stages of forming your professional development plan, discuss the plan with your manager. Your manager may have advice about skills that he or she thinks are going to be important or be aware of resources to which you could have access. Once you have set the goals for your development, prioritize which goals are most important. You may decide to first work on skills that would most help your organization meets its goals. You may want to start with areas you are interested in because you will be more motivated to learn. Or you might work on your weakest areas first if the weaknesses you identify are so important to your job that you will not be able to perform to standards unless you improve those skills.

Execute the Plan

Make time in your daily schedule to take part in professional development opportunities. If professional development activities are not scheduled, they become easy to overlook and forget. Look for opportunities that are right under your nose. Could you do something in a new way? For example, say that one of your goals is to provide more employee feedback. In the past, you have coached only when your employees needed correction. Instead, try each day to catch someone doing some good and praise him or her. Other ways to engage in professional development are:

- Develop a mentor-protégé relationship with a skilled manager. He or she can serve as a role model, as well as provide feedback on your performance and encourage your development.

- Take advantage of formal professional development opportunities available from your property or corporate offices. These could involve continuing education or other training classes.

- Look for opportunities to volunteer in your workplace. There is frequently more work to do than there are people to do it. Volunteering to learn new skills can enhance your career by making you more valuable to your organization.

- Work on earning professional hospitality certifications. Hospitality associations and other organizations offer certification programs at a variety of levels, from newly hired to senior managers. Certification provides a means of continuing and documenting your professional development over the length of a career.

U.S. Hospitality Organizations Offering Professional Certifications
 American Hotel & Lodging Educational Institute (AHLEI)
 Club Managers Association of America (CMAA)
 Convention Industry Council (CIC)
 National Restaurant Association
 National Tour Association (NTA)

Empowerment

Power—the ability to influence others' behavior.

Centralized Organization—an organization in which most decision-making authority is at top management levels.

Decentralized Organization—an organization where decision-making authority is distributed.

When you think of management, what is the first word that comes to mind? It is probably **"power"** or "authority." Power is the ability to influence others' behavior. Managers have the power to establish policies, such as dress code, or the power to make decisions about how guest interactions should be handled. However, not all managers have the same levels of power, and different companies have different power structures.

In **centralized organizations**, most decision-making authority is at top management levels. **Decentralized organizations** distribute decision-making authority. The degree of centralization or decentralization is determined by where decisions are made—at the corporate headquarters or at the unit level. Some large restaurant chains, for example, may give unit managers broad decision-making power in matters that affect their branches. However, a small hotel may have a highly centralized power structure if the general manager micromanages every department in the hotel.

There is no right or wrong approach to power structure. Just like management style, the degree of centralization or decentralization depends on what is best for the organization. In times of financial crisis, a high degree of centralization may be most appropriate. Top managers can take control and work out the crisis. Decentralization may be most appropriate for organizations that face fast-changing market conditions because they can usually respond faster and more effectively to change.

Centralized Structure

- President (1)
  - Senior VP (1)
    - Regional VPs (3)
      - District Managers (9)
        - Area Managers (25)
          - Restaurant Unit Managers (100)
  - Senior VP (1)
    - Regional VPs (3)
      - District Managers (9)
        - Area Managers (25)
          - Restaurant Unit Managers (100)
  - Senior VP (1)
    - Regional VPs (3)
      - District Managers (9)
        - Area Managers (25)
          - Restaurant Unit Managers (100)

Decentralized Structure

- President (1)
  - Senior VP (1)
    - Regional VPs (3)
      - Restaurant Unit Managers (100)
    - Regional VPs (3)
      - Restaurant Unit Managers (100)
    - Regional VPs (3)
      - Restaurant Unit Managers (100)

In order for decentralization to work, there has to be a high level of **empowerment** in an organization. Empowerment is a redistribution of power within an organization that enables managers, supervisors, and employees to do their jobs more effectively. The goal of empowerment is to enhance guest service and increase profits by passing decision-making responsibility, authority, and accountability to every level within the company. When employees are empowered, decision making, troubleshooting, and problem solving can happen much more quickly. Staff does not have to wait for information to move up the structure and for directives to come back down; information flows freely in every direction.

Decentralization and empowerment begin with changes in the leadership roles of top managers. Top-level managers must influence others to accept new responsibilities that accompany increases in power. They do this by involving managers, supervisors, and employees in defining the values, mission, and goals of the organization. Linking everyone with a shared vision helps them understand how their work contributes to the overall success of the company.

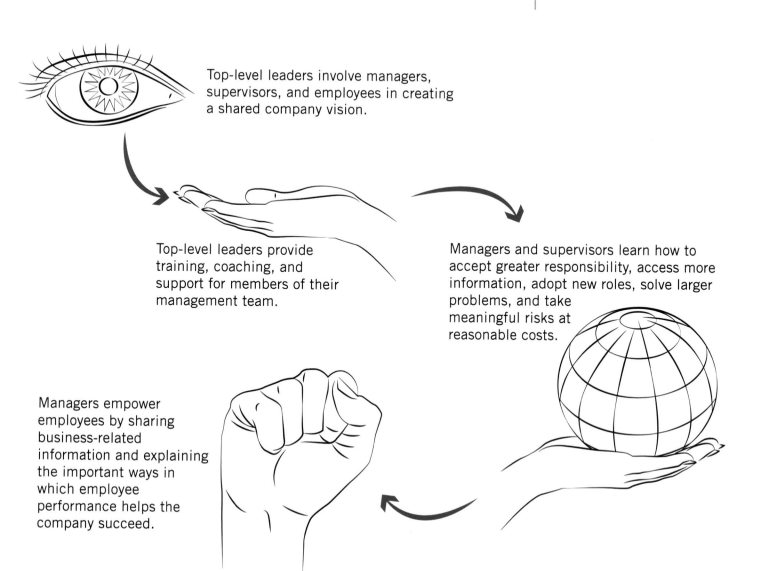

Top-level leaders involve managers, supervisors, and employees in creating a shared company vision.

Top-level leaders provide training, coaching, and support for members of their management team.

Managers and supervisors learn how to accept greater responsibility, access more information, adopt new roles, solve larger problems, and take meaningful risks at reasonable costs.

Managers empower employees by sharing business-related information and explaining the important ways in which employee performance helps the company succeed.

Showing Respect and Value for Diversity

Diversity—the human quality of being different or varied.

Demographics—the statistical data of a population, showing breakdowns of age, race, income, education, etc.

Diversity in the workplace is the presence of people who differ in age, race, national origin, gender, religion, sexual orientation, and other attributes. There are two major reasons for managers to be concerned with diversity. The first is **demographics**. A diverse workforce is a fact of modern life. If a company is not yet diverse, it soon will be. Simply throwing different people together does not create a productive work environment because cultural misunderstandings and prejudice can cause conflict, bad decisions, and poor performance. The second reason is that diversity is not just the right thing to do—it's good for business. A diverse workforce is uniquely poised to understand and respond to the needs of a diverse customer base.

Managing diversity means making all guests feel welcome and building a global workforce where individuals from various backgrounds with different experiences are respected and valued. Managers should focus on removing barriers that inhibit the creation of an inclusive environment.

Three main benefits of diversity in the workplace are:

- Increased productivity
- Improved quality of management
- Better service and new markets

Increased Productivity

People who enjoy coming to work generally produce more. People who believe that their work will be valued, or that their work will lead to advancement, are also inclined to work harder. In addition, research has shown that diverse groups are generally more creative and innovative than homogeneous groups, or groups that are composed of the same kind of people. When employees see a diverse group of leaders in an organization, they recognize that there is opportunity for everyone to experience professional growth. This, in turn, leads to employees who are more engaged and motivated to do their best work.

Improved Quality of Management

Including all employees in competition for managerial positions may open the door to highly qualified individuals who may have been unable to advance in the past due to discriminatory actions or policies. Exposure to colleagues from a variety of backgrounds can help managers develop new ways to solve workplace problems.

Better Service and New Markets

Multiculturalism in business is growing, and companies must embrace it to stay competitive. A customer is more likely to buy from someone he or she can identify with. A hotel that has no minorities at the front desk may be less attractive to an African-American or Hispanic group than one that does. A hotel gift shop that does not stock diverse periodicals may send a message that the hotel's management is not sensitive to the needs of different groups. Thus, a diverse organization is better able to understand what diverse customers need and to create loyalty with them.

Diversity within an organization can also result in larger shares of diverse markets. Before 2020, the market segments of women, African-American, Hispanic, Asian-American, and LGBT (lesbian, gay, bisexual, and transgender) customers are projected to grow by a large margin. In addition, as you will learn in Section 2.6, increased global tourism is expected to bring more diverse international audiences to American markets.

Hispanic 33.5%
Asian-American 31.1%
African-American 13.8%
LGBT 10%
Women 19.9%

Market Segment Growth by 2020

Bringing Diversity to Life

Leaders must embed diversity in the DNA of their organization. To do this, they must have "buy-in," or support, from every manager and employee. Many organizations have established diversity programs, which encourage:

- Keeping an eye on diversity in hiring practices by ensuring equal employment opportunity
- Giving minority-owned suppliers and contractors an equal opportunity to earn their business
- Documenting how diversity practices have been good for business to increase buy-in

Many laws have been instrumental in increasing diversity in American workplaces by providing equal employment opportunities and protection to all people. The U.S. Equal Employment Opportunity Commission (EEOC) is responsible for enforcing federal laws that make it illegal to discriminate against a job applicant or an employee based on the person's race, religion, sex, national origin, disability, or genetic information.

Equal Pay Act 1963
Requires that men and women in the same workplace be given equal pay for equal work.

Pregnancy Discrimination Act 1978
Prohibits discrimination against pregnant women.

Title VII of the Civil Rights Act 1964
- Bars discrimination on the basis of race, sex, religion, color, and national origin.
- Prohibits sexual harassment of an employee by a supervisor.

Age Discrimination in Employment Act 1967
Bars discrimination against people over 40. Some states have age discrimination laws that also protect people under 40.

1960   1970   1980

Family and Medical Leave Act 1993
Provides for mandated unpaid employee leave for up to 12 weeks for the birth, adoption, or serious illness of a child, or the serious illness of a parent or spouse, with a return to the same or equivalent job.

Americans with Disabilities Act (ADA) 1990
Prohibits workplace discrimination against people with disabilities.

Title II of the Genetic Information Nondiscrimination Act 2009
Bars discrimination against employees or applicants because of genetic information, such as genetic tests or family medical history.

1990   2000   2010

Global Guest Audiences

International tourism brings more than $150 billion to the U.S. economy every year. More than 63 million international visitors a year rely on the hospitality and tourism industry to provide them with world class guest service. Each visitor brings a unique blend of customs, perceptions, and expectations to every guest interaction. To get and keep this international business, hospitality and tourism leaders must be prepared to host global guest audiences.

It is leaders' responsibility to ensure that their organizations are prepared to meet the needs of international guests. As a manager, you should:

1. **Be proactive, not reactive.** It is better to anticipate and plan for special guest needs than to have to resolve complaints due to cultural misunderstanding.

2. **Do your homework.** Research international customs that might impact your business, whether general rules to follow or specific information about a particular group your organization is expecting to host.

3. **Create training programs and quick reference guides for staff.** Help employees stay informed about the cultures of your property's frequent international guests. Be sure that employees are aware of any special resources, such as maps or brochures in other languages. Make sure employees know where they can obtain translation services and other resources.

4. **Get employees involved.** Identify employees who speak other languages well enough to serve as translators. Ask staff to share their experiences in serving international guests. Brainstorm with employees ways to resolve complaints your company has received from international guests.

5. **Be a role model.** The best way to lead your staff to embrace global guest service is by modeling **inclusive** behavior and providing both domestic and international guests with exceptional service.

Creating a positive impression can create international publicity for your business through word of mouth or various technologies, including social media and travel websites.

Types of Tourism

In order to provide excellent service, it is important to know just who your guests are but also why they are traveling. People travel for different reasons, including recreation, business, or to visit friends and family. In recent years, several distinct types of tourism have become very popular.

Ecotourism: involves visiting fragile, pristine, and relatively undisturbed natural areas. It focuses on socially responsible travel and is often intended to educate tourists about the impact of human beings on the environment. Examples of ecotourism include going on a safari, taking a zip line adventure through a rainforest, bird watching, or visiting the Mayan ruins.

Agritourism: the practice of attracting visitors and travelers to agricultural areas for educational and recreational purposes. It shows people how their food is produced. Many small farmers use agritourism to help supplement their farming income. Agritourists can vacation on an olive farm in Tuscany, pick grapes at a winery, find their way through a corn maze, or work on a cattle ranch.

Culinary tourism: differs from agritourism in that it seeks to create a memorable eating and drinking experience — not necessarily focus on the source of the food. Culinary tourists might visit a winery or brewery, attend a food festival, or take a cooking class. Many cities have food tours of different neighborhood's cuisines.

Medical tourism: involves traveling to a different place, often across international borders, for medical treatment. People may travel to a location where medical care is less expensive or where they can receive alternative or experimental treatments. Some of the countries that are attracting medical tourism are India, Thailand, Philippines, Singapore, and Malaysia.

Heritage tourism: means traveling to experience the places, artifacts, and activities that represent the stories and people of the past. Heritage tourists can attend a Native American pow wow, take a cruise on a historic riverboat, or visit battlefields, historic homes, military forts, plantations, and other heritage sites. Heritage tourism also includes people traveling to places where they have family roots.

Foreign Arrivals to the United States, 2011

Country	In Millions
Canada	21.0
Mexico	13.4
United Kingdom	3.8
Japan	3.2
Germany	1.8
France	1.5
Brazil	1.5
South Korea	1.1
China	1.1
Australia	1.0

Source: American Hotel & Lodging Association, 2012 Lodging Industry Profile

Section 2.7

Welcoming Other Cultures

One of the benefits of working in the hospitality and tourism industry is the opportunity to serve and learn from different kinds of people from all over the world. However, sometimes misunderstandings and conflicts can arise due to employees' limited knowledge of or previous exposure to other cultures.

Various employees who may have contact with international guests include:

- Restaurant servers/bartenders
- Reservation agents/ticket sellers
- Room attendants
- Concierge
- Information booth operators
- Bus/shuttle drivers
- Cashiers
- Tour guides
- Fitness instructors
- Flight attendants

Management must set the tone for developing an international service style and provide training on how to handle common situations successfully.

Diversity

President Jimmy Carter signed a joint resolution in 1978 that declared May 4–10, 1979, as the first Asian-Pacific American Heritage Week. This was later extended by President George H.W. Bush in 1990 to a month-long celebration. The month commemorates the arrival of the first Japanese immigrant, a fisherman named Nakanohama Manjiro, to the United States on May 7, 1843, and marks the anniversary of the completion of the transcontinental railroad on May 10, 1869. Most of the workers who laid the tracks were Chinese immigrants.

Diversity Abroad and in Our Backyard

It is important to be aware that employees will encounter diversity from both international travelers and domestic guests. America is a mosaic of people from different races, religions, and cultural backgrounds. Some common cultural differences that might impact guest service and interactions include dress and eating habits, vocabulary and language differences, smoking customs, perceptions of time, regard for authority, and cultural or religious restrictions.

Verbal Communication—use of words.

Nonverbal Communication— use of visual cues, such as facial expression and eye contact.

Communicating with Other Cultures

Both **verbal communication** and **nonverbal communication** are important when interacting with guests from other cultures.

Verbal communication tips

1. Speak slowly and clearly, but do not patronize guests.
2. Speak at a normal volume.
3. Avoid slang, technical words, and acronyms.

Nonverbal communication tips

1. Minimize gestures, especially pointing, as it can be considered rude.
2. Never touch international guests.
3. Be aware of cultural differences in how eye contact and smiling are perceived.

A Manager's Checklist

Depending on available time and resources, there are a variety of ways a manager can prepare employees to welcome guests from other cultures, including:

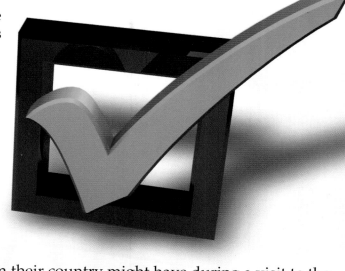

- ❑ Train all staff members who have contact with guests on welcoming other cultures and international travelers.

- ❑ Provide employees with information about the international guests who visit the property most frequently so they know what to expect.

- ❑ Invite speakers from countries from which you have frequent visitors to talk to employees about their countries. Ask speakers to describe difficulties a person from their country might have during a visit to the United States. You may also ask speakers to teach employees some basic phrases or greetings in their language.

- ❑ Provide incentives to employees who are willing to attend classes to learn a second language.

- ❑ Show employees how to convert American temperatures, weights, and measures into the metric system. Provide a printed reference guide or a link to a website that calculates conversions.

- ❑ Provide employees with a list of common terms in several languages for quick reference. Additionally, you may provide phrase books, bilingual dictionaries, or access to websites that offer translation.

- ❑ Keep a list of available foreign language resources in all departments.

- ❑ Make sure your property uses international symbols as well as English signs pointing out restrooms, telephones, exits, etc.

- ❑ Offer menus, maps, brochures, and other printed information in the languages spoken by your most frequent international guests.

- ❑ Keep on hand special items that guests might request, such as voltage converters, menu selections, eating utensils, or foreign language movies.

- ❑ Provide currency exchange for international guests.

- ❑ Offer a guide to tipping in the United States.

Apply Your Learning

Section 2.1
1. How has an increase in international travel changed the jobs of hospitality managers?
2. What are some ways a restaurant manager might plan for the needs of multicultural audiences?
3. How are consumers today different than 20 years ago? What tools do they use to make decisions?

Section 2.2
Match the name of the leadership theory to its description.

1. Employees exchange a certain level of performance for rewards, such as salary, bonuses, and time off.

2. Leaders recognize that the best leadership style will vary depending on the situation and can include directing, coaching, supporting, and delegating.

3. Leaders communicate a vision that inspires and motivates people to achieve something extraordinary.

4. Leaders are charismatic individuals who inspire loyalty and respect from their employees.

A. Personality-based leadership

B. Situational leadership

C. Transactional leadership

D. Transformational leadership

Section 2.3
1. List three reasons why professional development is important.
2. How can having a skilled manager as a mentor help you on your professional development path?
3. What tools can you use when conducting a self-assessment?
4. What are the benefits of professional hospitality certifications?

Section 2.4
1. In which types of organizations are decisions made at top management levels, centralized or decentralized?
2. A manager at a national car rental company decides to add more SUVs and all-wheel drive vehicles to the inventory based on local demand and road conditions. This car rental company probably has what kind of organizational structure?
3. What is the goal of empowerment?
4. What is the first step top-level leaders must take to instill a culture of empowerment in their organizations?

Section 2.5

1. What does the term "demographics" mean?
2. Why is it important to manage diversity?
3. How can diversity in the workplace increase employee productivity?
4. What is one economic benefit of diversity?
5. Which law prohibits discrimination against people with disabilities in the workplace?

Section 2.6

1. Why is international tourism important to the U.S. economy?
2. Name four ways managers can prepare to meet the needs of global guest audiences.
3. What can happen as a result of creating a positive impression on international guests?
4. From which three countries does the United States receive the most visitors?

Section 2.7

A group of business travelers from India is staying at your hotel and has requested that you cater lunch for a business meeting. Write a paragraph explaining how you would prepare your property and employees to host these international guests.

Hospitality Leadership Skills

This unit focuses on various processes that leaders must pay attention to in order to ensure their operations run smoothly. These include the:

- Guest cycle
- Guest experience
- Communication

It is essential that leaders learn the skills and processes involved in managing the guest cycle. They must empower their employees to find solutions to complaints and problems that arise in the course of the guest cycle. Managers must set the example in applying property standards to raise the level of guest service.

To effectively manage the guest experience, managers must develop strong communication skills. Hospitality and tourism leaders should be prepared to communicate internally with their peers and employees, as well as externally with guests and the media.

Chapter 3
Leadership and the Guest Cycle

COMPETENCIES

1. Identify the leadership skills and processes that lead to a seamless guest cycle.

2. Describe how employee empowerment contributes to effective guest recovery.

3. Explain how problem solving contributes to leadership processes in hospitality and tourism.

Gilles M. Honegger, CHA
Former Human Resources
President
ACCOR Group

Gilles M. Honegger, a native of Switzerland and a French national, was the former executive director of the Human Resource Corporate Office of the ACCOR Group. The Accor Group is a worldwide corporation based in Paris, France, that has 3,700 hotels, 3,000 travel agencies, and 170,000 staff members on five continents.

Mr. Honegger has had a long and varied career in the hospitality and tourism industry. He worked as a general manager, managing more than 20 large Accor properties on five continents. Mr. Honegger also headed the Institute Paul Bocuse, a French culinary institute, preparing a BA, a Master in Culinary Art and Hospitality Management, and a Doctorate in Food Business. He has always focused on the importance of continuing education and served as advisor and administrator to various hospitality educational organizations. Mr. Honegger served as advisor to the French Ministry of Education and various French universities, president of the Alternative Learning Society, and delegate to the European Union teaching and training board. He is a member of the International Restaurant and Hotel Association (IR&HA) and various gastronomic societies and clubs.

Mr. Honegger's various honors include the French Legion of Honour; Academic Palm Commander; French Agriculture Merit Commander; French National Merit, Academic Palms Officer; French Agricultural Merit; Ministry of Tourism Gold Medal; and Ministry of Education Gold Medal. His certifications include Certified Hotel Administrator (CHA), fellow of Institute of Hospitality (London), and fellow of the Tourism Society (London). He has also participated in civic service as a mayor of the municipality of a French town. Since he retired at age 65, Mr. Honegger has been honored to be posted as the president of the Competition for Master Craftsmen (M.O.F.) on 132 different specialties.

Section 3.1

Introduction

At the very core of the **guest experience** should be exceptional guest service. Creating a positive guest experience from the moment guests arrive until an employee wishes them a safe journey home will encourage repeat guest visits. The success of delivering the very highest level of guest service depends on how a property's leaders manage the guest cycle. This means that managers should:

- Understand the difference between typical and exceptional guest service
- Understand how great guest service can make your property more successful
- Empower your employees to solve problems, provide exceptional guest service, and successfully handle guest complaints
- Know the stages of the guest cycle and how to provide great guest service at each stage of the process

Managers must set the guest experience standards and act as the role model for employees. The process starts with knowing the level of guest service expected for the type of property you operate. Based on these expectations, you can set the standards for employee performance and create tools for measuring your property's success. Gathering information about how guests perceived their experience at your property can show where changes need to be implemented.

Guest Expectations

Luxury Property Guests	Business Travelers	Families

- White glove service
- Comfort and luxury
- Personalized attention

- Quick and efficient service
- Business tools
- Transportation options

- Package deals
- Suggestions for activities
- Kid-friendly amenities

Follow the Guest: Making the Cycle Seamless

Guests go through four distinct stages, referred to as the guest cycle, when they stay at or visit any hospitality and tourism business. The guests' perception of their experience will influence any future business they do with that company. Management should work to make the guest cycle a seamless experience, where interactions flow smoothly from one stage to another, creating an overall positive feeling of satisfaction. The ultimate goal of any company is to build **guest loyalty**. You can achieve this by making guests feel that you and your team are attentive to their needs.

Pre-Arrival

Pre-arrival is the time when the guest selects the hotel, restaurant, or tour and makes a reservation. This is the perfect time to collect information on guest preferences. For a hotel, this might include pillows, newspaper delivery, distance to elevators, floor level, or other special requests. For a restaurant, preferences might include table location or special occasion requests, such as flowers or a birthday cake. Airline passengers may have seat and meal preferences, or they might be traveling with infants, pets, or unusual baggage. Managers must ensure that a process is in place for recording guest preferences and ensuring those preferences are provided in the next stage of the guest cycle.

Guest Loyalty—the faithfulness guests feel to a property based on a positive guest experience; choosing to stay at the same property repeatedly.

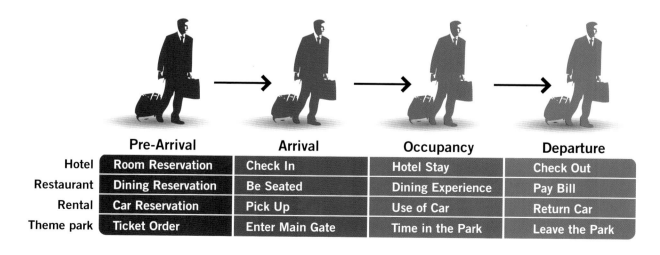

	Pre-Arrival	Arrival	Occupancy	Departure
Hotel	Room Reservation	Check In	Hotel Stay	Check Out
Restaurant	Dining Reservation	Be Seated	Dining Experience	Pay Bill
Rental	Car Reservation	Pick Up	Use of Car	Return Car
Theme park	Ticket Order	Enter Main Gate	Time in the Park	Leave the Park

Arrival

The arrival stage is the "moment of truth" when businesses have to deliver what was promised to guests. The manager's job is to make sure that guests form a positive first impression. Negative first impressions, once formed, are often very difficult to correct. It's best to start on a positive note. Since, in most cases, the manager will not have direct contact with guests, well-trained employees must provide exceptional guest service upon arrival. Employees should feel empowered to make on-the-spot decisions to improve guest service. Guest contact employees should be trained in how to:

• Greet and welcome guests

• Confirm and fulfill guest requests

• Mitigate circumstances in which requests cannot be fulfilled

• Handle difficult or demanding guests

• Delight guests with unexpected perks

Guests who have a positive experience during the arrival stage are going to be more disposed to enjoying their entire experience with your business. However, the loss of a guest's goodwill during this stage can create a pessimistic outlook on the remainder of the experience and may lead to the loss of the guest's future business.

Occupancy

Occupancy is the time the guest spends staying at a hotel, eating in a restaurant, relaxing at a spa, taking a guided rainforest tour, or exploring a theme park. During this stage, it is important to continue providing the highest level of service. Guests should not feel like you have forgotten about them once they checked into their room or sat down at their table. Always be on the lookout for ways to surprise your guests. Offering a complimentary taste at a restaurant, hosting a movie night in the hotel lobby, or providing directions and/or coupons to other local attractions are good ways to show that your company is engaged with guests' needs and their overall experience.

Managers can support their employees in providing great guest service during the occupancy stage by allowing them to be creative and encouraging them to contribute ideas for designing positive experiences. It is important to understand that a little money or time spent in this stage of the guest cycle can produce big returns in the future. Guests who have positive experiences will most likely become repeat customers and may recommend your business to family and friends.

Pineapple Fun Fact

Restaurant guests have come to expect a complimentary basket of bread on the table, but many restaurants today are realizing the drawbacks of this approach. Much of the bread simply goes to waste, or guests fill up on the free stuff and order less, both of which can hurt the bottom line. Instead, giving away a free bite at the beginning of a meal has become popular. These bite-sized tastes, called amuse-bouches, can highlight seasonal ingredients or a restaurant's specialties. A complimentary taste conveys a restaurant's spirit of generosity, surprises diners, and stimulates their taste buds.

Departure

During the departure stage, all guest service and guest accounting functions, such as settling the bill and leaving the business, are completed. The departure process can be hectic, so management must ensure that employees complete all transactions in a timely manner, whether it is hotel check-out or bringing the bill in a restaurant. A lodging property might consider investing in a free airport shuttle to help guests have a hassle-free departure experience.

Employees should be encouraged to solicit comments about the guest's experience. Institute a process for documenting these comments, and discuss them with employees during regularly scheduled meetings. Figure out where the guest experience fell short and brainstorm ways to improve service in the future. Managers can also directly connect with guests after departure by answering e-mails or responding to guest reviews on websites such as TripAdvisor.

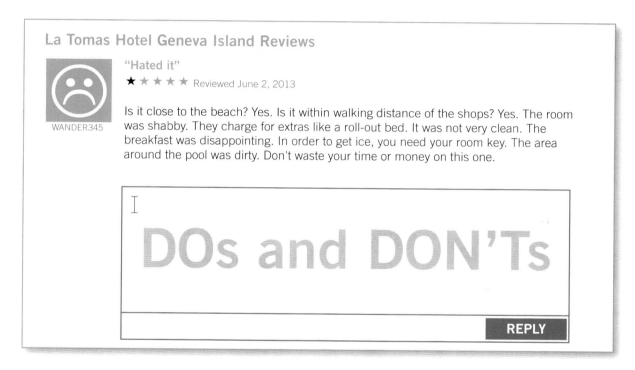

DO:
- Respond to a balanced blend of negative and positive comments
- Thank guests for their business and welcome them to come back in the future
- Take the time to carefully craft a response
- Sincerely apologize for any negative experience the guest had, regardless of fault
- Be selective about which comments you respond to—not every comment is a legitimate concern

DON'T:
- Be defensive or take comments personally
- Blame employees or the guest
- Respond only to complaints and negative reviews
- Blatantly sell your business in your response
- Discourage your staff from suggesting guests write online reviews

Guest Recovery

No matter how hard you try, even with outstanding training, clearly-defined processes, and a top-notch team of employees, things go wrong once in a while. But whatever the reason for the complaint, it is important to try and please the guests and send them home with a positive impression of your organization. Let them know that you value their comments and their loyalty. In addition, a less than perfect guest experience is an opportunity to learn how to prevent the situation from occurring in the future.

How you handle guest complaints often determines whether a guest will return to your establishment. Handle the experience quickly and efficiently, and you may have a customer for life. Handle the experience poorly, and you may find yourself in the midst of a negative word-of-mouth campaign that could reach thousands. Today, negative word-of-mouth campaigns can grow exponentially through social media.

96%

of guests do not complain to anyone who can help them.

95%

of guests will return if they feel their complaint was resolved quickly.

90%

of guests with unresolved complaints will never return.

There are four basic categories of guest complaints. You and your employees need to be able to respond and offer **guest recovery** solutions in order to appropriately resolve the issue.

Mechanical Complaints are caused by equipment malfunctions, such as problems with climate control, lighting, vending machines, key cards/door locks, and plumbing.

> Your response may be to offer a free meal or drink from the bar, offer a discount, or hand out a company logo item kept on hand for this purpose.

Attitudinal Complaints are caused by the poor treatment of a guest by an employee, usually in a one-on-one situation, which has angered or upset the guest.

> Your response may be to listen to what the guest thinks needs to be done to correct the situation and find a reasonable compromise. Follow up with coaching or counseling for the employee to ensure the behavior is not repeated.

Service-Related Complaints are caused by guests receiving cold food, having their requests or special needs ignored, or experiencing long waits for assistance from employees.

> Your response may be to provide guest recovery in the form of discounts or complimentary items. However, you must then find out the root cause of the service breakdown and address it by providing retraining or a change of procedures.

Unusual Complaints are unique situations caused by unexpected conditions that need to be handled on an individual basis. Many are a result of poor weather, power outages, or lack of desired amenities (pool, gym, outside seating).

> Your response may be to allow guests to vent their frustrations about the situation. You must learn to differentiate situations that warrant guest recovery from those when just providing a sympathetic ear will suffice.

Empowering Your Employees

Knowing when and how to empower employees to effectively handle guest recovery can be difficult for anyone in a leadership position. Determining the level of employee empowerment to train for can also be hard—employees should be able to handle most guest recovery situations on their own, but they should also know when a manager's involvement is needed.

How do you create employee empowerment that works?

- Hire talented people
- Share your vision of the guest experience with employees
- Trust your employees to do the right thing for your guests; encourage initiative
- Define and communicate parameters for empowered decision-making by employees
- Train employees
- Delegate effectively
- Listen to employee ideas and include employees in the decision-making process
- Keep employees motivated
- Provide the right resources
- Provide feedback; recognize and reward empowered employee behavior

Remarkable guest recovery means handling the service breakdown in a way that makes the guest even more loyal to your business after the issue has been properly resolved.

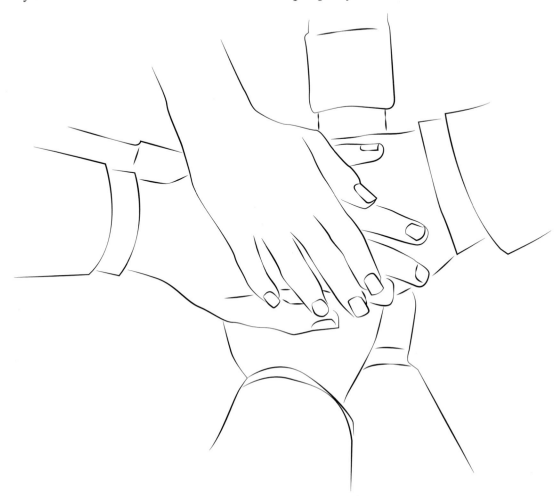

Problem Solving

Hospitality and tourism managers often say that a lot of their time—often too much of their time—is spent solving problems. It is true and for good reasons. Hospitality and tourism is an ever-changing, people-centered industry where providing excellent guest service is the organizational goal. And today's guests and employees all come from diverse backgrounds that create challenges and opportunities for hospitality leaders every day.

Issues or problems between employees, in operational processes, or between employees and managers, will all eventually affect guest service. When employees do not work as a team, some work may be duplicated, while other tasks may not get done at all, which can lead to slowdowns in service. Bad management practices can affect employee morale and motivation, resulting in employees who do not care about their jobs and provide sub-par service to guests. Breakdowns in processes affect employees' ability to do their jobs. If employees do not have the right tools or training at the right time, they will not be able to ensure a seamless guest experience.

Management's job is to try to identify and solve problems before they begin to impact guests. However, new and sometimes even experienced supervisors often have one of two reactions to problems: to ignore them and hope they go away, or to try to solve them without understanding the root cause of the problem. Managers must learn to look beyond the surface facts to understand the real cause of each problem. The root causes of most hospitality industry problems are:

1. **Working conditions**—Does the work involve some type of risk? Are safety practices in use? Do your employees have the right equipment and training to do their jobs?

2. **Processes**—Are you fully staffed, or are you short during busy times? Is turnover high? Are employees provided appropriate training? Do guest service issues cause challenges?

3. **The organization**—How do organizational or property-wide changes impact your operation and team? Do supplies and equipment pose operational challenges? Do you need better ways to conduct business? Are you always looking for improved work methods for the team to use? Is the work atmosphere one of inclusiveness that values diversity?

As a manager, you shouldn't feel that you must solve all problems by yourself. You, your employees, and your organization all benefit when you involve a diverse group of employees in the problem-solving process. Each employee brings a "fresh pair of eyes" to the problem, and managers who can tap into that talent will lead a more effective and efficient operation. When you use a team approach to problem solving, you:

- Respect and value diverse skills and experiences
- Improve employee morale and show the importance of teamwork
- Empower and promote initiative among employees
- Reduce resistance to change and encourage risk-taking

It makes good business sense to involve your employees in helping to solve problems that affect them. But not all problems will benefit from a team approach for a variety of reasons. Before you decide to create a problem-solving team, think about the answers to these questions:

1. Is it appropriate for your employees to help solve the problem? Does it involve anything confidential, such as personal employee data or proprietary company information?

2. Is it practical for your entire team to work on the problem, or should you select a few employees who are directly impacted by the problem to be on the team?

3. Do you have time in your schedule to be part of the problem-solving team? If not, how will you manage the team's efforts?

Six Steps to Problem Solving with a Team

1. Brainstorm to identify problems and root causes.

- Set a time limit on the brainstorming session.

- Don't let employees get sidetracked.

- Be sure that employees speak freely.

- Be sure all employees participate.

- Let your employees do the talking.

2. Prioritize problems and select a problem to solve. Analyze each problem individually to help you prioritize appropriately.

3. Develop possible solutions.

- Get input from everyone on the team.

- Examine the problem's effects on employees.

- State specific results you want to achieve.

- Brainstorm possible solutions.

4. Obtain feedback and test the solutions.

- Solicit responses from employees who would be affected by the solution.

- Conduct trial runs.

5. Implement the best solution.

6. Evaluate the results of the solution.

- Determine if the solution has solved the problem.

- If not, call your team back together and figure out why it's not working.

- Follow this process to find a better solution.

Apply Your Learning

Section 3.1

1. Why is it important for guests to have a positive experience?
2. What is the best way for managers to make sure employees follow the guest experience standards?
3. What level of service do business travelers typically expect?
4. How can collecting information about guests' perceptions of their experience at your property help you improve the guest experience?

Section 3.2

1. What is the role of management during the pre-arrival stage of the guest cycle?
2. Why is it important to make a good impression on the guest during the arrival stage of the guest cycle?
3. What can employees and managers do during the occupancy stage to ensure a positive guest experience?
4. True or False? Managers should respond to both positive and negative guest comments.

Section 3.3

1. What could happen if a company fails to handle a guest complaint efficiently and to the guest's satisfaction?
2. If a guest complains that the reservation agent was rude and unhelpful, what type of complaint is this?
3. How might a manager respond to a service-related complaint?
4. What can managers do to empower their employees to handle guest recovery situations?

Section 3.4

1. Give an example of a hospitality and tourism problem that might be caused by processes.
2. What are the benefits of creating a diverse problem-solving team?
3. When might it not be a good idea to use a team approach to problem solving?
4. What should happen next after a team has held a brainstorming session to identify a problem and its root causes?

Chapter 4

Managing the Guest Experience Cycle

COMPETENCIES

1. Describe why modeling inclusive behavior is an important skill for hospitality and tourism managers.
2. Identify how managers should apply property standards to the guest experience.
3. Identify the role of Guest Service Measurement (GSM) in managing the guest experience.
4. Explain how a manager leads a GOLD guest service team.
5. Describe the benefits of green practices and the role hospitality and tourism managers play in implementing them.

nickelodeon SUITES
RESORT

Louis Robbins, CHA
Managing Director
Nickelodeon Suites Resort

Louis Robbins is the managing director of the Nickelodeon Suites Resort in Orlando, Florida. Mr. Robbins is in charge of 600 team members who "Bring Nickelodeon to Life" every day. Nickelodeon Suites Resort was the first hotel in the world to receive the prestigious Certified Guest Service Property designation from the American Hotel & Lodging Educational Institute (EI).

Mr. Robbins has proudly served the hospitality community for 38 years, starting as a front desk clerk of a 60-room motel while he attended college. He graduated with Honors from Nova Southeastern University in Ft. Lauderdale, FL, while working as a general manager. Mr. Robbins has held general manager posts at Hilton Hotels and DoubleTree, where he focused on improving profitability, guest relations, and team member relations and satisfaction. During this time, he also guided his hotel through the devastation of Hurricane Andrew. Due to the outstanding successes of his team and its community involvement, the hotel won the DoubleTree Hotel Care Award for exceptional customer and team member satisfaction. Mr. Robbins was then promoted to area vice president for Embassy Suites Hotels in Florida and Puerto Rico and then to area vice president for Hilton Hotels of Florida, where he was responsible for 20 full-service hotels. He continued to focus on increased profitability, customer service, and team loyalty.

Mr. Robbins has always been extremely active within the community. He is a past president of the Central Florida Hotel & Lodging Association (CFHLA), has served on the board of CFHLA for over 17 years, and has acted as chair or vice chair of Bacchus Bash, where his committee has raised over $1 million to support hospitality education in Central Florida. He previously served on the executive committee and board of Visit Orlando. Mr. Robbins was the recipient of Promus Hotels General Manager of the Year and the Florida Hotel & Motel Association General Manager of the Year awards. He has also been honored as the Central Florida Hotelier of the Year.

Introduction

Hospitality and tourism guests have certain expectations. Consider the elements that would constitute an outstanding guest experience at a spa. The first impression of what kind of service the spa offers occurs when the guest calls to make a reservation. How gracious is the reservation agent? Does the agent sound genuinely interested in taking the reservation, or does he or she act as if the call were a nuisance? The next impression may be arriving at the spa. When the guest walks through the door, who greets him or her, and how? Is the greeter polite, welcoming, and concerned with the guest's needs? Does the property look clean and well-maintained? Do the employees adhere to the appointment time, or are they running behind? Do they interact with the guest, or do they ignore the guest and chat amongst themselves while doing manicures and pedicures? These are just some of the standards that are used when guests form opinions about a spa experience. If all of the parts of the process are performed better than expected—if reality exceeds expectations— guests rate the experience as exceptional. If reality matches expectations, guests rate the experience as satisfactory. But if the reality is less than what is expected, the guest experience is considered poor.

The expectations of the person receiving the service, not the person who is delivering the service, are the ones that count. Too often, managers assume that if they think they are providing a positive guest experience, then it must be so. Managers have a difficult time recognizing that their perceptions may differ considerably from those of their guests. To ensure that they are providing the best guest experience possible, managers must continuously monitor how well they are meeting guest expectations and respond to the results accordingly.

Pineapple Fun Fact

The Ritz-Carlton motto is, "We are Ladies and Gentlemen serving Ladies and Gentlemen." At the Ritz-Carlton, employees are the most important resource in the company's service commitment to guests. Every employee—from a top manager down to a busser—has an allowance of up to $2,000 per guest per day that can be used to enhance the guest experience. The allowance could be used for anything from sending champagne and cake up to the room for a guest's birthday to buying a new suit for a guest because the laundry could not get a stain out of the old one. Every employee is empowered to use his or her own judgment, without seeking permission from a manager, to create an outstanding guest experience.

Managing the Guest Experience: Being Inclusive

P art of providing a positive guest experience is making the guest feel welcome. The goal of every hospitality and tourism manager should be to make sure that guests from a variety of backgrounds feel comfortable. Following the R.A.V.E. principle can help managers and employees meet the diverse needs of their guests. R.A.V.E means learning to Respect and Value Everyone (R.A.V.E.) for where they come from, the personal beliefs and life experiences they may have, and the expectations they bring with them when they travel. It means being inclusive.

Inclusiveness must start at the highest organizational level and cascade down to all employees and guests. Managers can set the tone by modeling inclusive behavior. Through effective orientation and training programs, new and current employees can learn the importance of respecting and valuing each other and the property's guests. Hospitality and tourism organizations can realize a substantial benefit from successfully managing the guest experience to embrace inclusiveness. Guests who feel comfortable throughout their experience are more likely to return and to recommend the property to their friends and family.

Americans with Disabilities Act (ADA)

Discrimination under the ADA includes:

1. Denying or providing separate or unequal access to goods, services, and accommodations based on a disability.
2. A failure to have physical facilities that are accessible to individuals with disabilities.
3. A failure to provide auxiliary aids and services, where necessary, to ensure that individuals with disabilities have equal access to public accommodations.
4. A failure to make reasonable modifications to policies, practices, and procedures to ensure that individuals with disabilities have equal access to public accommodations.

There are a variety of special accommodations that hospitality and tourism businesses provide under the ADA, such as:

- Allowing service animals on the property
- Accessible guestrooms with walk-in showers
- Hand grips or bars for showers and toilets
- Wider doorways and aisles
- Lowered peepholes and door locks
- Teletypewriter (TTY) communication kits; Braille
- Buses and shuttles with the ability to kneel or lower to the curb
- Ramps or lifts

ADA

More than 50 million Americans are classified as having a disability. Many people with disabilities want to live, travel, shop, and access services independently. The Americans with Disabilities Act (ADA) of 1990 prohibits discrimination based on disability. The hospitality and tourism industry complies with the ADA by providing people with disabilities full and equal access to goods, services, facilities, and accommodations. Employees trained in providing service for guests with disabilities practice simple courtesy and respect, are aware of specific guest needs, and have a thorough knowledge of the facilities and services their property offers.

Guest Experience Property Standards

Guests have certain expectations when they interact with any hospitality and tourism business. Those expectations can be based on a variety of factors, including the type of property or business, the price, previous experiences, or recommendations. But before organizations worry about meeting these expectations, they must ensure that they are meeting guests' basic needs. These might include:

- **Safety and security**—guests need to feel that proper measures have been put in place to guarantee their safety.

- **Cleanliness**—walking into a clean hotel room or restaurant will immediately help guests feel comfortable.

- **Good repair**—all facilities and equipment should be fully operational.

- **Service**—basic courtesy and respect should be shown to each guest.

Taken together, these needs form a set of standards each property can follow. **Property standards** are the foundation of providing a great guest experience. Organizations can build on these standards to improve the guest experience, but if the foundation is not solid, the entire structure could crumble. Property standards could include anything from green practices to the temperature at which to wash dishes to how to greet guests when they walk in the door.

TERMS YOU SHOULD KNOW

Property Standards—basic requirements set to ensure safety, cleanliness, and good repair that all employees are expected to meet.

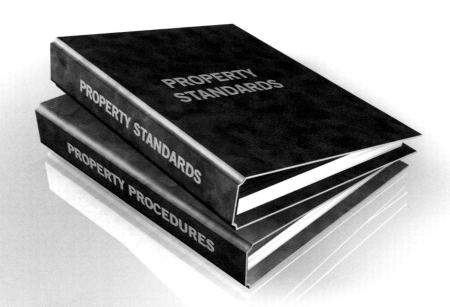

Standards + Procedures = Success

Property standards in hospitality and tourism businesses tend to be very similar. However, some organizations do a better job than others at meeting standards. One reason for this is that the procedures employees use to meet those standards can be very different, or sometimes nonexistent. For example, a property standard in a hotel might be to maintain clean bathtubs:

1. Bathtub is cleaned daily.
2. Bathtub is free of hair, soap scum, and mildew.
3. Fixtures are shiny and spot-free.
4. Water runs clearly through the drain.

Creating clearly laid out procedures is what empowers employees to meet the property standards every time. Procedures explain how to complete a task and should be presented in a logical order. Procedures for cleaning a bathtub might be:

1. Select the correct cleaning tools and chemicals.
2. Remove all hair and debris from the tub and drain.
3. Scrub the inside of the tub with cleaner and sponge.
4. Scrub the exterior of the tub and the plumbing fixtures.
5. Rinse thoroughly with hot water.
6. Dry all surfaces with a clean cloth.
7. Polish all fixtures with a dry, clean cloth.

Training to Meet Property Standards

Once solid property standards are in place, an effective training program should be implemented. Proper training will allow employees to meet property standards in a timely and efficient manner. Training will help employees have a clear understanding of:

- The property's standards
- Procedures to follow in order to meet standards
- How property standards are measured
- Why meeting property standards improves the guest experience

Training programs often fail because they don't provide the right information at the right time. The goal of training should be to give employees what they need in order to do their jobs without overwhelming them with unnecessary information. Training should take place not just in the classroom but also on the job on an ongoing basis. Delivering small pieces of information to employees at various points allows managers to practice good time management. It also gives them an opportunity to offer follow-up pointers, corrections, and suggestions. Property standards can and will fail if they are not properly reinforced. Effective training that does not end when the session ends will create a consistent guest experience. Once property standards are put into practice, a survey of the organization's progress should show an improved guest experience and an increase in guest loyalty.

Managing the Guest Service Measurement (GSM) Process

TERMS YOU SHOULD KNOW

Guest Service Measurement (GSM)—a process used to measure guest satisfaction.

Guest Comment Cards—a method for guests to provide feedback to businesses about the guest experience.

Hospitality and tourism businesses are constantly evolving to keep up with the needs and expectations of guests. For this reason, managers and employees must continually evaluate their products and services. The tool most commonly used to measure guest satisfaction is the **Guest Service Measurement (GSM)** process. GSM involves determining guest needs and expectations and whether they are being met through a process such as follow-up phone calls or **guest comment cards**. Comment cards can take the form of printed cards, online surveys, or feedback sections on company websites.

A well-executed guest comment card provides businesses vital information, shows that an organization cares about its guests, and offers guests a simple, hassle-free way to give feedback. Some hospitality and tourism businesses offer incentives to guests who fill out comment cards, such as complimentary items or discounts on the next visit, or birthday and anniversary "treats."

Guest comment cards might be available in a hotel room, on the table at a restaurant, or employees might direct guests to a website where they can fill out a comment card. The comment card must balance ease of completion with being able to provide useful information. A restaurant comment card might include sections for rating food quality, menu variety, price, service, and atmosphere on a scale of 1 to 5. A hotel comment card might ask guests about the speed of check-in and check-out, as well as have them rate the hotel's service, guestroom cleanliness, and amenities. Most comment cards include a section of short answer, open-ended questions, which can provide specific details about the guest experience. Comment cards can also provide additional data that can be used in marketing efforts, such as purpose of visit, first-time or returning guest, how guests heard about the company, whether they would return or recommend to friends and family, and even demographic information. This data can help managers refine their services to their target markets.

GSM is only helpful if used properly. The data collected must be analyzed to reveal weak spots in services. For example, if a hotel manager notices that a large percentage of guests are business travelers, he or she might follow up to see if the hotel's business center is meeting guests' expectations or if additional services need to be added. GSM can help identify which services are profitable and which are not. Managers can then use this data to eliminate services that do not justify the expense. In addition, GSM can be used to monitor guest responses to changes in services—has the change made a positive impact on the guest experience?

La Tomas Hotels

Guest Comment Card

Date of Stay _____   Room Occupied _____

Name/Address _____

_____

Please Rate Your Stay (please circle one)	Poor	Average	Good	Excellent
Reservation Accuracy	1	2	3	4
Check-in Speed	1	2	3	4
Check-out Speed	1	2	3	4
Accuracy of Bill	1	2	3	4
Guestroom Cleanliness	1	2	3	4
Room Service Quality	1	2	3	4
Restaurant Quality	1	2	3	4
Pool/Spa Quality	1	2	3	4

Are you likely to return?

_____

If we did not live up to your expectations, please let us know:

_____
_____
_____

If we exceeded your expectations, please let us know:

_____
_____
_____

Please share the name(s) of employees who helped make your stay memorable.

_____
_____

La Tomas, your dream team!

TOMA'S BISTRO
COMMENT CARD

Please Rate Your Visit (please circle one)	Poor	Average	Good	Excellent
Food Quality	1	2	3	4
Menu Variety	1	2	3	4
Service	1	2	3	4
Atmosphere	1	2	3	4
Cleanliness	1	2	3	4

1. What changes can we make to improve our restaurant?

_____
_____

2. What should we keep the same?

_____
_____

3. Would you recomment us to a friend?

_____
_____

Guest Service GOLD®: Leading a GOLD Team

The ability to provide the very highest level of guest service at all times is a talent that everyone in the hospitality and tourism industry must work to develop. Providing first-rate guest service is not about having one particular quality or skill—it's about creating a memorable guest experience. Remember, when you are with a guest, you have to be the strongest link in the chain. Exceptional guest service is the one element that ties together all the other parts of the business.

Professional Certification

The American Hotel & Lodging Educational Institute (EI) has developed a training and certification program called Guest Service GOLD® to help hospitality and tourism employees consistently exceed guest expectations. Employees who complete the Guest Service GOLD® training and pass the exam will receive the Certified Guest Service Professional (CGSP) designation. A property might also choose to become a Certified Guest Service Property or Certified Guest Service Partner by having all front-line employees receive their CGSP designations. Successful organizations will receive a CGSP property certification plaque to display prominently in recognition of their commitment to providing exceptional guest service.

Guest Service GOLD® focuses on seven key elements required to deliver excellent guest service on an ongoing basis. Providing guest service that goes above and beyond the typical should never have a start or an end. It should come from a desire to provide guests with the best the property has to offer. The seven elements of Guest Service GOLD® are:

1. **Authenticity:** Keep It Real

2. **Intuition:** Read the Need

3. **Empathy:** Use Your Heart

4. **Champion:** Be a Guest Hero

5. **Delight:** Provide a Surprise

6. **Delivery:** Follow Through

7. **Initiative:** Make the Effort

Leading the Way to GOLD

As a manager, you play a crucial role in the training efforts at your company. With the majority of training focused on new employees, the continued development of existing employees may sometimes be taken for granted. But everyone could use a refresher on guest service, the most important element of hospitality and tourism. Managers should focus on providing consistent, ongoing training to employees and keeping them motivated to continue providing a gold level of service. Here are a few ways to do this:

Hold pre-shift meetings. After employees complete the initial training, use these short meetings to remind employees of the most important elements of Guest Service GOLD®.

Inspire with personal anecdotes. Use stories from your own experience and career to inspire employees to perform at the highest level.

Encourage employees to share their stories. Employees may want to share a story about how they or a co-worker made a guest's experience special.

Be a resource to your staff. Ask staff if they have everything they need to do their jobs.

Observe employee performance. Create a checklist to help you keep track of how well each employee is performing. Give guidelines if you correct performance—tell people how they can do better.

Show employees that they are valued. Praise staff for a job well done. Make sure that your praise is meaningful and specific. If you hand out praise too often, it won't mean as much. But never using praise can have a negative impact on morale.

4.6

Managing Green Practices

TERMS YOU SHOULD KNOW

Carbon Footprint—the total greenhouse gas emissions caused by an organization.

Marketing research indicates that when making purchasing decisions, consumers are mindful of not just the value of a product or service but also of their personal values. Now more than ever, consumers of all kinds are demanding that the brands they buy, and the companies that make them, share their own personal, social, and environmental values. According to the Natural Marketing Institute's consumer trends poll, 83 percent of consumers are concerned with buying "green" products and services. To meet the demands of these consumers, the hospitality and tourism industry was one of the first to employ green practices. Industry leaders saw that in addition to their social and environmental impact, green practices can also save organizations money. Today, many guests look for hotels with green features, so it makes good business sense to invest in them.

The health and environmental benefits of green practices include:

- Improved air quality
- Reduced water and energy use
- Reduced **carbon footprint**
- Reduced exposure to dangerous chemicals
- Conservation of natural resources

The economic benefits of green practices include:

- Energy savings (electricity and water)
- Higher price point and increased profitability for green products and services
- Reduced waste disposal costs
- Increased market competitiveness

Green Practices

Greenhouse gases are emitted through the consumption of fossil fuels like oil, coal, and gas. When fossil fuels burn, they emit greenhouse gases like CO_2 that contribute to global warming. Many hospitality and tourism organizations today are working to reduce their carbon footprint by lowering their energy consumption or using renewable energy, planting trees and gardens, composting, recycling, using green building materials, purchasing fuel-efficient or hybrid vehicles, reducing corporate travel, and buying from local suppliers.

Leaders in every segment of the hospitality and tourism industry must be aware of the benefits of going green and ways to promote green practices in their organizations. The role of management is to:

1. **Identify the costs and benefits of green practices.** Some managers are hesitant to incorporate green practices into their organizations because the initial start-up costs may seem high. However, a thorough cost analysis will show that most green practices will provide a cost savings in the long run.

2. **Create a strategic vision.** Managers must develop strategic goals and a clear action plan, which will help set the direction for all other activities. One such goal might be to work toward and achieve a green certification. For example, many lodging and convention properties have achieved or are working toward LEED (Leadership in Energy and Environmental Design) certification, an internationally recognized green building program.

3. **Encourage company-wide participation in green initiatives.** It is essential to have "buy-in" from everyone across the organization, from upper management to front-line employees. Managers must focus on raising awareness and educating employees on the benefits of going green. Establishing a recognition or reward program for employees who demonstrate commitment to green practices can help get staff motivated.

4. **Manage the implementation of green practices.** Managers should strive to create a culture of **sustainability**. Every team member must be invested in the success of the initiative.

5. **Monitor the results.** Managers should track the costs and savings to understand how green initiatives impact the bottom line.

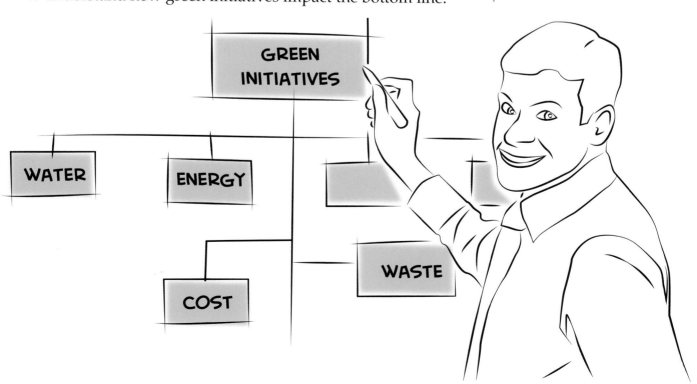

Apply Your Learning

Section 4.1
1. What are guest expectations?
2. What expectations would people have when going to a spa?
3. Why is it important for managers to work to meet guest expectations?

Section 4.2
1. What does R.A.V.E. stand for, and how does it apply to hospitality and tourism management?
2. Why is it important that guests feel comfortable?
3. What is the purpose of the Americans with Disabilities Act?
4. What special accommodations have hospitality and tourism businesses provided to comply with the ADA?

Section 4.3
1. How do property standards impact the guest experience?
2. What is the relationship between standards and procedures?
3. What should training programs on property standards cover?
4. Why is it important to continue training beyond the classroom?

Section 4.4
1. What is the role of a GSM process in managing the guest experience?
2. What information might be collected on a restaurant guest comment card?
3. What incentives do businesses provide to guests who fill out comment cards?
4. Why might demographic data be important when considering guest feedback?

Section 4.5

1. What is the CGSP designation? How does a hospitality and tourism employee get it?
2. What are the benefits of being a Certified Guest Service Property or Certified Guest Service Partner?
3. How can pre-shift meetings help managers keep employees on track?
4. What are some other ways managers can help their employees consistently provide the highest level of guest service?

Section 4.6

1. List three health and environmental benefits of green practices.
2. Explain how consumer demand for green products and services has affected the hospitality and tourism industry.
3. True or False? A carbon footprint is the responsible, long-term use of Earth's resources that meets the needs of the present without compromising the needs of future generations.
4. How can you reduce your carbon footprint in your everyday life? How can an organization such as a hotel or rental car agency reduce its carbon footprint?
5. Why might some leaders be hesitant to implement green practices in their business?
6. What is the role of management in the implementation of green practices in hospitality and tourism?

Chapter 5

Leadership, Employees, and Communication

COMPETENCIES

1. Describe the purpose of a mission statement.
2. Explain the importance of communicating the purpose and role of their job positions to employees.
3. Identify the steps involved in setting performance goals and ensuring that employee performance meets property standards.
4. Describe proper workplace etiquette for listening, speaking, and writing.
5. Explain communication strategies that can help managers deal with difficult employees.
6. Review the sources of conflict and describe basic strategies that can be used to manage conflict.
7. Define different aspects of guest communication.
8. Explain why media training for leaders in hospitality and tourism is necessary.

Hospitality Profile

**Carlos M. Molinet, CHA
Senior Vice President
Greater Fort Lauderdale
Convention & Visitors
Bureau**

Carlos Molinet is the senior vice president of the Greater Fort Lauderdale Convention & Visitors Bureau. In this role, he has oversight responsibilities for CVB operations, sales, and marketing. Mr. Molinet is a 25-year veteran of the hospitality industry. His experience has included general manager positions in such prestigious hotels as the Grand Bay Miami, Westin Providence, Wyndham Bel Age, Wyndham Old San Juan Hotel and Casino, and Palmas Del Mar Beach Resort. Mr. Molinet was recently general manager of the Hilton Fort Lauderdale Marina; director of operations for LXR Resorts and Hotels Fort Lauderdale; and the general manager of the Fort Lauderdale Grande.

Mr. Molinet is currently the chairman and immediate past president of the Broward Chapter of the Florida Restaurant & Lodging Association (FRLA), and he has also been inducted to the 2011-12 Executive Committee of the FRLA. He has served as the vice chair of the Beach Business Improvement District (BID) and was formerly the vice chair of the Beach Redevelopment Advisory Board for the City of Fort Lauderdale. He is a former member of the Broward County Tourist Development Council and a graduate of Leadership Broward Class XXVI.

Among his many industry awards and designations are Certified Hotel Administrator from EI, HSMAI's General Manager of the Year award in 2009, and the State Leadership Award from the AH&LA in recognition of his work with the Florida Restaurant and Lodging Association. As president and CEO of The Molinet Institute, he recently published his first inspirational book, *Running Through Life: From Adversity to Possibility*.

Introduction

Have you ever felt you just weren't getting your ideas across to a co-worker? Have you found your mind wandering while someone was speaking to you? If either of these situations sounds familiar, you've experienced a breakdown in communication. Hospitality and tourism leaders must communicate effectively as they interact with their own managers, peers, employees, guests, vendors, and numerous other persons. They must have excellent speaking, listening, and writing skills because almost all aspects of their work involve communication. The more effectively they communicate, the better they can perform their jobs and lead others.

Managers spend as much as 80 percent of their day engaging in some form of communication. Their ability to communicate often determines whether they succeed or fail as managers. Communication skills are important in every managerial activity, including recruiting, interviewing, training, evaluating, coaching, counseling, leading, and interacting with guests.

Managers must not only communicate with others about day-to-day issues like scheduling or guest needs, but they must also be able to communicate organizational information to employees. Everyone works better when they know why they are doing certain tasks and what the overall goals are. Managers must be able to communicate this information to their employees in a clear and concise way, while at the same time motivating them to perform to the best of their ability. Effective communication skills help managers resolve conflicts and deal with difficult people. Managers must also employ communication skills when representing their business to others, including members of the media.

Pineapple Fun Fact

Communication is about so much more than just the words we say. The act of communicating is made up of three elements—verbal communication, vocal variety, and nonverbal communication. Verbal communication, or the actual words you say, only accounts for 7 percent of all communication. Your tone of voice, volume, and rate of speech make up vocal variety, which accounts for 38 percent of communication. The remaining 55 percent is nonverbal body language, such as eye contact, posture, gestures, and facial expressions.

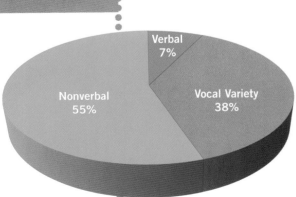

Purpose of the Mission Statement

Organizations function better when everyone—owners, managers, and employees—works toward the same goals; otherwise, there is bound to be confusion about where they are going and how they intend to get there. Forming a **mission statement**, or a description of the organization's reason to exist, can help focus everyone in the same direction. In times of fast change, growth, or hard times, everyone within the organization can turn back to the organization's mission for clarity and stability. Depending on the needs of the company, a mission statement can be short and simple or long and complex. Mission statements can contain some or all of the following elements:

TERMS YOU SHOULD KNOW

Mission Statement—a broad description of an organization's reason to exist.

- The nature of the organization (extended stay hotel, full-service restaurant, spa, historic tour company, airport shuttle service)
- The organization's purpose (to provide food, lodging, meeting space, recreation and relaxation, transportation)
- Major markets served (business travelers, families)
- Goal or desired image (to be the hotel of choice, to provide 100 percent guest satisfaction)

Here are some examples of mission statements from different hospitality and tourism organizations:

Mandarin Oriental Hotel Group

Our mission is to completely delight and satisfy our guests. We are committed to making a difference every day; continually getting better to keep us the best.

Wyndham Worldwide

We will be the global leader in travel accommodations welcoming our guests to iconic brands and vacation destinations through our signature Count On Me! service.

Panda Express

Deliver exceptional Asian dining experiences by building an organization where people are inspired to better their lives.

Carnival Cruise Lines

Our mission is to take the world on vacation and deliver exceptional experiences through many of the world's best-known cruise brands that cater to a variety of different geographic regions and lifestyles, all at an outstanding value unrivaled on land or at sea.

Values Statement—a description of the core values that should shape the culture of the organization and guide the behavior of individuals.

Vision Statement—a description of the future of the organization.

A **values statement** identifies the core values, common convictions, and acknowledged principles that unite an organization's management and staff. Some examples of company values are:

- Personalized guest service
- Environmentally safe practices
- Teamwork
- Respect
- Commitment to quality
- Individual worth
- Delivering shareholder value
- Ethical business practices
- Giving back to the community
- Continuous improvement

While the mission and values statements communicate the purpose of the organization and what it stands for, a **vision statement** describes where the organization wants to be at a specific point in the future. The vision statement helps managers focus their efforts on a long-range plan to move the company to where it wants to be. The following are examples of company vision statements:

Montage Hotels & Resorts

Montage will be the brand of choice for discerning consumers, our communities, our investors and our associates.

Smith & Wollensky Restaurant Group

To be recognized as the premier classic American steakhouse brand for business and social dining domestically and abroad.

Manchebo Beach Resort & Spa

At the Manchebo Beach Resort & Spa, located on the most beautiful white beach and turquoise blue sea of Aruba, we promise to preserve a safe and healthy environment for the island of Aruba, its people and visiting guests.

Spring Run Golf Club

Constantly striving to be the best bundled golf community in Southwest Florida.

Communicating Employee Purpose and Role

When new employees start their first day of work, they are nervous, but they are also excited. Their first impression of the organization begins with **orientation,** where they learn about the company and their specific positions. This is the perfect opportunity for management to foster pride in the organization and its goals. By creating a well-planned orientation and providing training, managers can communicate to employees that they are welcome and valued. Employees need to know that their presence in the organization is important and that their performance makes a positive contribution to the company's goals. There are many benefits to having employees attend orientation.

Orientation—the process of introducing new employees to the company and their jobs.

Orientations help:

- Reduce turnover
- Communicate expectations to employees
- Put new employees at ease
- Show how individual jobs fit into the overall company mission
- Employees feel invested in the company's goals

Types of Orientation

Orientation programs differ from company to company. As a rule, there are two types of orientation. A general orientation is an introduction to the company as a whole, including its values and philosophy, and helps new employees understand their purpose in the organization. A manager's role in the general orientation is to provide all employees with a consistent message. They should understand the overall goals of the organization and see how their specific job fits into those goals. A general orientation usually includes:

- Discussion of the company's mission and values
- Introduction to various departments
- Review of policies and procedures
- Discussion of guest and employee relations
- A tour of the property

The second type of orientation is a specific job orientation, which focuses on explaining the employee's role in his or her department. The manager's role during a job orientation is to begin building a relationship with the employee. During this time, the manager can establish his or her expectations and let the employee know how to meet those expectations. When each employee is aware of his or her role, the department and the company will run more smoothly. The specific job orientation explains what is expected of employees in terms of job performance. It helps employees quickly become productive members of the team and creates a more cooperative team environment. Employees are introduced to:

- Their responsibilities
- Safety information and key department policies and procedures
- The work environment and the location of necessary equipment
- The department's relationship to other departments
- People with whom employees will work on a daily basis

New Employee Orientation Checklist

Name of Employee: _____ Position: _____

Department: _____ Supervisor: _____

For each item below, put a check in the box and record the date the activity is completed or the information is provided.

Introduction
- ☐ _____ Welcome
- ☐ _____ Tour of the property

General Information
- ☐ _____ Our mission and values
- ☐ _____ Company structure
- ☐ _____ Policies and procedures
- ☐ _____ Salary/benefits/services

Your Position
- ☐ _____ Tour of department work area
- ☐ _____ Introduction to fellow employees
- ☐ _____ Review of task lists and job breakdowns
- ☐ _____ Job shadowing

I certify that all the above activities were completed on the date indicated.

Employee: _____ Date: _____

Supervisor: _____ Date: _____

Orientation Activities

As stated earlier, orientations differ depending on the company. Companies who hire large numbers of employees at one time may hold group orientation sessions, while smaller companies may have an individual orientation for each new hire. Some orientations might involve watching a video about the company or reading print or online materials. Others might be one-on-one sessions with a manager. Orientation may even include staying in the hotel or eating a meal in the restaurant where the employee is going to work. This can help employees understand the guest experience and the level of guest service they will be expected to provide.

The role of managers during the orientation process is to make sure that employees feel comfortable and to answer any questions employees may have. It is also important to evaluate the orientation process to make sure that it continues to be effective. This might involve having employees fill out evaluation forms after the orientation or talking informally with employees to ask what information they found helpful and what else might need to be included to help them understand their purpose and role within the company.

Setting Performance Goals

M anagers and employees should have a clear idea at all times of what they are trying to accomplish. Those who do are more likely to achieve their goals than those who do not. Research has shown that goal setting encourages high-level performance and fosters innovation in organizations. When employees are involved in the goal-setting process, they experience increased motivation.

As a manager, it is your job to communicate performance goals to employees to ensure that their performance meets standards. Setting effective goals is different from simply giving directions or telling employees how to do their jobs. Effective goals have the following characteristics:

- **Clear and specific**—Goals such as "Do your best" or "Improve" are not specific. However, "Increase food sales by $1 per guest over the next two months" is specific. Specific goals motivate; nonspecific goals do not motivate.

- **Measurable**—Goals should be stated in terms that can be measured. For example, the goal "Make guests happier" does not provide a way to measure whether the goal has been reached. "Decrease guest complaints by 10 percent over the next 6 months" provides a way to measure results.

- **Time limits**—If no deadline is given for achieving a goal, it might fall by the wayside. Phrases such as "as soon as possible," "high priority," and "right away" do not provide a time limit. Goals should include statements such as "by 2 p.m. every Friday," "in six months," and "by June 1."

Managers are involved in setting two types of goals with employees: self-improvement goals and performance goals. Self-improvement goals focus on gaining new skills or acquiring knowledge, while performance goals relate to achieving specific results at work. Having the right number of performance goals is important. Too many goals create confusion and stress, but too few goals do not provide enough of a challenge. Setting about five to nine goals has proven to be effective.

The process for setting performance goals with employees is as follows:

1. Establish performance goals that are clear, measurable, and have a deadline.
2. Specify the tasks to be completed to reach the goal.
3. Specify how the employee's performance will be measured.
4. Set priorities for multiple goals.
5. Establish a plan of action.

Encourage employees to participate in the goal-setting process. When employees help define the goals, they are more likely to work hard to attain them. Once performance goals have been set and the expectations for meeting them communicated to employees, managers must support their employees' attempts to reach those goals. Providing the necessary equipment, supplies, coaching, and other resources sends the message that managers want employees to succeed.

Performance Evaluations

Performance evaluations can help both employees and managers gauge how well employees are meeting performance standards. Regularly scheduled performance evaluations remind employees of their commitment to the company's mission and standards. Evaluations can take place on a monthly, quarterly, or annual basis. During this time, employees should be informed about the progress they are making toward attaining their goals. This information can motivate them further.

Feedback should be presented in a way that identifies the employee's strengths and areas for improvement. In all performance evaluations, the manager should provide support and encouragement. If improvement is needed, the manager and employee should discuss specific improvements the employee needs to make before the next evaluation session. The result of all performance evaluations should be improved employee-manager relationships, improved performance, and improved productivity.

TERMS YOU SHOULD KNOW

Performance Evaluation—a periodic review that evaluates how well employees are meeting performance standards.

Listening, Speaking, and Writing

Active Listening—requires the listener to be an active participant in the communication process.

Successful communication is a message that the speaker or writer sends and the listener or reader receives and that both parties understand and act on. Knowing how to effectively communicate is very important for managers and leaders because it often determines the extent to which the information they think they have communicated is actually understood. Most managers believe they communicate well, but in many cases they do not. Communication research found that while 95 percent of managers believe they have good communication skills, only 30 percent of their employees agree.

Listening

Most managers spend about 55 percent of their workday listening. They listen in meetings, while on the phone, when interacting with guests, and when receiving information from employees and other managers. Often, managers must make decisions based on the information they gather while listening to others. However, a recent study suggests that people understand and remember only 20 percent of what they hear. About 75 percent of the time that they are supposed to be listening, people are either distracted or preoccupied. Listening well requires hard work, but, fortunately, listening skills can be learned.

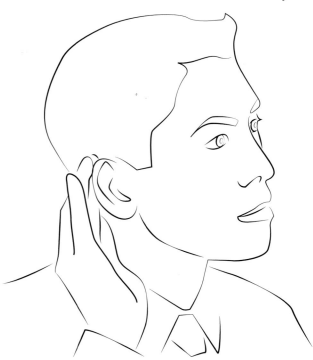

A good listener is an active listener. **Active listening** means participating in the communication process. Techniques to improve active listening include:

- Make eye contact
- Minimize outside distractions
- Ask appropriate questions
- Don't interrupt
- Interpret the speaker's feelings and emotions
- Show empathy
- Respond verbally and nonverbally

Speaking

When communicating with employees, guests, and fellow managers, remember to keep your speech professional. Just as you would avoid dressing too casually in the workplace, you should avoid expressing yourself too casually.

Voicemail

Voicemail is the busy manager's communication lifeline for managing incoming calls as well as contacting employees, other managers, vendors, and guests. Below is a list of how to use voicemail effectively:

- Record an outgoing message with pertinent information
- Update the outgoing message with out-of-office information and an alternate contact when necessary
- Set aside a time each day to listen to your messages, and return calls in a timely manner
- When leaving a message, include your full name, date of call, message, and phone number
- Speak slowly and clearly; avoid leaving long messages

Cell Phones

Here are some etiquette tips that can help managers use their cell phones in a professional manner:

- Respect your employees and guests by not answering the phone during a face-to-face conversation
- Place cell phone on silent or vibrate during meetings and training classes
- Avoid speaking too loudly and disturbing employees working nearby
- Follow and enforce company policy on personal cell phone usage

Writing

Have you ever heard the phrase, "Get it in writing"? This saying underscores the importance of written communication. When something is written down, it is on the record—you can refer back to it if needed. This is why it is essential for managers to be professional and clear in their writing. Most written communication in the workplace today takes place through e-mail. Here are some basic rules of e-mail etiquette for leaders:

- Follow all company e-mail policies
- Answer all questions thoroughly
- Use the Reply All feature sparingly and only when appropriate
- Follow up a verbal agreement with an e-mail for the record
- Use spell check
- Do not use emoticons or write in all capital letters

Managing Difficult People

One of the toughest challenges managers face is handling difficult employees. One difficult person can impact the morale and productivity of the entire team. Sometimes managers become overly focused on trying to "fix" the behavior of the problem employee. The secret is to be able to identify the reasons behind the difficult behavior in order to manage its impact on the workplace.

There are several different kinds of difficult people. Do you recognize any of them? Included with each description are tips for how to manage them.

Types	Characteristics	Tips
Dominator	▪ Act like they know it all, have done it all, and are experts at everything ▪ Try to tell others what to do ▪ Do not care about others' feelings or opinions	▪ Know your facts and ask for concrete information to back up their opinions ▪ Tactfully explain that you have already given team members their assignments
Blocker	▪ Oppose every idea or opinion ▪ Rarely contribute ideas of their own	▪ Introduce organizational changes slowly ▪ Ask them how they would solve the problem
Complainer	▪ Sarcastic and negative about every idea or opinion ▪ Want to feel important by making others feel ineffectual	▪ Ask solution-oriented questions ▪ Work to recognize instances when the complaints are legitimate
Volcano	▪ Explode without warning ▪ Throw temper tantrums or hurt others' feelings	▪ Stay calm; don't sink to their level by yelling back or arguing ▪ Do not tolerate hurtful remarks ▪ Hold them accountable for their actions
Martyr	▪ Act unhappy and put out most of the time ▪ Never complain or offer suggestions	▪ Ask questions that can't be answered with a "yes" or "no" ▪ Push for answers when they answer with silence
Wheeler-Dealer	▪ Only interested in what's in it for them ▪ Manipulate and gossip in order to cause tension between employees ▪ Hold back good ideas in meetings in the hope of being able to offer them individually to a manager	▪ Encourage a team atmosphere and reward good teamwork ▪ Set parameters for appropriate behavior and use corrective feedback when necessary

You can often spot difficult people as early as the interview process. Include "what if" questions and scenarios during job interviews to determine how a candidate might handle different situations. Think about candidates' ability to be flexible when working with others before you hire them. However, if difficult employees don't show their true colors until they are part of your team, there are ways to limit their effects on your department or organization.

1. Provide orientation and training that sets well-defined expectations for job performance, and be clear about what is acceptable and which behaviors will not be tolerated.

2. Show your value and respect for diversity by modeling appropriate behavior. Be aware of how you present yourself. Remain calm and firm during confrontations.

3. Avoid using the word "attitude," as in "Joe, I don't like your attitude." Instead, focus on specific behaviors or the quality of the work. For example, you might say that Joe used offensive language and did not complete the task that was assigned to him.

4. Document inappropriate behavior or incidents, as well as any training and coaching that took place. Explain what will happen when the next infraction occurs, and follow through on what you say. Make sure to follow company policy on disciplinary actions, such as verbal or written warnings and terminations. Know when it is appropriate to involve the human resources department.

5. Separate the person from the problem—stay focused on the issues instead of your feelings about the employee. Get to the root of what is causing the employee to be difficult.

6. Provide corrective feedback immediately after the behavior occurs. Include corrective actions the employee needs to take, and set a timeline for the corrective action to take place.

7. Use positive feedback to encourage or reward positive behaviors you wish to see repeated by your employees. Making employees feel special can motivate them to perform better.

8. Schedule follow-up discussions with the employee to review whether results have been achieved.

Conflict Management

Conflicts at work are inevitable. They might be as simple as a difference of opinion or a lengthy battle about how to handle a particular situation. Left alone, conflict may cause serious problems that prevent the team, the department, or even the company from reaching its goals. Every manager must be prepared to decide whether a conflict is a petty disagreement that will resolve itself or a true conflict that requires intervention. If properly managed, conflict can contribute to creative problem solving and promote teamwork by making employees focus on their work.

Conflicts in organizations occur for many reasons. These include:

Communication problems—Lack of information about the organization's resources, goals, roles, performance expectations, and work relationships is the most common source of conflict.

Limited resources—No hospitality and tourism operation has all the resources it needs. Limited resources, such as time, money, people, or equipment, can cause conflict between people in the same or in different departments.

Different goals—The main goal of any hospitality and tourism operation is to provide excellent guest service that will make the company financially successful. However, conflict can arise between different departments and individuals about how to make this happen.

Poor cooperation—Teamwork is based on cooperation. For example, guests at a restaurant cannot be seated unless someone buses and resets the table. When someone on a team does not complete an assigned task or completes it late, the chain of guest service is broken, and conflict may result.

Individual diversity—When employees fail to value and respect each other as individuals, conflict will occur. A diverse staff does not mean that employees will always be in conflict; however, it does mean that managers must take strong action on conflicts that result from inappropriate behavior by employees to other employees.

Organizational problems—Potential sources of organizational conflict are overlapping job responsibilities, change, vague job descriptions, or unclear company policies. Employees and managers can experience conflicts that create stress if they are not sure who is in charge or what their duties are.

There are two essential skills that managers must develop in order to effectively resolve conflicts:

1. Assertiveness: addressing a problem head-on and encouraging employees to talk about the conflict openly and honestly.

2. Negotiation: the process used to reach a solution, which may involve compromise or the use of persuasive tactics to reach the best outcome.

The manager's goal in conflict management is to reach a win-win outcome, or a compromise that everyone can live with. There are four steps to conflict resolution:

1. Recognize and define the conflict: define the "who, what, why, where, when, and how" of the problem.

2. Confront the individuals in conflict: approach the individuals and make them aware that you are here to help.

3. Develop a solution: negotiate a compromise both parties can live with.

4. Follow up on the conflict: check back to see if the solution is working.

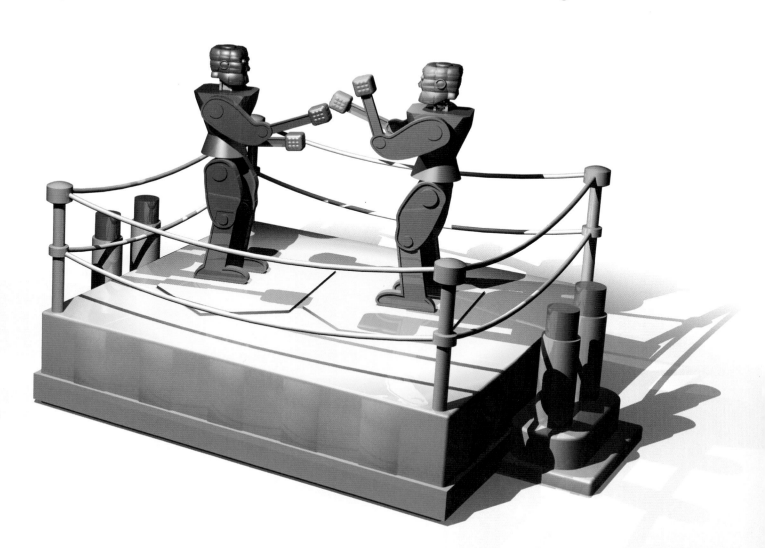

Guest Communication

Another important part of a manager's job is facilitating guest communication. There are several aspects to guest communication: how the hospitality and tourism organization communicates with guests, how employees communicate with guests, and what communication tools and technologies guests expect to have available during occupancy.

Brand Execution

One of the main ways that companies communicate with their customers today is through their websites and through social media such as Facebook, Twitter, or YouTube. These platforms are an opportunity for companies to engage with customers and to show who they are and what they offer. Although some companies see social media only as a marketing vehicle, it should actually be used as part of a larger **brand execution** strategy. Brand execution means delivering on the service promise to guests. Organizations can incorporate effective use of social media into their guest service strategy. Here are a few tips for companies to better use social media as a customer service tool:

1. Integrate social media into your existing customer service strategy.

2. Create a voice your audience can relate to.

3. Monitor social media outlets to spot issues and solve problems before they become crises. About 55 percent of customers expect a response the same day to an online complaint.

4. Customer service through social media involves dealing with criticism and complaints in public, often in front of an audience of millions. Always post a public response because it shows that the company is listening and responds to everyone.

5. Create a consistent process for dealing with social media requests. This ensures that the resolution is seamless on the customer side and that nothing falls through the cracks.

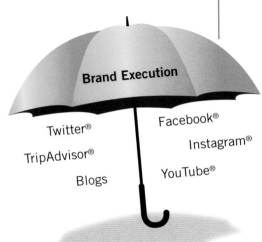

Brand Execution

Twitter®
Facebook®
TripAdvisor®
Instagram®
Blogs
YouTube®

Telecommunications Equipment and Guest Service

While guests are staying at a hotel, eating at a restaurant, or visiting a theme park, that organization's employees are using a variety of technologies and equipment to communicate with guests and make their visit more seamless and enjoyable. Employees communicate with guests by telephone and fax. In hotels, **private branch exchange (PBX)** systems are used to process calls. They include such functions as call waiting, call transfer, conference calls, voicemail, and **call accounting**. Guests can also receive automated wake-up calls.

Technology

Consumers often expect technology to be a part of their guest experience. They expect Wi-Fi to be available, to be able to make reservations and buy tickets online, and to be able to interact with companies through social media. Recent research has shown that about 50-90 percent of tourists all over the world prearrange their trips using the Internet, and 10 percent do so using mobile devices like smartphones and tablets. As many as 70 percent of all bookings are done online. The company's computer system is then used to process the reservation and create a guest account. Often, changes or cancellations to reservations can also be done online through this system.

Many hospitality and tourism businesses make use of mobile technologies to improve guest service. Restaurants use mobile devices to allow wait staff to send orders to the kitchen with the push of a button and to swipe credit cards at the table. Hotel and resort staff armed with a mobile device can check a customer in at the curb or in the lobby, print bar-coded tags for the guest's luggage, order room service, or look up local attractions right at the point of service. Some hotels are giving guests control of a large assortment of hotel-related activities—climate control, scheduling wake-up calls, ordering room service, making spa appointments, and printing boarding passes—with tablets like the iPad.

Mobile devices are a great tool for managers, too. They allow managers to track inventory, monitor wait times, view guestroom status, and access the schedule from anywhere. Managers can spend more time interacting with employees and guests and less time behind a desk.

ADA

ADA regulations require lodging properties to provide telecommunications devices for the deaf (TDD). Other names for these devices include teletypewriter (TTY) and textphone. TDD is a teleprinter, or an electronic device for text communication over a telephone line. With the increasing use of modern technologies such as e-mail, texting, and instant messaging, TDDs are becoming outdated. However, since not everyone has access to an Internet connection, or it is not available in some areas or countries, TDDs are still the only method for landline text phone calls. Just like texting, TTY uses abbreviations like BRB (be right back), MSG (message), R (are), and PLS (please).

Media Training

One aspect of a manager's job may be handling **public relations**. Public relations, or PR, can be defined as targeted communications that present your organization in a favorable light. Depending on the size of the organization and its available resources, public relations might be handled internally by management or externally by a PR firm. Public relations is part of an overall marketing strategy, and its main goal is to build brand recognition and attract new customers. Hospitality and tourism organizations relate with numerous publics, or groups of people, including:

- Guests
- Community leaders and residents
- Media outlets
- Suppliers and vendors
- Other segments of the travel industry
- Employees
- Shareholders and franchisees

Publicity

There are many misunderstandings about what public relations is and is not. For example, **publicity** is often confused for public relations. Publicity is having your business's name mentioned in a newspaper, in an industry blog, on the radio, or on television. Receiving such free press coverage is an important tool of public relations. However, publicity can be negative as well as positive—think of all the publicity surrounding cruise ship disasters. Unexpected positive publicity can result when a celebrity visits your establishment and talks to the media about his or her experience. Publicity can also be planned, such as getting the word out about planned expansions or special programs.

Public Relations Opportunities

Various occasions that present good public relations opportunities include anniversary dates, grand openings or expansions, accomplishments of employees or the company, special guests or events, receiving awards or certificates, new ownership/management, special displays, and community involvement. At these times, a company might reach out to members of the media.

Public Relations Resources

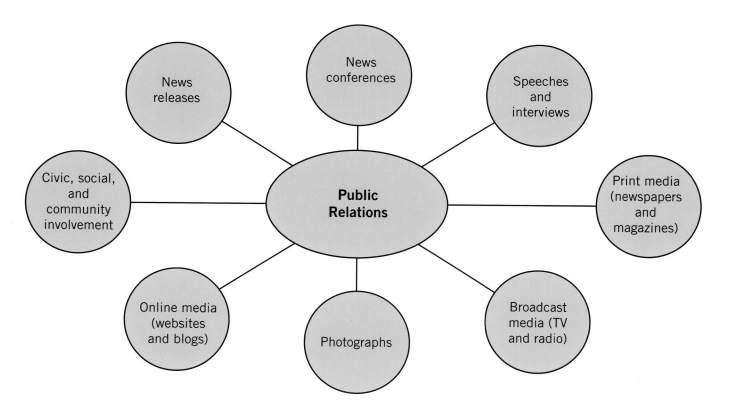

Media Relations

The variety of PR opportunities and outlets might make public relations seem like an easy job. However, dealing with the media is one of the most difficult tasks managers undertake because the media is very powerful. It reaches many consumers and can have an impact on how much business your company receives, so managers who interact with the media must receive media training. Above all, the media spokesperson should be prepared and knowledgeable. Whether the talk is about technical matters or corporate strategy, make sure the speaker has a firm grasp of the topic being discussed. The following are guidelines for managers or other spokespersons who have direct contact with the media:

1. **Schedule appropriately.** Except in emergency situations, try to schedule news conferences or interview times that will be convenient to the media organization. Media outlets operate in a deadline-driven environment. Provide information in a timely manner and respect deadlines.

2. **Tell the truth.** The information you provide should be honest and straightforward. Do not reveal confidential or proprietary information, but make sure that all your facts are correct. If you don't have the answer to a question, don't lie or invent information. Simply say, "I do not have that information at the moment; I will call and provide it to you today."

3. **Provide the facts and follow up.** Supply the key facts in writing to reduce the chance of being misquoted. If possible, follow up with media representatives to ensure all facts are accurate.

4. **Be concise.** People usually get into trouble with the media for what they say, not for what they don't say. Provide the facts in a concise and objective manner. The more you talk, the more likely you are to make a mistake.

5. **Maintain good media relations.** Your attitude should be friendly and open. Hostile, reactionary, or standoffish responses will damage your credibility and relationship with the media. Someone who dislikes you will not be eager to give you air time. If media representatives are visiting your establishment, make sure to provide ample parking, be on time, and stay organized.

Handling Emergencies

It is important to develop a public relations strategy for dealing with emergencies or other situations that can generate negative coverage, such as labor disputes, inappropriate behavior of staff or managers, or injuries or deaths on property. One of the most important strategies is to designate one spokesperson and prepare a message. This will ensure that the same information is presented to different media outlets and minimize the possibility that facts will be misrepresented. If the media raises difficult questions, the spokesperson should never reply with "No comment," but should provide reasons why he or she cannot answer. Some questions may need further investigation, and others cannot be answered for legal reasons (such as when the next of kin have not yet been notified). Employees who are approached by the media should refer all inquiries to the company spokesperson.

There may be times when a media report is slanted or contains misleading or incorrect information. In some cases, the mistake will not affect business, and it is best to let the story die. If the story is going to cause lasting damage, however, it is better to contact the media outlet to correct the error. Present your case and back it up with facts in a friendly, professional manner. Members of the media are just as concerned with being accurate as you are.

Apply Your Learning

Section 5.1
1. Why is it important for hospitality and tourism leaders to be effective communicators?
2. How much of their time do managers spend on communication-related activities?
3. Name five managerial activities that involve communication.

Section 5.2
1. What is the purpose of a mission statement?
2. Name the four elements a mission statement may contain. Provide an example of each.
3. Is the following an example of a mission, values, or vision statement?

   As a company, and as individuals, we value integrity, honesty, openness, personal excellence, constructive self-criticism, continual self-improvement, and mutual respect.
4. What is the difference between a mission statement and a vision statement?

Section 5.3
1. Define the term "orientation."
2. Name three benefits of having employees go through an orientation.
3. In which type of orientation would employees learn about the work environment and the location of necessary equipment?
4. Why is it important to communicate their purpose and role to new employees?

Section 5.4
1. What are performance goals?
2. Describe the three characteristics of effective performance goals.
3. What should managers do in the goal setting process after they specify the tasks to be completed to reach the goal?
4. What happens during performance evaluations?

Section 5.5
1. Why is effective communication essential for hospitality and tourism managers?
2. What is active listening?
3. List four techniques active listeners should use.
4. What should managers do if they receive a cell phone call while they are speaking to a guest or an employee?
5. What are some basic rules for e-mail etiquette for managers? Name at least two rules.

Section 5.6

1. How do difficult employees affect the department or organization?
2. What is the manager's main goal in dealing with difficult employees?
3. What are some characteristics of a martyr? What are the best ways to deal with this type of difficult employee?
4. When should corrective feedback be provided?
5. How can poor cooperation lead to conflict in the workplace?
6. What two skills do managers need to handle conflict resolution?

Section 5.7

1. How can hospitality and tourism businesses use social media to improve guest service?
2. What is used to process calls in most lodging properties?
3. How can mobile devices improve service in a restaurant?
4. What communication tools and technologies do guests expect to have available when they travel?

Section 5.8

1. What is the difference between public relations and publicity?
2. Why is it important for managers to receive media training?
3. What occasions might present good public relations opportunities? Name three resources that can be used for public relations.
4. Why is it important to be concise during interactions with the media?
5. What strategies should be used in emergency public relations situations?

Unit 3

Operational Leadership

▶ **Chapter 6**
Front Office Leadership

▶ **Chapter 7**
Managing Housekeeping Operations

▶ **Chapter 8**
Leadership and Facilities Management

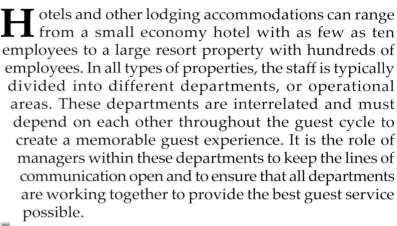

Hotels and other lodging accommodations can range from a small economy hotel with as few as ten employees to a large resort property with hundreds of employees. In all types of properties, the staff is typically divided into different departments, or operational areas. These departments are interrelated and must depend on each other throughout the guest cycle to create a memorable guest experience. It is the role of managers within these departments to keep the lines of communication open and to ensure that all departments are working together to provide the best guest service possible.

This unit will focus on leadership in the following operational areas: front office, housekeeping, and facilities management. It will explain how managers contribute to the successful operation of their departments, as well as to the overall guest experience and the property's profitability.

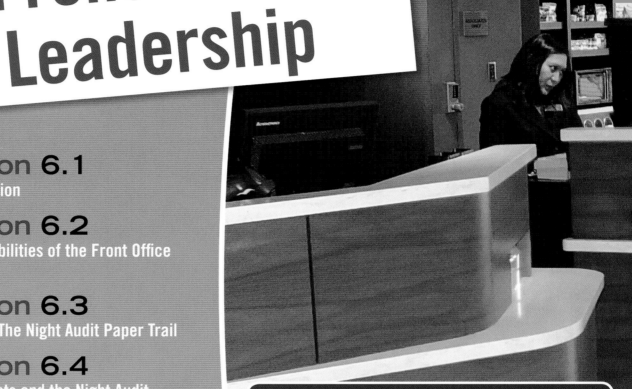

Chapter 6

Front Office Leadership

COMPETENCIES

1. Identify the key duties and responsibilities of the front office manager.
2. Identify the reports attached to the night audit process.
3. Describe how labor costs are managed by the front office.
4. Explain the role of job descriptions and specifications in measuring employee performance.
5. Summarize the role of the front desk in selling to guests.
6. Identify green practices that can be initiated and implemented by the front office.

Hospitality Profile

Anna Chiara Bersani
Front Desk Representative

Anna Chiara Bersani was born in Milan, Italy, in 1987. She received her degree in Public Relations & Advertising at the University of Milan in 2011, while she was working as an intern in an advertising company. After moving to the United States in 2012, Ms. Bersani attended a language course at the University Language Institute for four months. Soon after, she successfully applied to the Tulsa Technology Center, where she is enrolled in the Hotel & Lodging Management and the Event, Entertainment & Tourism Management programs.

While completing her coursework, Ms. Bersani began working as a front desk representative at the Courtyard Central Marriott in Tulsa, Oklahoma. Her responsibilities include checking in and checking out guests; making reservations and cancellations; cashiering; making room keys; telling guests about the hotel's facilities; providing guests with information about the city, nearby restaurants, and activities; and filling out maintenance request forms and contacting engineering staff about needed repairs. Ms. Bersani's goal is to become a hotel event planning manager.

Introduction

The front office is the most visible department in a hotel. Front office personnel have more contact with guests than staff in other departments. The front desk is usually prominently located in the hotel's lobby and is the focal point of activity for the front office. Guests come to the front desk to check in, check out, and to ask about the hotel's services, facilities, or the surrounding area. The front desk often serves as the control center for guest requests concerning housekeeping or engineering issues. In addition, it may also be the base of operations in an emergency, such as a fire or a guest injury. Other front office functions include answering the phones, making reservations, and receiving and distributing mail, messages, and faxes. Front office staff also performs cashiering duties. They are responsible for updating guest accounts and producing daily reports for management.

In addition to all of their other duties, front desk employees, in most cases, are the first and last (and often the only) contact guests have with hotel staff. The front desk agent's ability to make guests feel welcome and special has a tremendous impact on the quality of a guest's experience. Therefore, it is essential that front desk staff is well-trained and that morale is kept high so that interactions with guests and among staff members are always positive. This responsibility, and many others, falls to the front office manager.

Pineapple Fun Fact

A technology called Mobile Key may eliminate some of the functions of the front office, including assigning rooms and issuing key cards. Mobile Key allows guests to use their mobile phone to access their guestrooms, thus letting them bypass the front desk check-in procedure and go straight to their rooms. The technology is compatible with the smartphone operating systems and major electronic locking systems used today. Mobile Key is the greenest way to access a guestroom because it eliminates the need for toxic plastic key cards.

Responsibilities of the Front Office Manager

The front office manager position requires a very specific set of skills: a mix of superior customer service skills and a thorough understanding of hotel accounting. Although the organizational chart may vary depending on the size of the property, the front office manager usually reports to the assistant manager or the general manager and is responsible for managing some or all of the positions shown in the illustration below.

To become a front office manager, an employee typically must have at least a two-year college degree, as well as a minimum of one year of hotel front desk supervisory experience. He or she should also have experience with handling cash, accounting procedures, and general administrative tasks.

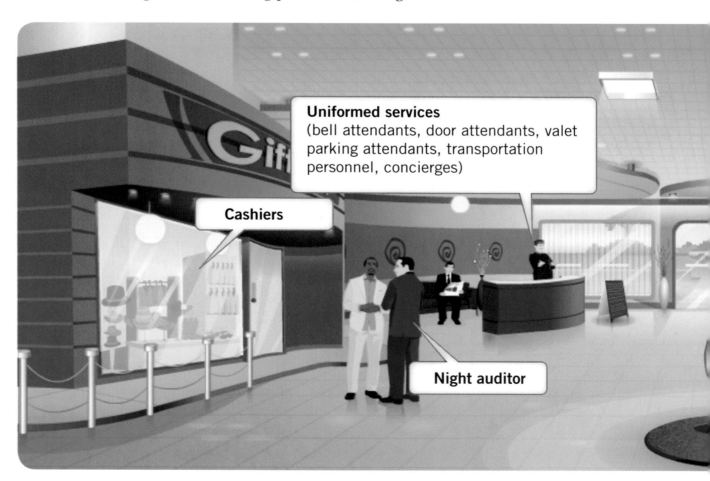

Uniformed services
(bell attendants, door attendants, valet parking attendants, transportation personnel, concierges)

Cashiers

Night auditor

The major duties and responsibilities of the front office manager include:

- Hire, train, schedule, supervise, conduct meetings, and evaluate the performance of front office personnel
- Maintain working relationships and communicate with other departments, such as housekeeping and engineering
- Maintain master **key control**
- Verify that accurate room status information is maintained and properly communicated
- Resolve guest problems quickly and courteously
- Work within the allotted budget for the front office
- Check cashiers in and out and enforce all cash-handling, check-cashing, and credit policies

Key Control—procedures that control access to property keys in order to increase guest security and privacy and to reduce the possibility of theft.

Telecommunications
(switchboard or PBX operators)

Front desk agents

Reservation agents

Forecasting

One of the most important functions of front office managers is **forecasting** the number of rooms available for future reservations. Forecasting is predicting the volume of business for a particular month, week, or day (or meal period for a restaurant). Forecasts are used to help manage the reservations process and guide front office staff in effective rooms management. Forecasting may be especially important on nights when 100 percent occupancy is possible. Occupancy forecasts help determine how much rooms are sold for, when rooms are taken out of inventory for maintenance, and how many employees are scheduled to work based on the expected volume of business.

Forecasting is a difficult skill to develop. The skill is acquired through experience and effective recordkeeping. Several types of information can be helpful in room availability forecasting:

- A thorough knowledge of the hotel and its surrounding area
- Occupancy data for the previous few months and the same period last year
- A listing of special events in the surrounding area
- The room availability of the most important competing hotels
- Plans for remodeling or renovating that would change the number of available rooms

Using such information, the front office manager needs to predict the:

- Number of rooms available for sale
- Number of walk-ins
- Number of expected stayovers
- No-show percentage
- Number of overstays/understays
- Number of expected check-outs

This data will allow the front office manager to produce a 3-day and a 10-day forecast. These forecasts may be helpful to other department managers as well. For example, the housekeeping department manager needs to know how many rooms the front office expects to be occupied to properly schedule room attendants. Restaurant managers must know the same information to better schedule service staff. The chef requires this figure to determine how much food to purchase.

ADA

Due to ADA requirements, hotels must keep track of guests with disabilities. One reason for this is to ensure that all disabled guests are accounted for in case of an emergency. This report is distributed to the various departments that need this information.

Reports: The Night Audit Paper Trail

A hotel is a 24-hour, seven-day-a-week business, and the front office operates continuously, with three shifts per day. The night audit occurs during the last shift, which is when the financial day at the hotel ends and a new one begins. The purpose of the night audit is to compare guest account transactions recorded in the property management system (PMS) or at the front desk against revenue center transactions, such as purchases at the hotel's gift shop or room service orders. This routine helps guarantee the accuracy, reliability, and thoroughness of front office accounting. An effective night audit increases the likelihood of correct account settlement.

Most of the manual work once performed by night auditors is now done automatically. The PMS can automatically post room charges and initiate the audit routine at a specific time. However, even in a fully-automated system, the night auditor must be able to manually verify all the posted entries to guest and non-guest accounts. In addition, he or she should be able to complete the audit by hand if the computer system is down. There are a variety of reports tied to the night audit process. These reports enable the night auditor to complete the process accurately and efficiently.

An automated PMS performs several audit functions continuously and can generate the following types of reports: reservation confirmation; revenue center summary; no-shows and expected arrivals and departures list; guest ledger report; room status report; non-guest billing statement; and specialty reports (group sales, frequent stays or VIPs, promotion sales, etc.). The following sections provide a closer look at some of the reports and their relationship to the night audit.

Audit Posting Formula

The posting formula for calculating or verifying account balances is the same for any account. The previous balance plus debits and minus credits gives the net outstanding balance.

Previous Balance	+	Debits	–	Credits	=	Net Outstanding Balance
PB	+	DR	–	CR	=	NOB

Here is an example of how to use the audit posting formula. Assume a guest account has a previous balance of $280 on which a further charge of $60 is made. The net outstanding balance becomes $340. This figure is transferred as the previous balance for the next transaction, which is a credit payment of $12.80. The credit is subtracted from the previous balance, leaving a net outstanding total of $327.20.

$280.00 + $60.00 - $0.00 = $340.00

Previous Balance	Debits	Credits	Net Outstanding Balance
$280.00	$60.00		**$340.00**
$340.00		$12.80	**$327.20**

$340.00 + $0.00 - $12.80 = $327.20

Guest Credit Limits

Part of the night audit process involves monitoring guest credit to identify any high balance accounts—accounts that have reached or exceeded assigned credit limits at the close of the business day. Night auditors must check credit company floor limits and the hotel's house limit. The floor limit is the maximum amount the hotel can charge to a guest's card without getting authorization from the credit card company. The house limit is the maximum guests can charge to their rooms. Night auditors must also be able to judge the guest's status or reputation as a potential credit risk. Once high-balance accounts have been identified, the night auditor must prepare a **high-balance report** for appropriate front office management action. Front office software can flag these accounts automatically.

Daily and Supplemental Transcripts

A **daily transcript** is a detailed report of guest accounts that had transactional activity on that particular day. Data on a daily transcript is broken down by revenue center, transaction type, and transaction total. A **supplemental transcript** tracks the day's transactional activity for non-guest accounts. Together, they detail all the transactions that occur on a single hotel day. These two reports are useful when trying to identify out-of-balance accounts. For example, the total of charged purchases reported by the hotel's restaurant should equal the total amount of restaurant charges posted to guest and non-guest accounts.

Preparing Reports for Management

The night auditor typically prepares reports about front office activities and operations. Due to the sensitive and confidential nature of the information in these reports, the night auditor must promptly deliver them to the appropriate managers. The **final departmental detail and summary reports** are prepared and filed for accounting division review. They can be used as proof to show that all transactions were properly posted and accounted for. The **daily operations report** summarizes the day's business and provides insight into revenues, receivables, operating statistics, and cash transactions related to the front office. This report is the most important outcome of the night audit.

Another important report is the **daily summary**, or flash report. It provides a snapshot of important operating statistics for the previous day, as well as month-to-date totals. Hotel managers often read this report at the start of a work shift. The daily summary may also show an occupancy and rate forecast for the new business day, which lets managers know of any changes that may have happened overnight.

Labor Costs and the Night Audit

Federal and state wage and hour laws apply to all hotel positions, including the front office. In addition, work hours in some properties may be modified by **labor union** contracts and rules. A 40-hour workweek is the typical workload for front office employees in most hotels. A front office employee may work any one of the property's work shifts, depending on the front office's needs and the staff member's availability. Traditional front office work shifts are:

☀	**Day shift**	**7 a.m. - 3 p.m.**
🌅	**Evening shift**	**3 p.m. - 11 p.m.**
🌙	**Night shift**	**11 p.m. - 7 a.m.**

The front office manager, just like the managers of other departments within the hotel, must control **labor costs**. He or she must balance the need to provide excellent guest service with the department's budget. There are several ways to manage front office labor costs.

A recent trend in front office operations is to provide a limited level of guest service during late night hours, thus reducing the number of employees required on the night shift. In mid-size and smaller hotels, the night auditor also serves as the front desk agent.

Part-time employees are an increasingly important source of labor for the hospitality and tourism industry. Many potential workers, such as students, parents of young children, and retirees, may not be available to work full time. Part-time workers give the front office flexibility to respond to fluctuating guest demands. For example, one front desk agent may work from 6 a.m. to 2 p.m. so that wake-up calls and check-outs can be handled more efficiently through the 7 a.m. shift change. Scheduling a front desk agent to work from 10 a.m. to 6 p.m. may allow for smooth processing of late-morning check-outs and guest arrivals during the time when evening shift staff are scheduled for a meal break. Using part-time workers can help reduce overall labor costs for the front desk because these workers are not eligible to receive benefits.

TERMS YOU SHOULD KNOW

Labor Union—an organization of workers formed for the purposes of protecting employee rights and for dealing collectively with employers about wages, hours, benefits, and working conditions.

Labor Costs—the sum of all wages paid to employees, as well as the cost of employee benefits and taxes paid by an employer.

Separation of Duties

In larger hotels, the front office may be organized according to functions, with different employees handling separate areas. This separation of duties can serve as an internal control to safeguard the integrity of front office accounting procedures. It ensures that no single individual is wholly responsible for all phases of a transaction. If the same front desk employee were allowed to sell a guestroom, post the charge, verify the posting, and collect the payment for the room, there would be no way for another staff member to detect mistakes or possible embezzlement. Instead, duties should be split among employees to maintain better control:

- Reservations agent sells the room
- Front desk agent performs the posting
- Night auditor does the verification
- Front office cashier collects the payment

Such a separation of duties may not be practical in a small hotel, where staff members are **cross-trained** and job duties are typically combined. For example, the front desk agent may also serve as the cashier and information clerk. In such situations, the front office manager must ensure the integrity of the accounting process through the other measures, such as the night audit.

Diversity

A front office that is operated by people from various races, ages, genders, and ethnic backgrounds reflects a property's value of diversity. Diverse guests feel more welcome at a diverse front desk. International guests may use the front desk to exchange currency, find a translator, or request other special assistance. Hotels that accommodate large numbers of international guests may even provide travel information and menus in various languages.

Measuring Employee Performance

Measuring and evaluating employee performance is one of a manager's toughest but most important responsibilities. Because front office employees are the face of a hotel and have the most frequent contact with guests, it is especially vital that front office mangers evaluate their staff to ensure that they are fulfilling their roles and providing the best guest service possible.

Job Descriptions

In order to measure something, you must have a measurement tool. A **job description** lists all the tasks that are required of a work position. It may also outline reporting relationships, working conditions, and necessary equipment and materials. Typically, front office managers write job descriptions for front office positions. A well-written job description can be used:

- In evaluating job performance
- As an aid in training new hires or retraining existing workers
- To prevent unnecessary duplication of duties
- To help ensure that each job task is performed
- To help determine appropriate staffing levels

Employee performance evaluations are often developed directly from job descriptions, which provide the basis for evaluating performance. Job descriptions can also be used for promotions by providing information required for determining if a current employee has the skills to perform the new job. In certain cases, job descriptions can be used for disciplinary action if employees are found not to be performing the duties outlined in the description.

Job Description—a summary of the duties, responsibilities, working conditions, and activities of a specific job.

ADA

The ADA states that people with disabilities are considered qualified for a position if they can perform the position's essential functions, with or without reasonable accommodation. Job descriptions, therefore, should list essential functions, and it is illegal for management to discriminate against an applicant with a disability who cannot perform a non-essential function. Proper job descriptions may open opportunities for qualified applicants who have disabilities covered under the ADA.

Job Specifications

Job specifications list the personal skills, qualities, and traits an employee needs to successfully perform the tasks outlined in the job description. Factors considered for job specifications are: formal education, work experience, physical requirements, and communication ability. Because of their high degree of guest contact, one of the job specifications for front office employees is extraordinary interpersonal skills.

Job Specification: Front Office Personnel

Our property considers the following traits important for the successful performance of front office work.

1. Professional Demeanor
   - Reports to work on time
   - Possesses maturity in judgment
   - Appears businesslike
   - Maintains control and composure in difficult situations
2. Congenial Nature
   - Smiles readily
   - Exhibits cordial and pleasant behavior
   - Is a people person
   - Possesses a sense of humor
3. Helpful Attitude
   - Is sensitive to guests' needs
   - Demonstrates creativity
   - Practices good listening skills
4. Flexibility
   - Willing and able to accept a different work shift if necessary
   - Understands others' points of view
   - Willing to try new ways of doing things; innovative
   - Works well with guests and hotel staff; a team player
5. Well-Groomed Appearance
   - Dresses appropriately; meets property standards for wear and care of uniform, jewelry, and personal grooming

---

Measurement Instruments

Most companies use some form of performance evaluations to gauge how well employees are meeting their goals and to help employees develop in their careers. Some hospitality and tourism companies now use software that measures employee performance in real time. It can measure data such as number of sales made, number of guests served, and time spent with each customer. This type of software can make performance evaluations a simple, ongoing process rather than a stressful annual event. Managers can align their corporate strategy with day-to-day employee activity or integrate reward programs with employee performance. Although knowing they are being evaluated every day can cause some initial stress for employees, in the long run it can actually increase staff engagement and accountability.

One traditional evaluation approach is a graphic rating scale. Using the rating scale, managers typically rate employees on 10 to 15 criteria using a scale that ranges from 1 to 5, with 1 being exceptional and 5 being poor. The criteria cover such items as quality of work, quantity of work, dependability, interaction with people, job knowledge, and attention to detail. Ratings on each item are added together and averaged to arrive at a score for each employee.

Employee Rating Scale

	Exceptional		Average		Poor
Attendance	1	2	3	4	5
Teamwork	1	2	3	4	5
Problem solving	1	2	3	4	5
Guest service	1	2	3	4	5
Communication	1	2	3	4	5

Using the rating scale above, a manager might give an employee the following scores:

- Attendance: 4
- Teamwork: 2
- Problem solving: 3
- Guest service: 3
- Communication: 3

Averaged together, these scores give the employee an overall score of 3.

Section 6.6

Guests and the Front Desk

Most guest-employee contacts are potential sales situations, but few staff members strive to make the most of these encounters. Whether checking in a guest, serving a room service meal, or managing the details of booking a large conference, many employees tend to focus entirely on the task at hand. Thus, they might miss opportunities to go beyond merely fulfilling a guest request to deliver truly outstanding service. Believe it or not, "sales" and "outstanding service" go hand in hand.

Front desk personnel are perfectly poised to raise the bar of guest service through suggestive selling. The front desk is a revenue center—a department that generates revenue for the property through the sale of products or services to guests. Front office managers should stress the importance of selling to front desk employees and help them work on their sales skills.

From the moment they make eye contact with a guest walking into the lobby until their final farewell at check-out, front desk agents create an impression that "sells" guests on your property. Suggestive selling is a form of guest service in that it shows guests that you want them to have a pleasant stay by offering them accommodations that will better meet their needs and enhance their comfort. In addition to creating a positive guest service environment that attracts and retains business, front office employees can also impact the bottom line by using suggestive selling techniques to interest a guest in a more expensive room than the one originally booked.

Managers can use the following training techniques to help front desk agents upsell guestrooms:

1. Make sure all agents know the kinds of guestrooms, facilities, and services available at the property. Participating in a property tour will increase agents' confidence by enabling them to accurately describe what they are selling.

2. Teach employees to translate the property's features into benefits. A feature is a characteristic or amenity; a benefit is how the feature addresses a guest's needs. For instance, a suite with a separate sitting area is a feature. For a business traveler, the benefit of such a room is the ability to meet with clients in the room.

3. Have employees practice their selling techniques using role-play exercises. In order to match guests with the features that will benefit them, front desk agents must know how to correctly "read" guests. For example, a family with kids who've been cooped up in the car all day might like a room near the pool. The agent could also suggest the deluxe guestroom with more space for children to play.

4. Keep agents informed of any promotions the property or chain is offering so they can suggest special promotions that may meet guests' needs. Guests like to feel that they are getting a deal.

5. Encourage front desk employees to promote the property's services—gyms, business centers, complimentary breakfast—even if they don't add to the bottom line. Giving guests information they need to have a pleasant stay is another way of providing great guest service that will keep them coming back again and again.

Green Practice Programs for Guests

Being green can have many different applications in the lodging industry from encouraging guests to reuse towels, to recycling waste, to using wind-generated electricity, to cooking with organic ingredients, to using environmentally-safe cleaning agents, to installing rooftop solar panels. Some of these practices will be discussed in greater detail in later chapters. The front office can also participate in green programs. More importantly, front office employees play a large role in educating guests about the hotel's green programs and features.

The traveling public appears to be increasingly interested in patronizing hotels that invest in environmentally-friendly buildings, equipment, processes and techniques.

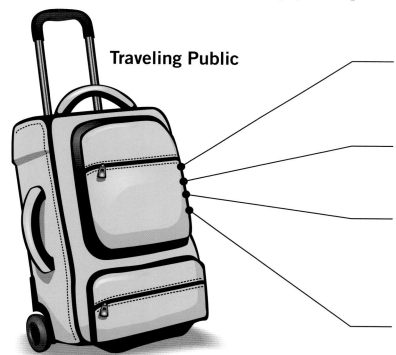

Traveling Public

Per a 2012 **TripAdvisor** study, 71 percent of U.S travelers said they plan to make more **eco-friendly** choices and 50 percent are willing to pay more for them.

About 65 percent of **Travelocity** customers said **green ratings** influence their selection when prices are the same.

Per the 2010 **Global Business Travel Association's** executive update, 30 percent of corporate travel managers said they include **green initiatives** in their policies and proposal requests.

More than 51 percent of meeting planners will hold meetings only in **green venues**.

Green Practices

Environmentally-conscious meetings are a growing trend. The Convention Industry Council, Environmental Protection Agency, and other organizations provide guidelines for green meetings. The greening of a meeting can be accomplished in many ways, including not pre-filling water glasses at banquet tables, collecting name tags and badge-holders for reuse when meetings end, providing recycling bins inside the exhibit area, and using compostable cups and other green materials.

Selling Green

Reservation agents should be thoroughly versed in the hotel's green features and programs. During the booking process, agents can take a moment to tell guests about their property's green initiatives and address any questions or concerns guests might have. This is also a good opportunity to inform guests about any green discounts the hotel offers to guests, such as discounts for electric or hybrid certified vehicles. In addition, some hotels provide visitors the opportunity to buy **carbon offsets** to offset the carbon emissions footprint generated by their travel. Guests can do so by making a contribution to organizations that fund projects that reduce the emission of greenhouse gases, such as Carbonfund and MyClimate. Carbon offset providers balance out a person's carbon impact by ensuring that somewhere else on the planet, an equivalent amount of carbon dioxide is reduced as a result of his or her offset purchase. In 2011, $576 million of carbon offsets were purchased by individuals, second only to 2008's record of $776 million.

Being Green

Front office managers and employees can do their part in contributing to the property's green efforts. The following list provides ideas for green practices that can be implemented by the front office:

- Display the property's environmental policy at the front desk and in guestrooms. Educate guests about the policy.

- Use both sides of paper when printing or making copies. Make discarded paper into message pads.

- Buy recycled paper goods for use in guestrooms, kitchen, housekeeping, and other areas of the hotel. If possible, purchase goods that are easily **biodegradable**.

- Use electronic files rather than paper ones.

- Do not deliver newspapers to each occupied room unless requested. Have the newspapers available in the lobby instead.

- Implement a recycling program for cans, bottles, cooking oil, phone books, plastic containers, computers, printer/toner cartridges, cardboard, newspaper, plastic, and other items. Place recycling containers throughout the hotel, including the guestrooms.

- Use biodegradable key cards that will completely decompose in a landfill or compost within 18 months; or use corn key cards that are manufactured from domestically-grown, 100 percent biodegradable, and annually-renewable corn.

- Shut down office equipment such as photocopiers and computer monitors when not in use.

- Reduce unwanted mail by requesting removal from direct mail lists.

TERMS YOU SHOULD KNOW

Biodegradable—objects made from organic material, such as plant and animal matter, that are capable of being broken down into harmless products by microorganisms.

Apply Your Learning

Section 6.1
1. Which hotel employees have the most frequent contact with guests?
2. What do guests do at the front desk?
3. What role does the front desk serve in emergencies?
4. Why is it so important that the front desk staff is well-trained and morale is kept high?

Section 6.2
1. Name four positions for which the front office manager is responsible.
2. What qualifications are required to become a front office manager?
3. What is key control?
4. What are the front office manager's responsibilities with regard to cash, checks, and credit?

Section 6.3
1. How does the night audit increase the likelihood of correct account settlement?
2. What is the purpose of a high-balance report?
3. Which two reports are useful when trying to identify out-of-balance accounts?
4. Which report summarizes the day's business and provides insight into revenues, receivables, operating statistics, and cash transactions related to the front office?
5. Use the audit posting formula to calculate the net outstanding balance for the following scenario. Ms. Carlson's account has a previous balance of $440. She has charged $90 at the hotel restaurant and made a payment of $55.70.

Section 6.4
1. What are the three traditional front office work shifts?
2. How can front office managers use part-time workers to manage labor costs?
3. Why is it important to maintain a separation of duties at the front desk?
4. What is one way to limit labor costs in the night hours?
5. Define the term "labor union." Explain how it applies to front office management.

Section 6.5

1. Name two uses for a job description.
2. How is a job description important in ADA hiring practices?
3. What are some examples of job specifications for front office positions?
4. What is the benefit to using software that measures employee performance in real time?
5. Explain the goals of performance evaluations.

Section 6.6

1. How can suggestive selling improve guest service?
2. How can a property tour help front desk agents be better salespeople?
3. Why should front desk agents be informed of any sales promotions your property or chain is offering?
4. Why is it important to promote the property features and services that do not add to the bottom line?

Section 6.7

1. What are some ways of making meetings green?
2. What are carbon offsets? Why might hotels wish to partner with carbon offset organizations?
3. What are the benefits of using biodegradable or corn key cards?
4. Name three front office green practices related to paper.
5. How does being green "sell" a property to guests?

Chapter 7
Managing Housekeeping Operations

COMPETENCIES

1. Identify which positions report to the executive housekeeper.
2. Identify the duties and responsibilities of the executive housekeeper.
3. Explain how the housekeeping department manages the budget process.
4. Identify methods housekeeping management can implement to control labor and linen expenses.
5. Describe how the executive housekeeper develops, communicates, and monitors performance standards for housekeeping staff.
6. Explain how the training of housekeeping staff is conducted.
7. Discuss housekeeping management's role in promoting sustainable green practices.

PALMERHOUSE
A HILTON HOTEL

**George Sous
Housekeeping Manager
The Palmer House Hilton**

Born and raised in Amman, Jordan, George Sous has long been interested in pursuing a career in hospitality. He earned a B.A. in Marketing from the University of Jordan. After immigrating to Chicago, Illinois, with his family, he enrolled in Harold Washington College to pursue a degree in Hospitality Management. During his time at Harold Washington College, Mr. Sous was able to earn different certifications from the National Restaurant Association and the American Hotel & Lodging Association, and he was selected as one of the recipients of the Gerald Roper Scholarship. He has also twice been awarded the Illinois Hotel & Lodging Association (IHLA) Scholarship.

After completing a Rooms Internship at the Palmer House, Mr. Sous enrolled in the Hilton Management Training Program, where he cross-trained in five departments, including catering, sales, events, food and beverage, and accounting and finance. He was offered an opportunity to work full time as a housekeeping manager at the Palmer House, and he hopes to transition to a front office manager position. Mr. Sous is pursuing his studies in an MBA program at Roosevelt University, with a concentration in Hospitality Management. In addition, he is a member of the Roosevelt University Hospitality Association executive board and an active member of the IHLA Under 30 Gateway.

Introduction

Efficiently managed housekeeping departments prepare guestrooms for arriving guests and maintain everything in the hotel so that the property is as fresh as the day it opened for business. Most housekeeping departments are responsible for cleaning:

- Guestrooms
- Hallways
- Public areas, such as the lobby and public restrooms
- Pool and patio areas
- Management offices
- Storage areas
- Back of house areas, such as employee locker rooms

Housekeeping employees of hotels offering mid-range or world-class service are generally responsible for cleaning additional areas, such as:

- Meeting, banquet, and dining rooms
- Convention exhibit halls
- Hotel-operated shops
- Game rooms
- Exercise rooms

Pineapple Fun Fact

There are an estimated 52,214 lodging properties in the United States, with a total of 4.8 million guestrooms available for sale each day. That's a lot of rooms to clean! For example, if the average room attendant cleans 15 rooms a day, and each guestroom has 8 pillows, then each room attendant changes an average of 120 pillow cases per day!

Other housekeeping employees work in the hotel's linen and laundry rooms. Add to this the management staff of housekeeping departments, and it's easy to see why there are usually more employees working in the housekeeping department than in any other hotel department. In fact, more than 877,980 people in the United States work as housekeeping cleaners or room attendants, with the largest percentage employed in hospitality and tourism. Other industries that employ housekeeping staff are hospitals, nursing care facilities, and facilities for the elderly.

Top States for Housekeeping Employment

1. California
2. Florida
3. Texas
4. New York
5. Illinois

Source: United States Department of Labor, Bureau of Labor Statistics, 2011

The tasks performed by a housekeeping department are critical to the smooth daily operation of any hotel. There are many management opportunities in the housekeeping department. Depending on the size of the hotel, the housekeeping department may have only one or several levels of management. For example, a large hotel may have a director of housekeeping overseeing an executive housekeeper in charge of rooms and an executive housekeeper in charge of public spaces. Another housekeeping manager may be in charge of uniforms and banquet linens. These managers would, in turn, oversee floor supervisors, project supervisors, and other assistant supervisors.

Organizational Chart for a Large Mid-Market Hotel

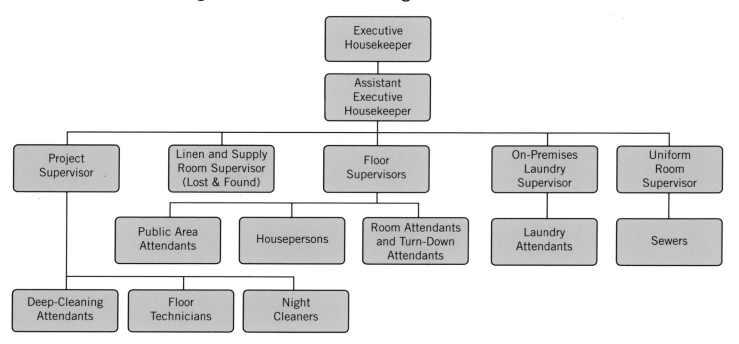

Being the Executive Housekeeper

Area Inventory List—all items within each area of a hotel that are the responsibility of housekeeping.

Frequency Schedule—indicates how often items on area inventory lists are to be cleaned or maintained.

Deep Cleaning—the process of taking a room out of inventory and cleaning it more thoroughly than during regular daily maintenance.

Like all other managers in a hotel, the executive housekeeper uses available resources to meet the objectives set by top management executives. Planning is the executive housekeeper's most important management function. Without adequate planning, every day would present one crisis or another. Constant crises decrease employee morale, decrease productivity, and drive expenses higher. Also, without the focus that planning provides, the executive housekeeper can easily become sidetracked by tasks unrelated to meeting the hotel's objectives.

Planning

Planning the work of the housekeeping department begins with the executive housekeeper creating **area inventory lists**. These are lists of all items within each area that will need housekeeping's attention. Area inventory lists are long and extremely detailed. Since most properties offer several different types of guestrooms, separate inventory lists may be needed for each room type. The list should follow the order in which room attendants will clean items and in which supervisors will inspect them. This enables the executive housekeeper to use the inventory lists as the basis for developing cleaning procedures, training plans, and inspection checklists.

Frequency schedules show how often items on area inventory lists are to be cleaned or maintained. Some items must be cleaned every day. Others must be cleaned or maintained on a weekly, biweekly, or monthly schedule. These items become part of a **deep-cleaning** program and are scheduled as special projects. Whenever possible, special cleaning projects should be scheduled when occupancy is low. Also, deep cleaning must be flexible. For example, if maintenance schedules repair work on several guestrooms, the executive housekeeper should make an effort to schedule around these projects. Most guestrooms are deep cleaned between two and four times a year depending on occupancy levels. Higher occupancy results in more wear and tear on the furniture and fixtures in guestrooms. Therefore, a hotel with higher occupancy will need to deep clean its guestrooms more often than one with lower occupancy.

Sample Frequency Schedule

Special Projects	Frequency	
	Per Week	Per Month
1. Wash down tile walls in restrooms	1	
2. Strip and wax the following:		
Restrooms (as necessary)		1
Basement hallway	1	
Lounge, lobby, and stairs		1
3. Shampoo the following:		
Registration area		1
Stairs		1
Restrooms		1
All dining rooms		2
All lounges		1
Coffee shop		1
Meeting rooms		1
Guest elevators		1
Employee cafeteria (as needed)	2	
4. Spot shampoo the following:		
Front entrance		2
Side entrance		2
Front desk area		2
5. Wash windows in pool area		1
6. Dust louvers in pool area		1
7. Clean guest and service elevator tracks	1	
8. Polish kitchen equipment		1
9. Polish drinking fountains	1	
10. Clean outside of guest elevators	2	

Collaborating with the Front Office

Teamwork between housekeeping and the front office is essential to daily hotel operations. The front desk agent cannot assign guestrooms until the rooms have been cleaned, inspected, and released by the housekeeping department. Typically, rooms are recycled for sale according to the following process.

Each night, a front desk agent creates an **occupancy report**. It lists rooms occupied that night and indicates guests who are expected to check out the next day. The executive housekeeper picks up this list early the next morning and schedules the occupied rooms for cleaning. As guests check out of the hotel, the front desk notifies housekeeping about the change in room status. Housekeeping gives these rooms top priority so that clean rooms are available for arriving guests. The executive housekeeper assigns guestrooms for cleaning based on their status. The chart on page 128 defines typical room status terms used in the lodging industry.

Housekeeping Status Report—shows the current housekeeping status of each room.

Room Status Discrepancy—a situation in which the housekeeping department's description of a room's status differs from the room status information being used by the front desk to assign guestrooms.

Room Status	What It Means
Early make-up request	These rooms should be cleaned first to meet guest needs.
Vacant and dirty	Cleaning vacant rooms before stayover rooms helps arriving guests get into their rooms more quickly. These rooms are also called check-out rooms and should be cleaned early in the shift.
Stayover	The guest is not checking out today and will remain for at least one more night. These rooms can be cleaned later in the shift.
Late check-out rooms	The guest has requested to check out later than the standard time. The room should not be cleaned until the guest has checked out.
DND (Do Not Disturb)	The guest has requested not to be disturbed. Check back on this room later in the shift.
No service	The guest has requested that the room not be cleaned. Do not put this room on the schedule today.
Vacant and ready	The room has been cleaned and inspected and is ready for an arriving guest.

At the end of the shift, the executive housekeeper prepares a **housekeeping status report** based on a physical check of each room in the property. This report shows the current housekeeping status of each room. It is compared to the front desk occupancy report, and any discrepancies are brought to the attention of the front office manager. **Room status discrepancies** can affect the hotel's ability to meet guests' needs and maximize rooms revenue. If a room is clean and ready for sale but the front desk agent does not know it, the agent may turn away business needlessly.

Green Practices

New guestroom key-card systems allow the front desk to track when a room is occupied. These key-card systems also helps control energy usage and costs. As guests enter their room, they place the card in a key-card reader, which initiates "comfort" mode. This mode turns on the lights and the heating or air conditioning and allows guests to control the thermostat. As guests take the card and leave, the system initiates "energy saving" mode. The lights turn off after 15 seconds, and the heating or air defaults to a predetermined temperature. Such a system can provide about 25-40 percent savings on guestroom energy costs.

Sample Housekeeping Status Report

| Housekeeper's Report | | | | | | A.M. | |
| Date _____ , 20 _____ | | | | | | P.M. | |

ROOM NUMBER	STATUS	ROOM NUMBER	STATUS	ROOM NUMBER	STATUS	ROOM NUMBER	STATUS
101		126		151		176	
102		127		152		177	
103		128		153		178	
104		129		154		179	
105		130		155		180	
106		131		156		181	
107		132		157		182	
108		133		158		183	
120		145		170		195	
121		146		171		196	
122		147		172		197	
123		148		173		198	
124		149		174		199	
125		150		175		200	

Remarks:

_____

_____

_____

_____

Housekeeper's Signature

Legend:
- ✓ - Occupied
- 000 - Out of Order
- —— - Vacant
- B - Slept Out (Baggage Still in Room)
- X - Occupied, No Baggage
- C.O. - Slept In but Checked Out Early A.M.
- E.A. - Early Arrival

Promptly notifying the front desk of the housekeeping status of rooms is a tremendous help in registering guests who arrive early, especially during high-occupancy and sold-out periods. In a computerized room-status system, housekeeping and the front desk have instant access to room information. When a guest checks out, a front desk agent enters the departure into the system. Housekeeping is then automatically alerted that the room is vacant and ready to be cleaned. Next, housekeeping attendants clean the room and notify the housekeeping supervisor that the room is ready for inspection. Once the room is inspected, the inspector enters this information into the system. The front office is notified that the room is available for sale.

Building a Budget

Fiscal Year—a 12-month period, which may not necessarily coincide with the calendar year, over which a company budgets its spending. Also known as the financial year or budget year.

Cost per Occupied Room—the expenses required to operate each occupied room in the hotel, which include salaries and wages and the usage rates for recycled and non-recycled inventory items.

Since housekeeping is not a revenue-generating department, the executive housekeeper's primary responsibility in achieving the property's financial goals is to control the department's expenses. This can be accomplished through careful budget planning. The budget projects the revenue the hotel anticipates receiving and the expenses required during the **fiscal year**.

Planning the Budget

The process of planning an annual operating budget generally takes several months and requires cooperation from managers across all departments. The first step in budget planning is to forecast room sales. As you learned in Chapter 6, occupancy forecasts are usually developed by the front office manager. The forecast is based on past room sales, as well as on information from the marketing department about the expected effect on sales of various special events, advertising, and promotions.

Once occupancy levels are predicted, the executive housekeeper can use those figures to determine expected costs. These expenses are expressed in terms of **cost per occupied room**, which includes the salaries and wages for housekeeping staff, cleaning supplies, guest supplies, laundry, and linens required to clean that room. By specifying expense levels in relation to room sales, the budget actually expresses the level of service the hotel will be able to provide. If the budget for housekeeping is cut, some services will have to be eliminated or downgraded.

Using the Budget as a Control Tool

Each month, the hotel's accounting department produces statements that show each department's actual expenses. The executive housekeeper compares these numbers with the amounts in the budget. If there is a discrepancy, the executive housekeeper must determine why it exists. One explanation could be that the actual occupancy levels varied from what was predicted. If the number of occupied rooms was lower than expected, the department's actual expenses should also decrease. If the occupancy levels were higher than expected, there would be an increase in expenses. Small variations from the budget are normal; however, any major deviations should be investigated. The executive housekeeper should be ready to formulate a plan to get the department back on budget if needed. This might require re-examining staffing or standard practices within the department.

Budgeting Labor and Linen Expenses

Nearly all the expenses the executive housekeeper is responsible for are directly dependent on the number of occupied rooms the housekeeping department will have to service. The main expenses of the housekeeping department are:

Salaries and Wages—Using the occupancy forecasts, the executive housekeeper can determine the number of labor hours needed for each job category per budget period. Then, he or she can multiply the number of hours by the position's per-hour wage. By adding the calculations for all the positions together, a total wage cost can be determined for each budget period.

Employee Benefits—The costs of employee benefits depend on the number of labor hours expected to be scheduled, the types of job classifications involved, and the property's policies regarding benefits. The human resources department can help the executive housekeeper plan benefits expenses.

Outside Services—If the hotel employs outside contractors for major cleaning projects or for laundry services, then the costs of those services are averaged throughout the budget period.

In-House Laundry—The cost of laundering room linens and uniforms can be budgeted based on occupancy levels. Multiplying the cost of laundry operations per occupied room by the number of occupied rooms forecast for each budget period will provide the total for laundry expenses.

Operating Supplies—This category includes non-recycled items such as guest supplies and amenities, cleaning supplies, and small equipment. The executive housekeeper can budget for the costs of these items on the basis of cost per occupied room.

Uniforms—The cost of new and replacement uniforms, as well as laundry or dry-cleaning costs for uniforms, must be included in the housekeeping budget. These costs can vary greatly depending on employee turnover and new hires. The executive housekeeper must create an annual plan for uniform replacement based on the number of employees and the cost for each uniform piece.

Linens—Like uniforms, linens are a recycled inventory item, meaning that these items can be cleaned and reused. However, their lifespans are ultimately limited, and new linens must be purchased throughout the year as older linens are removed from service due to loss, damage, or wear. The budget costs of replacing linens are also tied to occupancy, as higher occupancy means linens will wear out faster. The following section explains the annual linen purchase in more detail.

Fixed Staff Positions—must be filled regardless of the volume of business.

Variable Staff Positions— filled in relation to changes in hotel occupancy.

Labor Costs

Labor is the greatest single housekeeping expense. The first step toward budgeting for labor costs is to determine which positions within the housekeeping department are fixed and which are variable depending upon occupancy levels at the hotel.

Fixed staff positions are those that must be filled regardless of the volume of business. They are generally managerial and administrative and may include:

- Executive housekeeper
- Assistant executive housekeeper
- Supervisor
- Department clerk (day and afternoon shifts)

Employees in these positions are usually scheduled to work at least 40 hours a week, regardless of the occupancy level at the hotel.

Variable staff positions include:

- Room attendants (day and afternoon shifts)
- Housepersons (day and afternoon shifts)
- Inspectors
- Laundry attendants
- Lobby attendants

The number of employees scheduled to work in these positions is determined primarily by the number of rooms occupied during the previous night (or expected to be occupied, based on past history and existing reservations). Generally, the higher the previous night's occupancy, the more employees must be scheduled to work the next day. The number of housepersons and lobby attendants needed for any given shift may also vary in relation to meeting room and banquet functions and convention and restaurant business.

Linen Replacement

After salaries and wages, linens are the next highest expense in the housekeeping budget. The initial purchase of linens for the hotel will greatly influence the costs of replacing lost or damaged linens. The fabric type, size, and color influence both price and lifespan of linens. Colored items are usually more expensive and have shorter lifespans than white ones since the colors fade through repeated washings. The lifespan of linen is measured in terms of how many times it can be laundered before becoming too worn to be suitable for guestroom use.

Physical inventory records show the executive housekeeper how long the existing stock of linens will last and how much of each type of linen needs to be reordered to maintain par levels. Linens are purchased annually, with deliveries scheduled quarterly to ensure there is enough storage space. Also, ordering large quantities is often less expensive.

Formula for Annual Linen Purchase

$$\left\{ \textbf{Par Stock Level} - \text{Linen on Hand} = \textbf{Annual Order} \right\}$$

The executive housekeeper must carefully select suppliers and linen products to ensure the hotel receives good value for the money spent. Buying cheaper linen that wears out quickly can actually cost more in the long term because the linen has to be replaced more frequently and poor linen quality can lower guests' perceptions of the property. Durability, laundry considerations, and purchase price are the main criteria to use in selecting linen. The laundering costs over the lifespan of a linen product can be determined by multiplying the item's weight by the hotel's laundering cost per pound, then multiplying again by the number of launderings the item can withstand before wearing out. With this information, a cost per use can be calculated to evaluate alternative linen purchases using the following formula:

Formula for Cost per Use

$$\left\{ \frac{\textbf{Purchase Cost} + \text{Lifespan Laundering Cost}}{\textbf{Number of Lifespan Launderings}} = \textbf{Cost per Use} \right\}$$

Managing Housekeeping Performance Standards

The executive housekeeper can begin to develop performance standards by answering the question, "What must be done in order to clean or maintain the major items within this area?" Standards are required-quality levels of performance. Performance standards are not only what must be done, they also describe in detail how the job must be done.

One of the primary objectives of planning the work of the housekeeping department is to ensure that all employees carry out their cleaning tasks in a consistent manner. The keys to consistency are the performance standards that the executive housekeeper develops, communicates, and manages. If performance standards are not properly managed, the productivity of the housekeeping department suffers because employees will not be performing their tasks in the most efficient and effective manner.

The most important part of developing standards is understanding how cleaning and other tasks are carried out. Employees who actually perform the tasks should be asked to contribute to creating the standards that will eventually be adopted by the entire housekeeping department.

Well-written standards are useless unless they are applied. Performance standards must be communicated to employees through ongoing training programs. The executive housekeeper is responsible for making sure that standards are being applied consistently. The best way to check this is through inspection. Daily inspections and regularly scheduled performance evaluations should be followed by specific on-the-job coaching and retraining. The executive housekeeper should review the department's performance standards at least once a year and make appropriate revisions as new work methods are implemented.

Diversity

Cultural diversity is very common in housekeeping departments, especially in major U.S. urban centers. A variety of languages may be spoken by the housekeeping staff, and some employees may not be able to communicate well in English. Executive housekeepers must be aware of these diversity issues so they can tailor training programs and department communications to the specific needs of their employees.

Training Housekeeping Staff

One of the executive housekeeper's responsibilities is to ensure that housekeeping employees receive proper training. Although other supervisors or the training department may do the actual training, the executive housekeeper's job is to make sure training programs are in place and that employees participate in the training. Whether training a new group of employees or experienced staff members, a four-step training method works best. The four steps are: prepare, present, practice, and follow up.

Prepare

Preparation is essential to successful training. Otherwise, the training may be out of sequence and key details may be missing. The foundation for training employees and preventing performance problems is **job analysis**. Job analysis involves three steps: identifying job knowledge, creating a task list, and developing a job breakdown for each task performed by each housekeeping position.

1. **Job knowledge:** identifies what an employee needs to know to perform his or her job. For example, room attendants need to know knowledge for all employees, such as bloodborne pathogens and ADA information; knowledge for all housekeeping employees, such as courtesy and security; and knowledge for room attendants, such as unusual guest situations and deep-cleaning techniques.

2. **Task list:** the tasks should reflect the total job responsibility of the employee. If possible, the tasks should be listed in the order they are performed on a daily basis. The tasks should be observable and measurable.

3. **Job breakdown:** the format can vary by property but should include a list of equipment and supplies needed to perform the task, as well as steps, how-tos, and tips explaining the methods of performing the task.

TERMS YOU SHOULD KNOW

Job Analysis—determining what knowledge an employee must have, what tasks each employee needs to perform, and the standards at which he or she must perform them.

Clean the Toilet

Materials needed: *gloves, goggles, cleaning supplies, a damp sponge, a toilet bowl brush, dry cloths, a pen, and a room assignment sheet.*

STEPS	HOW-TOs
1. Put on protective gloves and goggles.	
2. Flush the toilet and make a note on your room assignment sheet if it does not flush and fill properly.	
3. Spray cleaning solution on the inside and outside of the toilet, the walls beside and behind the toilet, and under the vanity.	
4. Clean the area around the toilet.	❑ Using a sponge, wipe the walls around the toilet. ❑ Wipe the pipes leading to the toilet. ❑ Wipe the wall under the vanity and the drain pipe. ❑ Wipe the top, lid, seat, and outside of the toilet.
5. Clean the inside of the toilet.	❑ Use a toilet bowl brush to scrub the inside of the toilet bowl. Be sure to clean under the rim and the seat. ❑ Rinse the brush in the toilet when you are done and flush. This brush should only be used for cleaning the toilet.
6. Polish the toilet.	❑ Use a dry cloth to wipe the outside of the toilet. Polish the walls and pipes at the same time.

The next step in preparing for training is analyzing what employees need to know. New employees have to be trained in all the tasks, but they can't realistically be expected to learn everything before their first day on the job. Therefore, the executive housekeeper must prioritize the tasks to be learned 1) before working alone on the job; 2) within two weeks on the job; or 3) within two months on the job. Current employees may sometimes need refresher training in a particular area, or the entire department might require training on a new task or procedure.

Present

If possible, give employees time to prepare for training by providing them with an overview of what will be covered in the training at least one day in advance. Using the job breakdown as a training guide, show employees what to do, how to do it, and why the details are important. When explaining each step of the training, demonstrate it. Make sure employees see exactly what is being shown and have an opportunity to ask questions. Be sure to take enough time when presenting the training and repeat as necessary to ensure that all employees understand. Avoid using jargon because employees who are new to the industry may not understand it.

Practice

Trainees should try to perform the tasks alone. Immediate practice results in good work habits. Have each trainee demonstrate each step of the task presented during the training session. This will indicate whether trainees really do understand. Compliment the employee if the task is done correctly, and gently correct him or her when it is not. Bad habits formed during this stage of the training may be very difficult to break later. Be sure that the employee understands not just how to perform a task but also the purpose of each step.

Follow Up

There are a number of things managers can do to follow up on training:

- Provide opportunities for employees to offer feedback on the training.
- Continue coaching on the job.
- Give positive feedback when employees are performing the job well and corrective feedback to help employees improve.
- Evaluate employees' progress using a checklist. Provide further training for tasks that have not been mastered.

Managing Housekeeping Green Practices

Just-in-Time Buying—the practice of buying products just before they are needed.

Housekeeping managers today play an important role in ensuring their properties are wisely using resources, preventing waste, and contributing to an environment that is safe to live in. Given how much of the property housekeeping employees see and touch every day, they are in an ideal position to identify potential green opportunities. The executive housekeeper in particular is responsible for a wide variety of green management duties, including:

Communication: Housekeeping managers must communicate information about the property's green initiatives to staff and guests. It is also helpful to create a formal process for employees and guests to provide feedback on green practices.

Training: The annual cost of energy and water for a hotel can be reduced by as much as 10 percent by training employees to operate the hotel efficiently. It is essential to train housekeeping and laundry attendants to follow the hotel's green policies.

Purchasing: The executive housekeeper can implement green practices in purchasing, including buying in bulk, using local suppliers, buying more durable supplies for longer use, and **just-in-time buying** to reduce waste. Sometimes, employees may use more of a product if there is a large quantity of it on the shelf, while they are more likely to conserve it if there is a small amount.

Green practices can be implemented in many ways within the housekeeping department.

Water Conservation

- Implement towel and linen reuse programs in guestrooms.
- Install low-flow faucets, shower heads, and toilets in guestrooms.
- Install automatic faucets and toilets in public restrooms.
- Switch to water-efficient washing machines.
- Wash only full loads of laundry.

Energy Efficiency

- Turn off heating and cooling systems, coffee makers, hair dryers, televisions, radios, and other appliances in unoccupied guestrooms.
- Use natural lighting while cleaning guestrooms.
- Limit the amount of hot water used for cleaning.
- Close draperies and shades when leaving guestrooms.
- Use the coolest temperature setting for washers.

Waste Management

- Place recycling receptacles in guestrooms for paper, glass, and cans.
- Purchase toilet paper, tissues, and paper towels with recycled content.
- Reuse retired linens by turning old sheets into laundry bags and stained tablecloths into napkins.
- Donate old linens, clothing hangers, and other items to homeless shelters, humane societies, veterinarian offices, thrift shops, etc.
- Purchase items that use reduced packaging or for which the supplier takes the packaging back and reuses it.
- Use dispensers for amenities instead of single-use disposable bottles.

Indoor Air Quality

- Use High Efficiency Particulate Air (HEPA) filters and replace them regularly.
- Clean air handler units and coils at least annually.
- Eliminate moisture or standing water that promotes mold and mildew growth.
- Use environmentally preferred cleaners.

Cleaning Chemicals

- Purchase biodegrade, low toxicity, and low volatile organic compounds (VOCs) cleaning products because they are safer for employees and guests.
- Use as little of the chemical as possible to achieve the desired result.
- Dispose of chemicals properly through the waste management system, not the storm sewer system.
- Clean up chemical spills safely and as quickly as possible to prevent them from soaking into surfaces or entering the ventilation system.

Apply Your Learning

Section 7.1
1. In addition to guestrooms and public areas, which additional areas might housekeeping employees be responsible for cleaning in mid-range and world-class hotels?
2. What industries other than hospitality and tourism employ housekeepers and room attendants?
3. Name three levels of management positions in the housekeeping department.
4. What are the top two states for housekeeping employment? Why do you think this might be?
5. What public areas might the housekeeping department have to clean?

Section 7.2
1. How does the executive housekeeper use frequency schedules?
2. Planning the work of the housekeeping department begins with creating _____.
3. Which type of rooms should be cleaned first?
4. Why is it important to promptly notify the front desk of the housekeeping status of rooms?
5. What is a room status discrepancy? Why is it important to correct it as soon as possible?

Section 7.3
1. What is the difference between a fiscal year and a calendar year?
2. What does the executive housekeeper use to calculate expected costs for the budget?
3. What is included in the cost per occupied room?
4. Why is it important to ensure that the housekeeping department's actual expenses are in line with budgeted costs and actual occupancy levels?
5. What should happen if the executive housekeeper finds that expenses have majorly deviated from the budget?

Section 7.4
1. What is the greatest housekeeping department expense?
2. Which type of positions must be filled regardless of business volume?
3. How is the lifespan of linen determined? Explain your answer.
4. What must the executive housekeeper take into account when selecting linen to purchase?
5. Name three variable staff positions in the housekeeping department.

Section 7.5

1. Why is it important that employees perform tasks in a consistent manner?
2. Who should participate in developing performance standards? Explain your answer.
3. How can the executive housekeeper make sure that performance standards are being applied?
4. What is the best way to communicate performance standards to employees?

Section 7.6

1. What are the three steps of a job analysis?
2. Which step of the training process involves trainees trying to perform the tasks alone?
3. Which training document includes a list of equipment and supplies, steps, how-tos, and tips explaining the methods of performing the task?
4. What are some things managers can do to follow up on training?
5. What might happen if employees form bad work habits during training?

Section 7.7

1. Why are housekeeping employees crucial to identifying green opportunities within a hotel?
2. How can just-in-time buying help reduce waste? Explain your answer.
3. Explain how housekeeping management's purchasing decisions can affect green practices at a property.
4. List three ways that the housekeeping department can limit employee and guest exposure to harmful chemicals.
5. How can housekeeping employees contribute to the hotel's energy efficiency? Write a short paragraph explaining steps they can take to save energy.

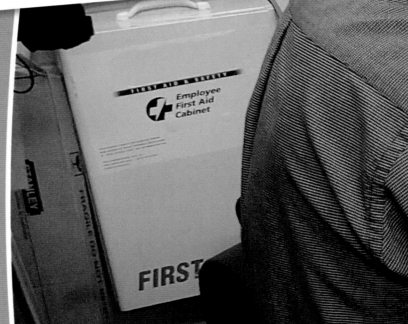

Chapter 8

Leadership and Facilities Management

COMPETENCIES

1. Summarize the duties and responsibilities of the chief engineer.

2. Analyze how ADA improvements affect the budgetary process.

3. Identify various measures facilities managers can take to manage and conserve energy.

4. Describe common emergency systems and their associated maintenance procedures.

5. Explain the benefits of using green building materials.

6. Identify ways the facilities management team can reduce a property's carbon footprint.

HD SUPPLY
HOSPITALITY SOLUTIONS

Geoff Feingold, CMHS
Director of National
Accounts
HD Supply

Geoff Feingold has more than 23 years of hospitality industry experience. Since 2001, Mr. Feingold has held leadership roles within the hospitality division of HD Supply, formerly The Home Depot Supply and Maintenance Warehouse. He was a national account manager for the first five years and then was promoted to director of national accounts. Prior to his role at HD Supply, he served as director of quality assurance for Wyndham Worldwide, as well as in other positions for the company's franchise services and property openings departments.

Mr. Feingold has also held positions on several industry association committees, including the American Resort Development Association (ARDA) Suppliers Council and AH&LA's Extended Stay Council. In 2011, Mr. Feingold began a two-year term as chairman of the AH&LA Allied Executive Committee (AEC).

Section 8.1

Introduction

The hospitality and tourism industry of today relies on well-designed and well-maintained facilities as a key element of its business. Guests want a safe and comfortable environment in which to conduct business, entertain, relax, dine, and sleep. The hotel, restaurant, club, or spa is their home away from home, and they usually want it to be better than home. Facilities play critical and varied roles in the hospitality and tourism industry, including:

- **Guest satisfaction:** Facilities can provide an appealing environment that contributes to the ambiance, experience, and comfort of the guest. In the case of destination resorts, theme restaurants, casinos, theme parks, and water attractions, the facilities themselves are the attraction.

- **Manufacturing plant:** Facilities house and interconnect the equipment and systems that allow the operation to function. Power and communication cables, elevators, and kitchen or laundry equipment are part of the manufacturing role of facilities. The facilities are also the workspace of the employees. Back of house areas need to be efficient, comfortable, and safe.

- **Market identity:** Characteristic roof shapes, signs, colors, and other trademark elements create an image for various hospitality and tourism businesses and help draw customers. Travelers quickly learn to identify various businesses by the appearance of their facilities.

- **Industry growth:** In an era of e-commerce, the hospitality and tourism industry remains a business that requires a unique "space" (facility) to produce and deliver its service. While some growth can be achieved by higher prices and more customers served, growth mostly comes through the addition of facilities, such as a chain restaurant adding more locations.

It takes a team of people from various backgrounds to create the right blend of facilities to meet guest needs. Facilities are created by the combined efforts of construction workers, architects, engineers, interior designers, and craftspeople. They are then cleaned by housekeeping staff. The facilities management department, however, holds the primary responsibility for making sure all facilities are maintained and remain in proper working order.

 ## Pineapple Fun Fact

There are many theme parks and themed restaurants around the world. One theme park with distinctive facilities is the LEGOLAND® brand of parks, with locations in the United States, United Kingdom, Malaysia, Denmark, and Germany. The parks' rides are all LEGO themed, and many are made to appear as if they are built out of LEGO bricks. Each park includes a Miniland area with models of landmarks and scenes from around the world made from millions of LEGO bricks. Both U.S. locations feature a water park, and the LEGOLAND® California Resort will soon include a LEGO-themed hotel.

Function of the Chief Engineer

F acilities managers in charge of lodging properties may have one of a variety of titles, such as chief engineer, director of engineering, director of property operations, or director of facilities. Their responsibilities may vary as well. Small, economy lodging properties have chief engineers who do much of the work themselves and require more technical than managerial skills. At larger properties, the chief engineer is more of a manager, controlling a large budget and staff. In commercial buildings, facilities managers may also oversee housekeeping and security activities.

Facilities staffing varies with the age of the property, services offered, and the types of systems it has. Staffing also depends on whether most repairs and renovations are covered by in-house staff or contract services. In lodging, staffing levels of 2.5 to 4 facilities staff per 100 rooms is the average.

Job Title: Chief Engineer

Job Description: Manages and coordinates the work of a skilled engineering staff, placing particular emphasis on guest satisfaction and maintaining the property in good working condition.

Responsibilities:

Technical

- Current on all safety and sanitation policies and procedures
- Familiar with chillers, cooling towers, chemical treatments, water systems, boilers, refrigeration systems, compressors, etc.
- Strong energy management background
- Strong skills in HVAC, electrical, mechanical, plumbing, carpentry, etc.

Managerial

- Interviewing, hiring, and training employees; planning, assigning, and directing work; evaluating employee performance
- Instilling a guest service and "can-do" attitude in all employees
- Ability to sell concepts and ideas to management, peers, and employees
- Ability to lead by example and hands-on approach to management

---

Cost Control

Cost control is one of the top priorities of the chief engineer. Hospitality and tourism facilities generate several types of costs. First, the facilities must be designed, developed, and constructed. Once occupied, they must be operated. Eventually, they must be renovated and modernized. Each of these phases has its own unique expenses.

Costs of Development and Construction

Even a 100-room economy hotel can cost several million dollars to build, while a large luxury property could cost several hundred million dollars. These costs include construction; furniture, fixtures, and equipment (FF&E); development, including fees (architectural, consultant, legal, accounting) and payments (surveys, feasibility studies, insurance, soil tests); and financing. Hotels also have pre-opening costs, which include employee salaries, training, advertising, promotions, and office expenses.

Hotel Development Costs

Cost Category	Percent of Total
Construction	60-65
FF&E	15-18
Development	10-12
Financing	8-10
Pre-opening	3-4
Working Capital	1-2
Reserve for Opening Shortfall	3-5

*Excluding land, which can be 10 to 20 percent of the final total.

A facility that is constructed with appropriate quality and good budget control should have predictable maintenance and operating costs. However, one that was poorly designed or built with cost overruns or cost-cutting due to poor budget planning, poor project management, or poor construction practices will face major problems in the first few years of operation.

Capital Expenditures (CapEx)—the money used by a company to improve long-term physical assets such as property, buildings, or equipment. These are expenditures over a minimum dollar amount for the purchase of items and equipment expected to last more than one year.

Costs of Operation

The two main categories of facilities operation are maintenance and utilities. Lodging properties refer to maintenance as property operation and maintenance (POM) and restaurants refer to it as repair and maintenance (R&M). Restaurants typically spend more on utilities than hotels, but restaurant costs are lower because they do not include labor.

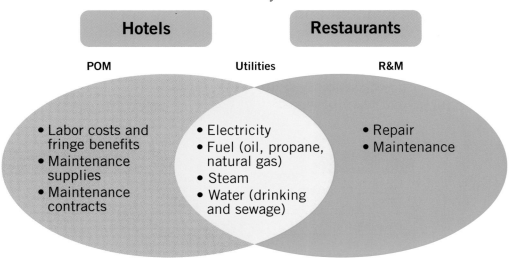

Hotels

POM

- Labor costs and fringe benefits
- Maintenance supplies
- Maintenance contracts

Utilities

- Electricity
- Fuel (oil, propane, natural gas)
- Steam
- Water (drinking and sewage)

Restaurants

R&M

- Repair
- Maintenance

POM and utilities costs vary based on occupancy—the higher the occupancy, the more of a building is heated and cooled and the more equipment is operated. Weather plays a large role in determining utilities costs. In addition, the costs of POM will generally correlate to the construction costs of a property. That is, the more you spend to build the property, the more you spend to maintain it.

Costs of Renovation and Modernization

One of the jobs of the chief engineer is to plan for and implement **capital expenditures (CapEx)**. CapEx can include replacing worn-out furniture or equipment, as well as replacement due to changing technology or market demand. In addition, CapEx covers franchise product demands and regulatory requirements such as the ADA.

Budgeting to Meet ADA Requirements

M any factors must be taken into consideration when planning and designing a new property or renovating an existing property. Hospitality and tourism businesses are subject to a variety of regulations, from zoning codes to health standards to sign ordinances. Buildings must comply with local building and fire codes. The aim of these codes and regulations is to keep guests safe. Construction or renovation budgets must account for meeting these regulations

The chief engineer must also confirm that the property is in compliance with the ADA. One lengthy section of the ADA deals with public accommodations, including lodging. Non-compliance with the law leaves properties vulnerable to lawsuits either from individuals or the U.S. Department of Justice, the government body tasked with enforcing ADA compliance. Many properties set aside a part of the budget for meeting ADA requirements.

To help new lodging properties comply with the law, the U.S. Department of Justice has identified these five steps:

1. Obtain copies of the ADA requirements and give them to your architect and building contractor.

2. Tell your architect and building contractor that you expect your new facility to comply with the ADA.

3. Make sure the building plans do not contain common ADA mistakes.

4. Make sure the facility is being built according to the ADA requirements as shown in the building plans.

5. Inspect the facility at the completion of construction to identify ADA mistakes and have them fixed.

Common ADA Accommodations at Lodging Properties

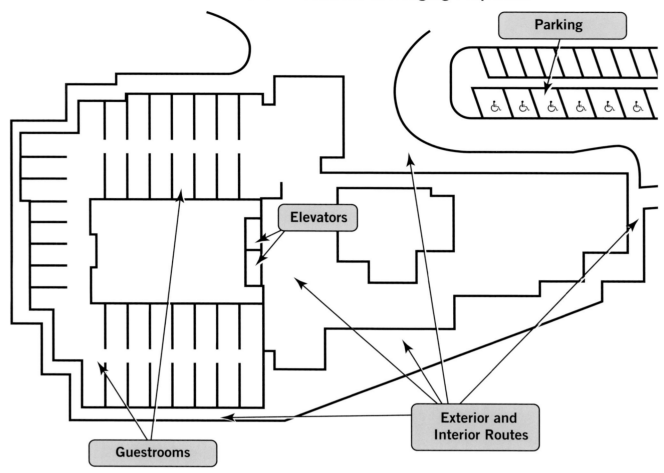

Guestrooms

- Door width of at least 32 inches
- Visual notification devices, including fire alarms
- Lowered light switches
- Roll-in shower

Elevators

- Wheelchair accessible
- Audible floor indicators and Braille control signals

Exterior and Interior Routes

- Wheelchair-accessible sidewalks, walkways, and hallways
- Ramps for those unable to climb stairs

Parking

- Accessible parking spaces
- Van-accessible spaces

Energy Management

Energy includes usage of electricity, fuel, water and sewage, and steam. By-products of energy usage include carbon dioxide and particulate matter. Energy management and conservation attempt to reduce energy usage, resulting in cost savings and a reduction in environmental pollution. Examples of **energy management** actions are:

- Keeping records of energy usage and costs
- Properly maintaining equipment
- Using proper operating methods and records

Energy Management

The facilities manager should monitor energy usage and the amount paid for energy. Using computerized controls, facilities managers can obtain records of energy usage over time as well as instantaneous usage. Another helpful monitoring strategy is using **submetering**, which allows for usage to be matched to specific operations, such as the laundry.

Proper maintenance of equipment is key to achieving top performance. Cleaning, lubricating, and aligning equipment makes it operate more efficiently. Facilities staff and other employees must be trained in how to properly operate equipment to maximize efficiency because efficient use leads to lower overall costs.

Energy Management— measures taken to achieve the minimum possible energy use and cost while maintaining comfort levels.

Submetering—monitoring the energy consumption of individual equipment or operational areas.

Waste Energy—the energy, such as heat, produced as a by-product of energy consumption.

Energy Conservation

Opportunities for energy conservation and cost savings include:

- Improving efficiency
- Reducing operating hours
- Reducing the load being supplied
- Recovering and reusing waste energy
- Using the least costly energy source

The amount of energy used by any equipment is significantly influenced by the efficiency of the equipment. Facilities managers must decide whether the benefits of updating old, inefficient equipment outweigh the energy costs of operating outdated equipment. Another way to save energy is reducing operating hours, that is, turning equipment off. For example, turning off indoor and outdoor lighting, computers, and copiers for part of the day can prevent unnecessary energy usage.

Reducing energy loads is an often-overlooked option. Window film can reduce solar heat gain, low volume shower heads and toilets reduce the amount of water required, and roof insulation can cut down on heating and cooling costs. Hospitality and tourism operations have a number of opportunities to recover and use **waste energy**. One option for all commercial buildings is recovery of heat or cold from exhaust air, or air that is removed from an air-conditioned space and discharged to the outdoors. Pre-heating or cooling the building's incoming air via the exhaust air is a way to recover and reuse waste energy. Heat can also be recovered from exhaust air and discharged water from the laundry. Some facilities have found ways to produce some of their own power from solar or steam. In addition, careful recordkeeping and research can lead to finding a less costly energy source. It may be worthwhile to hire an outside company to conduct an audit of the utility bills.

Emergency Systems Planning

Because of their knowledge of the facility and its systems, facilities managers play a leadership role in property emergency planning. If a catastrophic event causes damage to the facility, the staff must be prepared to secure the facility from further damage and restore the facility to proper operation. Facilities have a variety of emergency systems to ensure guest and employee safety during emergencies. These include:

- Power
- Lighting
- Communications

Power

Emergency power systems supply power to the building during temporary interruptions. They are generally required for all types of hospitality businesses except possibly very small food service establishments. Among the items that might be connected to this system are lighting, fire detection and alarm systems, fire pumps, and public safety communications systems. The two main types of emergency power systems are:

- Battery backup units: standby power supply (SPS) or uninterruptible power supply (UPS)
- Generators

Emergency power systems must be properly maintained and tested to make sure they will operate correctly when needed. Maintenance may include:

- Checking the charge and fluid levels of batteries
- Checking proper ventilation of battery rooms
- Cleaning battery terminals to prevent corrosion
- Testing generator systems

Lighting

Emergency lighting exists in most public buildings and areas. Think about exit signs in a movie theater or emergency lights on an airplane. These lighting systems are necessary in the event of a power failure to guide people to the exits. Emergency lighting requirements for a property will be specified in local building codes, with which facilities managers must comply.

Emergency lighting systems should have their own power source, independent of the regular lighting system. In the event of a power failure, the emergency lights should come on after no more than 10 seconds and must provide light for 1.5 hours. Exit signs operate 24 hours a day and must be kept in good working order. There are a number of options to reduce energy usage from exit signs, including using LEDs, low-wattage incandescent lamps, compact fluorescent lamps, and self-luminous signs.

Communication

To provide information to guests in case of an emergency, lodging properties should install voice and visual alarm and communication systems. Emergency voice alarm communication (EVAC) systems combine a warning alarm with a pre-recorded message providing guests with information about proper procedures to follow in case of a fire or other emergency. The systems allow property staff or the fire department to override the message to provide additional instructions.

To notify hearing-impaired guests of fires and other emergencies, visual signaling devices are used. They consist of strobe alarms located in guestrooms, in hallways, and on hotel exit signs. Voice alarms and other communication systems must be periodically tested for proper operation.

ADA

Guests with disabilities are often at greater risk during emergencies. They may be unable to hear warning signals or to exit a building quickly. In addition to visual alarm systems, new hotels are required to have fire sprinklers and a rescue assistance area on each floor where guests who are unable to use stairs should wait to be evacuated. These areas should connect directly to an exit, such as a fire stair; be large enough for two wheelchairs; and be out of the path of other emergency exits.

Managing the Facility's Green Practices

Buildings have an impact on the environment. In addition to their physical footprint, hospitality and tourism facilities produce waste and pollution. As hospitality operations work to reduce their effect on the environment, facilities managers have a large role to play because they can impact everything from building materials to energy usage to waste management practices.

Greener buildings can return millions of dollars each year to the bottom line. They are more efficient in lowering operating costs, protecting guest and employee health, improving productivity, and addressing market needs.

Using Alternative Materials

Facilities managers have an opportunity to incorporate alternative, or green, materials into renovation and building projects. Green building materials are non-toxic, reusable, recycled, sturdy, or sustainable. Using local materials whenever possible eliminates the need for transportation, which reduces air pollution, saves fuel, and lowers overall costs. These purchases also support the local economy.

Flooring

Bamboo has become a popular choice for green flooring because it is a natural material that replenishes very quickly. Cork is also a renewable material. It is harvested from the bark of the cork tree, which continues growing and keeping the air clean. The cork grows back and can be re-harvested every nine years. Other green flooring options include recycled carpet tiles, recycled rubber, wool carpeting, tile made from recycled glass or porcelain, and **reclaimed** wood. Reclaimed wood is wood that was previously used in another structure that has been disassembled and used to make floors, furniture, and a variety of other things.

Insulation

In the past, asbestos was often used for insulation, but it has been banned due to the health hazards it poses. Good sustainable choices for insulation include those made from recycled paper, wood pulp, soy, cotton, denim, recycled plastic, or cork.

Roofing

Metal roofing materials are long-lasting and durable, and they have solar reflective qualities which make them effective in hot climates. Living roofs are covered in grass or other plants, and some even contain rooftop gardens. They eliminate the need for manufactured roofing materials, provide insulation, create a habitat for wildlife, and reduce the **urban heat island** (UHI) effect. UHIs form in areas where natural surfaces such as soil and vegetation have been replaced by built surfaces that do not allow solar radiation to be absorbed and released as water vapor.

Glass

Double-paned windows filled with air or argon gas provide insulation that saves energy. Windows can also be covered in solar film to reflect heat.

Cement

Light-colored cement will reflect heat and help reduce temperatures, especially in urban areas. Porous cement allows water to absorb into the soil rather than run off and pollute waterways.

Fabric

Eco-friendly fabrics include those made from natural fibers, such as cotton, jute, wool, soy, hemp, bamboo, and sisal. They can be used to make rugs, furniture upholstery, window treatments, and wall paneling.

Engineering the Property's Carbon Footprint

In the past, hotels have used a variety of methods to calculate their carbon footprint, which was confusing for customers and government agencies. In response to a growing need to standardize how carbon emissions are calculated, a group of international hotel chains came together to take part in the Hotel Carbon Measurement Initiative (HCMI). Led by the World Travel & Tourism Council and the International Tourism Partnership, this initiative seeks to provide a standard way of measuring a property's carbon footprint. There are four pieces of data needed to calculate a hotel's carbon footprint:

1. Energy consumption data for 12 months using meter readings or invoices

2. Area data for guestrooms and corridors, meeting space area, and total area

3. Area of private space (back of house) and total area which is air-conditioned/heated within that space

4. Carbon emissions or energy consumption data from the hotel's supplier if the hotel outsources its laundry

The following practices implemented by facilities management can help reduce a property's carbon footprint:

- Use renewable energy
- Reduce overall energy and water use
- Plant native or drought-tolerant landscaping
- Recycle in guestrooms and employee areas
- Buy products with recycled content
- Improve insulation and fit draught excluders on windows
- Use hydrocarbon refrigeration
- Harvest rainwater or use reclaimed water for irrigation and toilets
- Use alternatives to fossil fuels, such as biodiesel, for vehicles

Green Practices

Scandic Hotels, based in Stockholm, Sweden, has a goal to become carbon neutral by 2025. This means that the chain plans to reduce its carbon emissions to zero. So far, Scandic has managed to cut its emissions in half by using only renewable energy from wind and water for electricity in all its Nordic locations. Scandic's guestrooms feature water-saving devices and a three-bin recycling system. Older gas stoves in the kitchens are being replaced with induction ovens. The company has also overhauled its travel policy, focusing on train travel and lowering emissions from company cars.

Apply Your Learning

Section 8.1

1. What role do facilities play in market identity for hospitality and tourism businesses?
2. Can business growth happen only through increasing prices or serving more customers? Explain your answer.
3. Why are facilities more important in the hospitality industry than in other industries?
4. What are the criteria for back of house facilities?
5. Think of a hospitality and tourism business with facilities you easily recognize. Write a brief description of the facility design.

Section 8.2

1. Compare and contrast the responsibilities of chief engineers at small and large properties.
2. Approximately how many facilities employees are needed per 100 rooms of a lodging property?
3. What percentage of hotel development costs is construction?
4. What does "POM" stand for? What is included in POM costs?
5. List three examples of capital expenditures a hotel might make.

Section 8.3

1. Why must properties comply with the ADA?
2. What is the first step facilities managers for new lodging properties should take to ensure ADA compliance?
3. What should facilities managers do at the completion of construction?
4. Name two features of ADA-compliant elevators.
5. What kinds of showers should ADA-compliant bathrooms have?

Section 8.4

1. List three examples of energy management actions.
2. Explain the term "submetering" and how it contributes to energy management practices.
3. Why is it important to properly maintain all equipment?
4. How can waste energy be recovered and reused? Provide two examples.
5. What is the purpose of energy management and conservation?

Section 8.5

1. Why do facilities managers play an instrumental role in property emergency planning?
2. What are the two main types of emergency power systems? Which other critical systems depend on emergency power systems in the event of a catastrophe?
3. List three energy efficient lighting options that can be used for exit signs.
4. What kinds of communication systems are used to notify hearing-impaired guests of an emergency?
5. What is an EVAC system? Why might it be necessary for the fire department to override its pre-recorded message?

Section 8.6

1. What are the benefits of using alternative building materials?
2. What makes cork a sustainable flooring option?
3. What is the urban heat island effect and how can it be reduced?
4. Name one of the pieces of data needed to calculate a property's carbon footprint.
5. What is the purpose of the Hotel Carbon Measurement Initiative?

Unit 4

Managing Food and Beverage Operations

There are nearly one million food and beverage operations in the United States alone. These operations can be independently owned, part of a chain, or located in a hotel or some other lodging operation. In addition, various specialty markets—transportation, recreational, business/industry, educational, healthcare, corrections, and military—have their own food and beverage operations that have unique operating processes and challenges.

This unit will focus on managing various types of food and beverage operations. Chapter 9 will explore food and beverage service leadership, including such topics as staffing, menu management, purchasing, sanitation and safety, and controlling costs. Chapter 10 will discuss managing banquets and other types of catered events, from booking to getting ready for service to delivering the service.

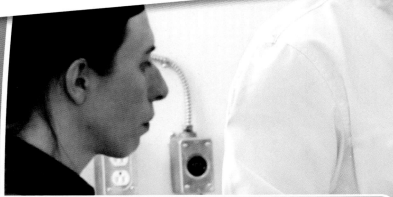

COMPETENCIES

1. Identify the organizational structures of various food and beverage operations, and describe how restaurants attract and retain staff.

2. Explain the steps involved in menu planning and menu design, and explain the value of periodic menu evaluation.

3. Describe procedures and issues involved with purchasing, receiving, storing, issuing, and controlling food and beverage operation supplies and equipment.

4. Describe the process of planning the design and choosing the décor of food and beverage operations, and summarize the cleaning process.

5. Describe the critical role of food sanitation in food and beverage operations, and outline workplace safety responsibilities of managers.

6. Discuss labor and revenue control, and explain how food and beverage managers forecast sales.

7. Explain how food and beverage operations are addressing requests for healthier food options, sustainable foods, and food allergy issues.

Jason Lyon
CEO
The Common Man

Jason Lyon is the CEO of The Common Man family of restaurants. He began his career with The Common Man as a dishwasher at the age of 14. Over the years, he worked his way up through many positions, including prep cook, server, bartender, general manager, executive general manager, and director of operations. In 2000, Mr. Lyon became the CEO, overseeing the daily operations of The Common Man family. He balances his administrative role with a hands-on approach. Mr. Lyon finds the most rewarding aspect of being CEO is being able to work within each restaurant, mentoring and coaching management teams and employees. He has a great passion for quality food and over-the-top hospitable service. He also plays a key role in ensuring all Common Man family members are invested in giving back to their local communities, spearheading community donations and charitable events at all locations.

Mr. Lyon has a degree in business finance management with an economics minor from Plymouth State University. He was inducted into the Inaugural PSU Business Hall of Fame in 2009 and is a member of Delta Mu Delta. He frequently speaks locally and nationally about The Common Man's philanthropic efforts and counsels businesses and organizations on making charitable giving part of their business models.

Mr. Lyon is Foodservice Management Professional (FMP) certified, ServeSafe certified, TEAM certified, and is a Plymouth State University business student mentor. He is a current board member of the New Hampshire Lodging & Restaurant Association (NHLRA), serving on the organization's Marketing, Membership, and Government Affairs committees. He is also on the board of directors for the national Council of Hotel and Restaurant Trainers (CHART) and a two-time conference team member.

In 2012, Mr. Lyon was appointed by New Hampshire's governor to the NH Legislative Youth Advisory Council.

Introduction

When you hear the term *food service*, do you picture a dining room with starched white tablecloths in an expensive restaurant, a truck stop on a busy highway, or a concession stand in a sports stadium? How about dietary services in schools, colleges, hospitals, nursing homes, and other institutions? Are you aware that military food facilities and country clubs are also part of the food service industry? As you can see, the food service industry is vast, encompassing every type of food and beverage operation that provides meals to people away from their homes and sometimes even in their homes.

Food and beverage industry developments and trends are constantly changing as the needs and expectations of consumers evolve. Food and beverage managers must stay abreast of these trends so that changes and improvements to the business can be made. For example, menus must continually evolve so they can feature menu choices that guests want. Catering to changing guest needs can help a restaurant stay profitable.

U.S. Restaurant Industry

More than **$630 billion** in sales

Industry employs **12.9 million** people

10% of the total U.S. workforce

The nation's **2nd largest** private sector employer

Expected to add **1.4 million** jobs in the next decade

The following developments and trends are currently making an impact on the food and beverage services industry:

- Wholesale food prices are on the rise and are expected to continue to increase in the near future. As one-third of sales in a restaurant go toward food and beverage purchases, fluctuations in food prices are significant to a restaurant's bottom line.

- Technology use continues to increase in restaurants, with many food and beverage operations experimenting with online ordering, electronic ordering using tablet computers, and at-table or wireless electronic payment options.

- Social media continues to be an effective marketing tool in attracting 20-something consumers. Restaurants can reach out to consumers through e-mail or text messages with daily specials, or make them available on Facebook and Twitter.

- According to the National Restaurant Association (NRA), nearly three-quarters of consumers say they are more likely to visit a restaurant that offers locally-produced food items, and more than half of all restaurants currently offer locally-sourced produce. Many restaurants are offering ethically-sourced foods, including meat, because they think "it's the right thing to do."

- The NRA reports that about three-quarters of consumers are trying to eat more healthfully at restaurants. Restaurants are offering more healthy menu options and smaller portions.

- In the spirit of creating community, more restaurants are offering free Wi-Fi, encouraging people to linger and mingle.

- Food quality, customer service quality, and value are the top attributes consumers look for when choosing a table-service restaurant. For quick-service restaurants, customers are looking for food quality, value, and speed of service when picking where to dine.

- Many restaurants are focused on reducing energy consumption. Darden, a company that includes Red Lobster and Olive Garden, plans to reduce energy and water use by 15 percent within five years.

Pineapple Fun Fact

Food trucks started years ago as coffee carts or lunch wagons that delivered food to construction workers. In recent years, they have become one of the hottest trends in the restaurant industry. These mobile eateries are now offering a variety of gourmet options and fusion cuisine. Food trucks use social media, especially Twitter and Facebook, to let customers know about their offerings and locations. They are most popular in large cities, such as New York, Los Angeles, and Seattle, where operators see them as a way to beat the high costs of real estate. Due to their small size and ability to move to various locations, food trucks were instrumental in helping to feed people in areas hardest hit by Hurricane Sandy in New York and New Jersey in October 2012.

Organization and Staffing of Food and Beverage Operations

The food service industry is labor-intensive, meaning that a large number of people are required to do the work necessary to meet guest needs. Staff members in food service operations are just as valuable as guests, in the sense that, without them, the restaurant fails: there is no one to do the work, no work gets done, no guests come, and the restaurant must close its doors. A motivated staff is the key to success in any food and beverage operation. Managers must lead wisely and well if their food and beverage organizations are to be successful. Hiring and retaining staff members who are able to provide quality service is an important element of this success.

Food service employees fall into three general categories: managers, supervisors, and entry-level production personnel. The way a food service organization is structured affects its ability to meet its goals. For example, if supervisors have to oversee the work of too many employees, they are less likely to be able to provide each employee with the necessary attention and training.

A food and beverage operation's organizational chart will vary depending on the size of the operation and whether it is independently owned, part of a chain, or an institutional organization, such as a school or hospital. The organizational charts on the next page show the possible organization of a large restaurant and a hospital.

Organizational Chart for a Large Restaurant

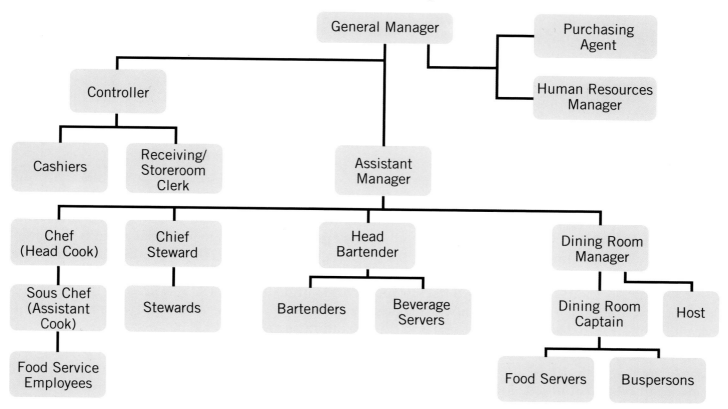

Organizational Chart for a Hospital Food Service Operation

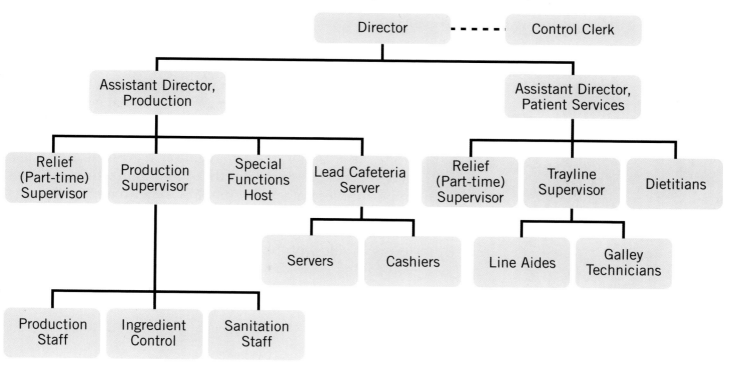

Attracting and Retaining Food and Beverage Staff

On average, one in five people change jobs each year; however, that number is closer to one in two in the hospitality industry. To do a better job of retaining staff members, restaurants must begin by recruiting and selecting the right people. This process involves recruitment, selection, orientation, training, and retention. It is designed to find people who are the very best fit within the culture and philosophy of the restaurant. Managers should choose staff members not only based on experience but also on the service attitude required for the position.

Managers can ask their best staff members to recommend individuals to recruit. Spreading the word will help attract the very best talent. Interviewers should show excitement about the restaurant, the opportunities available there, and the people who work there to encourage potential recruits. Having a positive attitude will attract positive people to the organization! When selecting a candidate, the manager should consider how the person's attitude and professional goals fit in with the organization. The selection process should also include a background check and a drug test, if required by the company. Effective orientation can reduce turnover because it gives new staff members the tools they need to become familiar with their new positions and the operation as a whole.

The most effective way to train staff members is by using job instruction training. This process includes writing training objectives, showing the trainee what to do, having the trainee practice performing the position responsibilities, and providing feedback once the trainee begins to work independently. Having high staff morale will help an organization retain its best staff. To build morale, managers must be able to communicate and listen to staff needs, wants, and expectations. Managers should check in with their staff members on a regular basis to assess morale. Other ideas for retention are planning friendly competitions, hosting an annual outing, working as a team to give back to the community, or reimbursing employees for work-related education expenses.

Attracting and Retaining Restaurant Managers

Learning how to be a good manager takes time. One of the most important skills a manager can have is the ability to train staff members, so they, in turn, can go on and train others. Promoting staff to supervisor and manager positions from within allows the organization to grow its own talent and shows staff members that the organization provides opportunities for advancement. Another retention strategy is to provide manager incentives, in the form of bonuses, for good performance. Performance might be measured in terms of sales, profit, guest satisfaction, staff satisfaction, controlling expenses, or other factors.

Menu Management

The menu is like a restaurant's business card—it defines an operation's concept and communicates that concept to guests. A menu is one of the single biggest influences on an operation's development of a loyal guest base and a positive return on investment of energy, money, time, and other resources. One of the goals of menu development, then, is to influence the behaviors and emotions of the guests reading the menu. From influencing guests to select the more profitable items on the menu to making them feel good about their menu choices, the menu serves as a statement of the restaurant's theme. It's a plan for the entire food and beverage operation, and it should be carefully developed with guest needs and expectations in mind.

Menu Planning

To produce a memorable menu—one that will please guests and help achieve the goals of the operation—there are several objectives a menu planner must meet. The menu must:

- Meet or exceed guest expectations
- Attain marketing objectives
- Meet quality standards
- Be cost-effective
- Be accurate
- Achieve a balance between traditional and innovative menu items
- Be appropriate for the operation's facilities

Selecting Menu Items

Choosing items to feature on the menu is a complicated process with many variables. Planners must balance costs with guest needs and expectations. After menu planners have considered these and other factors, they can select the items they wish to offer in the following categories:

- Appetizers
- Soups
- Salads (side and entrée)
- Entrées
- Desserts
- Beverages (alcoholic and nonalcoholic)

Fixed Menu—does not change from day to day but may feature daily specials.

Cyclical Menu—changes daily for a certain number of days until the menu cycle repeats itself.

À la Carte Menu—offers and prices each food item on an individual basis.

Prix Fixe Menu—offers a complete meal with several courses for one price.

Menu Engineering—evaluating the menu by studying the popularity and profitability of menu items.

Menu Types

Menu planners must also decide on which meal periods to focus. The three traditional meal periods are breakfast, lunch, and dinner. While some food and beverage operations do most of their business at breakfast and lunch, others are primarily dinner houses. Some restaurants may choose to feature each meal period on a separate menu. Others may have a combination menu. There is also a wide range of specialty menus, including: children's, senior citizens', alcoholic beverages, dessert, room service, take-out, banquet, poolside, afternoon tea, and many others.

Another way to classify menus is to determine whether they are fixed or cyclical. A **fixed menu** does not change from day to day, although it may feature daily specials in addition to the regular items. A **cyclical menu** changes daily for a certain number of days until the menu repeats itself. These types of menus are often found in schools, healthcare facilities, and other types of cafeterias. Another popular classification is based on the pricing structures of menus. Many restaurants use an **à la carte menu** that offers and prices each item on an individual basis. Guests may select from a variety of different salads, entrées, vegetables, desserts, and beverages that are all individually priced. A **prix fixe menu**, on the other hand, offers guests a fixed price meal that includes several courses.

Electronic Menus

Increasingly, menus are appearing on the screens of various electronic devices, including big-screen televisions, smartphones, and tablets. Touch screen menus located at the tables in some restaurants can transmit orders directly to the kitchen and accept table-side payments.

Menu Formats

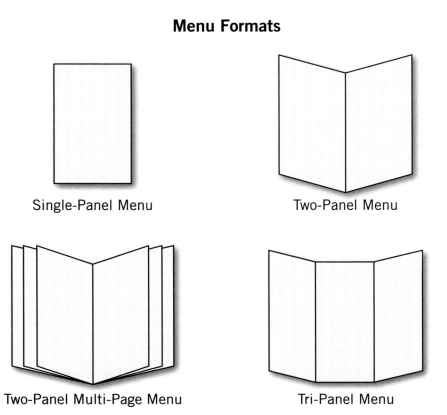

Single-Panel Menu

Two-Panel Menu

Two-Panel Multi-Page Menu

Tri-Panel Menu

Menu Design

Menus are sales tools, so they must be designed to grab the attention of guests quickly. A well-designed menu complements an operation's overall theme, blends with the interior décor, and helps sell the most profitable menu items. The following are the top ten rules for successful menu design:

1. **Speak plainly.** Use terms that are familiar to the reader; carefully select text to appeal to those who read it.

2. **Say what is important.** Because of various restrictions, such as diets and allergies, guests need to know whether menu items contain ingredients like wheat, pork, nuts, dairy, or shellfish.

3. **Do not be afraid to be descriptive**. The use of appealing adjectives, such as "crispy," "fresh," and "sizzling," paints a mental picture of the item in the guest's mind.

4. **Say it correctly.** Whenever a description, point of origin, or government grade or preparation technique is used on the menu, it must be accurate.

5. **Describe accompaniments.** Include a description of all items that accompany the main dish.

6. **Remember, "less is more."** Describe only those ingredients that add significantly to the flavor and value.

7. **Maintain a sense of perspective.** Do not try to recommend everything; focus on signature menu items, with no more than two or three per menu category.

8. **Spell it properly.** If you wish to create an image of being the expert, make sure everything on the menu is spelled correctly and uses correct grammar.

9. **Punctuate properly.** Remember to use a comma between items in a series, such as "breadcrumbs, mushrooms, and fresh parsley." Another common mistake is to use an apostrophe to indicate plurals; an apostrophe should only be used in contractions (isn't, don't) and possessives (chef's).

10. **Follow the rules of good typography.** Select a paper color, ink color, font, and point size that can be read in the level of lighting in the dining area. Leave sufficient blank space between items and sections to make the menu easy to follow.

Changing the Menu

No matter how well-planned and designed they are, menus should be evaluated periodically. **Menu engineering** allows managers to study the popularity and profitability of each menu item. Managers can evaluate the menu by asking pertinent questions or using menu management software. The following factors can influence menu changes:

External
- Guest demands
- Economic factors
- Competition
- Supply levels
- Industry trends

Internal
- Operation's meal pattern
- Concept and theme
- Operational system
- Menu mix

Purchasing Supplies and Equipment

F ood and beverage operations require a wide variety of supplies and equipment in order to serve guests properly. If the operation is part of a chain, purchasing is typically done centrally by staff at the chain's headquarters. This centralized approach often results in lower prices for bulk orders. Managers at independent operations must do their own purchasing.

Purchasing is more than just placing an order. Purchasing practices have a direct impact on the operation's bottom line. Therefore, it is very important to purchase the *right* product at the *right* time from the *right* distributor for the *right* price. The following are some common supplies and equipment food and beverage operations must purchase.

Supplies	
China	
Glassware	
Flatware	
Disposable items	
Uniforms	
Linens	
Furniture	

Equipment	
Holding tables (food warmers)	
Coffee urns and makers	
Refrigerators and freezers	
Dishwashers	
POS systems	
Handheld terminals	
Electronic pocket pagers	

Establishing Quality

Managers must decide what types and quality of supplies and equipment can best meet guest needs. For example, just as you would not use expensive china in a quick-service operation, you would not use plastic flatware in a full-service restaurant. Whenever possible, managers should consider purchasing manufacturer's brands that are available from more than one distributor. **Open-stock items** are much easier to replace than **custom-made items** produced by a single distributor.

Establishing Par Levels

Restaurant supplies are maintained at what are known as par inventory levels, or stock levels. Managers must set the par levels and decide the minimum level that each item can be allowed to reach before an order must be placed to build the item's inventory back up to its established par level. The minimum level is called the reorder point. If par levels are set too high and supplies are overstocked, problems with cash flow, theft, or wasted storage space can occur. In contrast, if par levels are set too low and there aren't enough supplies on hand, guest and staff member frustration and dissatisfaction can result. There are so many different kinds of food and beverage operations that it is impossible to generalize about specific par inventory levels that should be maintained for a given item. It is the responsibility of the general manager of each independent operation to determine par levels based on the type of operation, the number of seats, operating hours, and many other factors.

Sample Par Levels

Item	Par Inventory Level
Plates	3 per seat
Bowls	2-3 per seat
Flatware	1½ to 3 place settings per seat
Glasses	3 per seat
Uniforms	3 per each service staff member
Linens	4 times the number used during a busy shift

Receiving and Storing

The process for receiving and storing food and beverage supplies can be summarized as follows:

1. Check incoming products against the **purchase record** to ensure that what was received matches what was purchased.

2. Check incoming products against the standard purchase specification form, which lists specific quality requirements for items.

3. Check incoming products against the delivery invoice. The type and quantity of products the operation receives should match what it is being billed for.

4. Record in writing any discrepancies between what was received and what was ordered. Record any errors in price or corrections for damaged items that are returned to the distributor.

5. Move items to secure storage areas after delivery and receipt.

Issuing

Service supplies are transferred from storage areas to kitchen and dining areas as they are needed. This process is called **issuing**. Because space for the storage of supplies in dining areas is often limited, managers must ensure that the proper quantities of service supplies—and no more—are available in these areas. Depending on the size of the operation, supplies may be requisitioned, or ordered, from storage by the general manager, assistant manager, host or hostess, or another staff member. It is important to establish and follow issuing procedures in order to prevent waste or shortages in the kitchen and dining areas.

Controlling

Service supplies are costly; therefore, managers must properly control them. The primary control problems with food and beverage supplies involve misuse, waste, breakage, and theft. Creative staff members improvise when they do not have the materials to do their work efficiently. They might use a napkin as a potholder, thus ruining the napkin. To prevent misuse of supplies, managers must purchase proper supplies and equipment. Careless staff may waste items, such as throwing away unopened food packets or accidentally throwing flatware in the trash. Close training and supervision can help reduce this problem. Managers must also train staff to properly handle breakable items because these items are expensive to replace. Managers should also beware of theft by guests and staff members and implement programs to reduce theft, such as offering items with the operation's logo for sale.

Facility Design, Décor, and Cleaning

A total dining experience consists not only of food and beverages but also of the restaurant's design and décor. The design and décor must complement the cuisine and service. The design and layout of a food and beverage operation also has an impact on its appeal to guests and on the productivity of employees. Managers must consider the design of all areas of the operation, including the kitchen, storage areas, the dining room, and the bar or lounge area. However, even the most attractive design and nicest décor mean nothing if the food and beverage facility is not kept clean. Not only is cleanliness one of the top guest expectations, it is also a legal issue: food and beverage facilities must comply with local sanitation laws.

Design and Layout

Designers must approach the design from the guest's perspective. They must consider elements such as noise, lighting, color coordination, and use of space. They must also be aware of government safety regulations, which govern such factors as emergency exits, how many guests a space can accommodate, and ADA accommodations. Design also affects service. A poor layout may prohibit service staff from completing their work efficiently. The following factors should be considered in food and beverage facility design:

- **Traffic flow:** There should be an efficient flow of guests, staff members, products, supplies, and trash through a facility. Kitchen design must also take into consideration the distances staff have to walk and the heights of employee work areas.

- **Food safety and sanitation:** Sinks should be located in areas where they are most likely to be used. To avoid cross-contamination, clean and dirty items should not come into contact with each other, and, if possible, raw and cooked items should be refrigerated separately.

- **Sustainable design:** Green features can be incorporated into the design. Facilities should consider purchasing ENERGY STAR rated appliances or even applying for LEED certification.

Décor

The dining area environment must be compatible with an organization's theme, menu, and service style. The furniture, decorations, and staff uniforms must all work together to support the overall theme. For example, in a gourmet restaurant, it may be appropriate for the manager to wear a tuxedo. In a Mexican or other ethnic restaurant, uniforms and decorations may reflect the national heritage of that particular culture. However, managers must remember to remain practical and not get carried away. They should purchase products that can withstand wear and tear and make sure that any delicate decorations are out of reach and well-anchored. When choosing a food and beverage operation's décor, it is essential to think about:

- Color
- Flooring
- Wall coverings
- Decorations
- Lighting
- Ventilation
- Noise
- Music
- Furniture
- The exterior

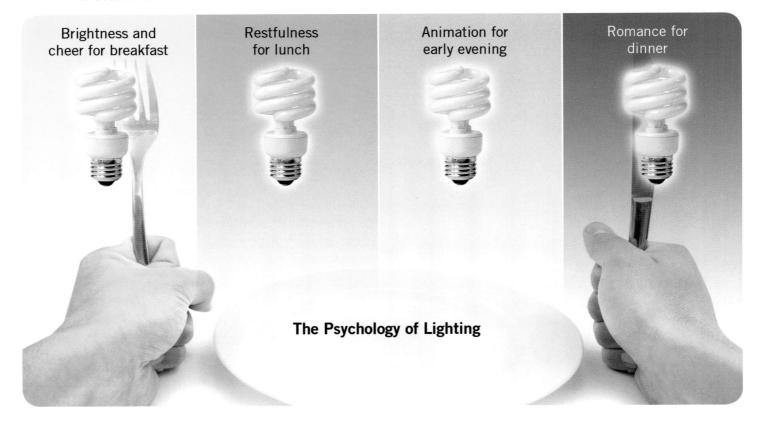

Brightness and cheer for breakfast | Restfulness for lunch | Animation for early evening | Romance for dinner

The Psychology of Lighting

Cleaning

One of the first things guests notice about a restaurant is its cleanliness. If the tabletops and the items stored there are not clean, guests may get the feeling that other areas of the operation—such as the kitchen—are not clean. Cleaning is important not only because dirty facilities create a negative impression on guests, but also because food safety depends on cleanliness. In addition, the useful life of fixtures, furniture, and equipment will be longer if they are regularly cleaned and maintained.

For cleaning to be effective, cleaning standards and procedures must be put into place and be part of orientation and ongoing training programs. Checklists are an effective way to ensure that all the items receive the proper attention. Cleaning schedules will let employees know how often items must be cleaned.

Managing Sanitation and Safety

Sanitation and safety are two topics food and beverage managers cannot ignore. If an outbreak of foodborne illness is traced to an operation, the costs in human suffering, productivity (if employees become ill), medical and hospital expenses, legal expenses (including claims settlement), negative publicity, and lost business can be devastating. The costs in human suffering and medical and legal costs can also be significant if a worker or guest is injured on the property because of unsafe conditions.

Sanitation must be addressed at each stage of the food-handling process. Serious illness and even death can be caused by the failure to follow simple, basic food sanitation procedures. Safety concerns are just as vital. Food service managers have a personal, professional, and legal responsibility to provide safe conditions for employees and guests.

Sanitation

The Hazard Analysis Critical Control Point (HACCP) system seeks to eliminate safety risks in food processing by identifying the specific hazards at each important point in a food production system. The key to successful use of the HACCP system is staff training. For each preparation step they perform, staff members must know which control points are critical and what the critical limits are at these points. Management must routinely follow up to verify that everyone is complying with the critical limits. The seven HACCP principles should be incorporated in the process:

Step 1: Hazard analysis. Identify significant hazards and develop preventative measures for a process or product to ensure safety. A thorough analysis includes a review of ingredients, processing, distribution, and intended product use.

Step 2: Identify critical control points (CCPs). Steps including cooking, chilling, recipe control, and prevention of cross-contamination are CCPs that might apply to a specific recipe.

Step 3: Establish critical limits/preventative measures. Proper cooking, holding, and storage temperatures are examples of standards that must be incorporated into food-handling procedures.

Step 4: Establish procedures to monitor CCPs. These procedures help identify problems, assess the results of corrective actions, and provide written documentation for HACCP plans.

Step 5: Establish necessary corrective action(s). This helps to identify reasons for deviations from HACCP plans and helps to ensure that critical CCPs are controlled.

Step 6: Establish an effective recordkeeping system. Plans must detail hazards at each CCP, specify monitoring and recordkeeping procedures, and outline implementation strategies.

Step 7: Establish procedures to verify that the HACCP system is working. Plans must be reviewed and verified, CCP records must be studied, and managers must determine that decisions for controlling damages have been effectively made when production deviations occur.

In addition to the production cycle, managers must ensure food safety during purchasing, receiving, storing, and issuing. Buyers should ensure that food is obtained from sources that comply with all local, state, and federal sanitation laws. All foods must be checked to make sure they meet quality standards when they are received. Food should be stored as soon as possible after receiving, at the correct temperature, and should be issued on a first in, first out (FIFO) basis. In other words, foods that are in storage the longest should be used first.

Food safety procedures also include proper cleaning and sanitizing of dishes, flatware, pots, pans, cooking surfaces, and the facility itself. Cleaning removes dirt from surfaces, while sanitizing reduces harmful microorganisms to acceptable and safe levels. In addition to the kitchen, regular cleaning must be performed on floors, walls, sidestations, and restrooms.

Safety

Safety relates to the prevention of accidents, especially those that can harm guests, employees, and others. Most accidents are caused by someone's carelessness and can be prevented. The most common types of food service accidents are burns, cuts, falls, lifting injuries, and equipment accidents. Managers must ensure that staff is properly trained in the prevention of these types of accidents and injuries. If an accident does occur, the manager should fill out an accident report. Then, an accident investigation should:

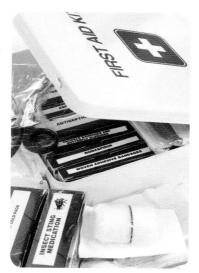

1. Assess exactly what happened.

2. Determine why the accident occurred.

3. Suggest what should be done to prevent recurrences.

4. Follow up to ensure that preventative action has been taken.

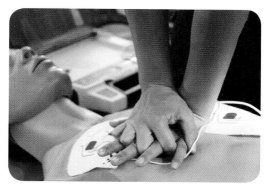

Every food and beverage operation should have a clear policy on how to handle emergencies such as injuries to staff members or guests. First aid kits should be available and conveniently located. All staff members should know where first aid supplies are stored and be trained in how to use them to treat minor injuries. Because of the nature of the business, food and beverage staff must be prepared to handle incidents that involve choking. The Heimlich maneuver is often used to save choking victims. It is a good idea to have at least one person who is certified in cardiopulmonary resuscitation (CPR) on duty at all times.

Management's Role in Sanitation and Safety

Food and beverage managers have the ultimate responsibility for developing, implementing, and monitoring the operation's sanitation and safety efforts. Their role includes the following:

- Incorporating sanitation and safety practices into operating procedures
- Ensuring that sanitation and safety concerns take priority over convenience
- Training employees in sanitary and safe work procedures
- Conducting sanitation and safety inspections
- Completing accident reports, assisting in investigations, and ensuring that problems are quickly corrected
- Assisting in treatment and seeking medical assistance for injured employees and guests when necessary
- Reporting necessary repairs or maintenance, changes in work procedures, or other conditions that are potential problems

Labor and Revenue Control

Staffing Guide—a worksheet showing the number of labor hours that must be worked as the volume of expected business changes.

Every dollar in excessive labor costs represents a dollar subtracted from the bottom line. For example, if a restaurant consistently exceeds its labor costs by $100 per week, that adds up to $5,200 per year off the bottom line. How much revenue would the restaurant have to generate to make up that amount to the bottom line? Much more than $5,200! If the restaurant's profit margin is 12 percent (.12), the restaurant would have to generate $43,333 in gross sales to make $5,200 in profit:

$$\$43,333 \times .12 = \$5,200 \text{ (rounded)}$$

Labor Control

Labor expenses in both the kitchen and service areas are really investments in the guests' overall dining experience. As a general trend, labor costs per hour have been rising in food and beverage operations, in part due to rising minimum wages mandated by law. However, higher wages may also mean that the operation is attracting and retaining more qualified staff members. It is the responsibility of the operation's managers to achieve a proper level of staffing. When scheduling, they should aim to achieve a balance between the needs of staff, guests, and the owner. If staff levels are too low, staff members feel rushed and overworked, and guests are more likely to have a negative dining experience. Staff levels that are too high may lead to reduced tips per server, which can lead to decreased morale. In addition, high staffing levels will greatly increase labor costs and reduce restaurant profits.

Labor standards and **staffing guides** are critical to maintaining labor control. Labor standards help determine the amount of time required to perform assigned tasks, such as rolling silverware in napkins, setting up the buffet, or cleaning the dining area after a shift. Using this information, a staffing guide can be developed, which tells managers the number of labor hours needed for each position according to the volume of business forecasted. The staffing guide is a tool for both planning work schedules and controlling labor costs. When the number of actual hours exceeds the number identified by the staffing guide, managers should analyze where the difference came from and make adjustments.

Sample Restaurant Staffing Guide

Position	Number of Meals				
	50	**75**	**100**	**125**	**150**
Food Server	8.5 5:00-9:30 7:00-11:00	9.5 5:00-9:30 6:30-11:30	16.0 5:00-9:30 6:30-11:00 7:00-10:00 7:30-12:30	16.0 5:00-9:30 6:30-11:00 7:00-10:00 7:30-12:30	19.0 5:00-10:00 6:00-11:00 6:00-11:00 7:30-11:30
Bartender	9.0 4:00-1:00	9.0 4:00-1:00	9.0 4:00-1:00	9.0 4:00-1:00	9.0 4:00-1:00
Cook	7.0 4:00-11:00	14.0 3:00-10:00 5:00-12:00	14.0 3:00-10:00 5:00-12:00	14.0 3:00-10:00 5:00-12:00	16.0 3:00-11:00 4:00-12:00
Busperson	– –	2.0 7:30-9:30	4.0 7:30-9:30 7:30-9:30	5.0 7:00-9:30 7:30-10:00	7.0 7:00-9:30 7:30-10:00 7:30-9:30
Host (Manager serves as host on slow evenings)	– –	3.0 6:00-9:00	3.5 6:00-9:30	4.0 6:00-10:00	4.0 6:00-10:00

Forecasting Sales

Another important aspect of controlling labor costs is being able to forecast sales. To schedule the right number of production and service staff, managers must know approximately how many guests to expect, what they are likely to order, and when they are likely to arrive. Sales forecasts are also used to purchase, receive, store, issue, and produce menu items to serve the estimated number of guests. If too much food is purchased for the actual business volume, it could spoil, cutting into the operation's bottom line. Forecasts are usually based on historical averages for each meal period and then adjusted for current conditions. For example, such conditions as road construction in the area, a local event, or a special dining promotion can affect the forecast. Two common forecasting methods are the moving average method and the weighted time series method.

Moving Average Method

$$\left\{ \text{Moving Average} = \frac{\text{Activity in Previous n Periods}}{n} \right\}$$

If the numbers of Tuesday dinners served over the past three weeks have been 285, 270, and 260, respectively, the three-week moving average would be determined as follows:

$$\left\{ \text{3-Week Moving Average} = \frac{285 + 270 + 260}{3} = 272 \text{ (rounded)} \right\}$$

Weighted Time Series Method

This method places a greater value on the most recent data. For example, if we are forecasting the number of next Tuesday's dinners, we could assume weights of 3, 2, and 1 for the prior Tuesdays, with 3 assigned to the most recent Tuesday, and so on.

1. Multiply each week's number of dinners sold by its respective weight and total the values:

$$\left\{ (285)(3) + (270)(2) + (260)(1) = 1{,}655 \right\}$$

2. Divide the total by the sum of its weights:

$$\left\{ \frac{1{,}655}{3 + 2 + 1} = \frac{1{,}655}{6} = 276 \text{ (rounded)} \right\}$$

Revenue Control

Guest check systems are designed to ensure that the kitchen produces only items that were actually ordered and that revenue is collected for all items served. The majority of restaurants use electronic point-of-sale (POS) technology. However, when automated systems crash, it is important to be able to use a manual guest check system.

Before entering an order, the server "opens" the guest check in the system by inputting her identification number. Once a guest check has been opened, it becomes part of the system's open check file. An automated POS allows managers, at any point during service, to monitor the status of any guest check, including voided items, outstanding checks, and the servers responsible. Once payment is received, the guest check status changes from open to closed.

Processing Payment

Processing payments is an important revenue control function. Managers must ensure that a process is in place to protect guest information and prevent fraud and theft. Staff must follow all the guidelines for processing credit card payments. To prevent credit card fraud, some restaurants have instituted tableside payment using handheld devices. In most food and beverage operations, individual servers are responsible for collecting payment. Whenever feasible, a dedicated cashier should handle the payment to ensure a separation of duties.

- With a **server banking system**, servers and bartenders use their own banks of money to collect payments from guests and retain the collected revenue until they check out at the end of their shifts.

- With a **cashier banking system**, guests pay the cashier, the bartender, or the food and beverage server (who then pays the cashier or the bartender who has cashiering duties).

Staff members responsible for revenue collection are issued cash banks at the starts of their shifts. They count their opening banks to make sure they contain the appropriate amounts of each type of currency. At the end of their shifts, they count the banks again and record the amount of revenue collected.

TERMS YOU SHOULD KNOW

Server Banking System— servers and bartenders use their own banks of money to collect payments from guests and retain the collected revenue until they check out at the end of their shifts.

Cashier Banking System— guests pay the cashier.

Nutrition and Sustainable Foods

Consumers are increasingly making lifestyle choices and changes that contribute to healthier living. Food and beverage operations are selling less alcohol today than they did a decade ago. More guests are choosing smaller portion sizes and demanding foods that are low in fat, sodium, cholesterol, and sugar. Vegetarian, vegan, and pescetarian menu items are appealing to a growing number of restaurant patrons. A pescetarian excludes poultry, beef, and pork from his or her diet but includes fish and other seafood. In addition, some local and state governments have passed laws that ban trans fats and require operators to include calorie counts on menus.

Food Allergies

Some guests may need to avoid certain foods because they have a food allergy. According to the World Allergy Organization, 220-520 million people may suffer from food allergies worldwide. A food allergy involves a reaction of the person's immune system. Signs of a food allergy include itching, hives, vomiting, or abdominal pain. More severe food allergies can even result in death. Many allergic reactions are caused by milk, eggs, legumes, nuts, shellfish, and wheat. Guests typically know which foods they are allergic to and ask about ingredients before they place their order.

Eating away from home can pose a significant risk to people affected by food allergies. Research suggests that close to half of fatal food allergy reactions are triggered by food served by a restaurant or other food service establishment. Therefore, it is important that food and beverage staff and managers take food allergies seriously and recognize that there are no shortcuts to accommodating persons with food allergies. Food and beverage managers should research ways they can create menu choices to accommodate allergies. It may be useful to create a plan for dealing with guests with allergies for staff members to follow.

Organic and Sustainable Foods

An increasing number of guests prefer to see **organic foods** or other sustainable food options at restaurants. The term organic refers to plants or animals that have been raised without the use of chemicals. Sustainable foods are those that have been grown or raised locally or without harming the environment. They are healthy for consumers and animals, fair for workers, and support the local community. Examples of sustainable foods include:

- Grass-fed and antibiotic-free meat
- Eggs from cage-free chickens
- Fish and seafood that is not endangered
- Organic or heirloom produce
- Fair trade coffee

Some restaurants have discovered a new market of guests who will pay a premium for the generally higher-priced organic foods. Others incorporate sustainability and green practices into their operations because they feel it's the ethical thing to do.

TERMS YOU SHOULD KNOW

Organic Foods—plants or animals raised without the use of chemicals.

Apply Your Learning

Section 9.1
1. Name three institutions that offer food service.
2. Why must menus constantly evolve?
3. What percentage of the U.S. workforce is employed in the restaurant industry?
4. How is social media being used by the restaurant industry?
5. According to the NRA, what two consumer trends are on the rise?

Section 9.2
1. Why are staff members in a food and beverage operation so important?
2. How should interviewers act when trying to recruit new staff members?
3. What kind of attitude should managers look for in potential recruits?
4. What can an organization do to retain its best staff?
5. Explain the benefits of promoting employees to management positions from within.

Section 9.3
1. Explain the role of the menu in the food and beverage sales process.
2. Compare and contrast fixed menus and cyclical menus.
3. What must managers take into account when planning the menu? Provide four examples.
4. Explain the term "menu engineering."
5. Name two internal and two external factors that might influence menu changes.

Section 9.4
1. What kinds of supplies and equipment must food and beverage operations purchase? Give two examples of each.
2. Why should managers consider buying open-stock items instead of custom-made items?
3. What is the first step in the receiving process?
4. What can happen if par inventory levels are set too high?
5. What are the primary control problems with food and beverage supplies?

Section 9.5
1. True or False? Designers must approach facility design from the employees' perspective.
2. List three aspects of décor that food and beverage facility designers must think about.
3. What kind of lighting would be most appropriate for an operation serving breakfast?
4. Provide two reasons why cleaning is important.
5. How can cleaning schedules impact the cleaning process?

Section 9.6

1. What are the implications for a food and beverage operation if an outbreak of a foodborne illness is traced back to it?
2. What are critical control points?
3. What does FIFO stand for? How does this concept apply to safety in issuing?
4. What are the most common types of food service accidents?
5. Place the four accident investigation steps in the correct order.

_____ Determine why the accident occurred.

_____ Follow up to ensure that preventative action has been taken.

_____ Suggest what should be done to prevent recurrences.

_____ Assess exactly what happened.

Section 9.7

1. How do food and beverage managers use sales forecasts?
2. What is the difference between the moving average method and the weighted time series method of forecasting sales?
3. Calculate the 5-week moving average for next Saturday's brunch given the following number of Saturday brunches sold in the past five weeks: 300, 275, 320, 290, 305.
4. How does an automated POS help the manager maintain revenue control?
5. What elements distinguish a server banking system from a cashier banking system?

Section 9.8

1. What kinds of foods are guests choosing today compared to the past?
2. What effect do government regulations have on the types of foods served in restaurants?
3. Name three signs of a food allergy.
4. What should managers do to prepare for dealing with guests with allergies?
5. What does the term "organic foods" mean?

Chapter 10

Managing Banquets and Catered Events

COMPETENCIES

1. Outline the types of positions available to event planners, and describe the benefits of banquets and catered events for food and beverage operations.

2. Explain how banquets and catered events are booked and planned, and describe function books, contracts or letters of agreement, and function sheets.

3. Summarize how banquet and catering operations prepare to provide service to clients during an event, from setting up function rooms to scheduling staff members, and preparing, plating, and storing food.

4. List challenges that managers and staff members face during banquets, and list examples of protocol issues.

5. Describe the types of controls that banquet managers must practice, and explain how guest comments can be collected and used.

Hospitality Profile

Zubin D'Souza, CHA, CFBE
Executive Chef
Waterstones Hotel and Club

Mr. Zubin D'Souza is the executive chef at the upscale boutique Waterstones Hotel and Club in Mumbai, India. His role is to oversee the food and beverage offerings for the property's elite clientele. Mr. D'Souza has had a long and varied career in the catering and food and beverage industries, with expertise in food preparation, kitchen management, and training delivery. This extensive experience and Mr. D'Souza's global viewpoint stem from his leadership positions in restaurants and hotels in India, Ethiopia, Hong Kong, and Scotland.

Mr. D'Souza has a bachelor's degree in Business Administration and various industry certifications, including Certified Hotel Administrator (CHA) and Certified Food and Beverage Executive (CFBE) from EI. He has published five cookbooks that explore specialty foods in India. Mr. D'Souza has been honored with the Best Appetizer Award at the International Food & Wine Show in Mumbai and the Leader of the Month Award from the JW Marriott, Mumbai.

Giving back to society is important to Mr. D'Souza. Through his work, he has supported the Hong Kong Cancer Fund, where he has conducted cooking classes for cancer survivors and created a cookbook to honor these brave individuals. He has also worked to help reduce his organization's carbon footprint through recycling and composting programs in the kitchen.

Introduction

Special event planning, or event management, has become a popular career track in a number of hospitality schools due to the growing demand for professional management. Individuals, companies, and charitable, social, and trade organizations rely on trained and experienced people to create and execute their events.

Event Planning

Hospitality school graduates have numerous opportunities for careers in event planning. They can join an organization's event department, work for a company specializing in producing special events, or become an independent planner. Many hotels and convention centers hire event planners to handle planning for special events held on premises, such as weddings, company parties, and meetings. Some independent event planners specialize in one kind of event (weddings, for example), while others take on any type of event—personal, cultural, leisure, or organizational. Weddings and birthday parties are personal events, while an art show is an example of a cultural event. Leisure events include concerts and organized recreational activities. Events produced for businesses or charitable groups are classified as organizational.

Event planners coordinate every aspect of the event. In some cases, they may select the city or the hotel, or another venue where the event will be held. Since event planners must deal with other contractors, such as decorators, florists, caterers, audiovisual companies, and transportation companies, they must have some knowledge of those functions. Creativity and organization are important traits for an event planner. Many clients expect the planner to recommend a unique location or create a one-of-a-kind event.

Pineapple Fun Fact

Banquets were a popular form of entertainment during the Middle Ages. Medieval banquets contained several courses and a large number of different dishes. Those of higher rank usually dined on three courses, while attendees of lower rank got fewer courses and smaller portions. One of the most elaborate feasts in history celebrated George Neville becoming Archbishop of York in 1465. The banquet lasted several days, and the list of provisions included 4,000 pigeons, 2,000 chickens, 400 swans, six wild bulls, 1,000 sheep, 2,000 pigs, 200 pheasants, 4,000 dishes of jelly, 4,000 baked tarts, 300 tuns of ale (about 75,000 gallons), 100 tuns of wine, and many other items. Medieval-style banquets and weddings are still popular today, with many food service operations offering medieval-themed events.

Banquets and Catered Events

This chapter will focus mostly on special events that involve banquets or catering. Banquets and catered events can represent a substantial amount of revenue for food and beverage operations and hotels. In the United States alone, banquets and catered events generate billions of dollars in revenue each year. Banquets and catered events are part of many office events, meetings and conferences in hotels, anniversary celebrations, family reunions, bar and bat mitzvahs, retirement parties, and so on. The return on sales for a banquet is typically 35-40 percent, while the return on sales in a regular dining room is only 10-15 percent. You can see from this difference that banquets and catered events can greatly add to a food and beverage operation's bottom line.

A banquet and catering operation can be an independent business, part of a large commercial or noncommercial food and beverage operation, or a department within the food and beverage division of a lodging property. In all of these various forms, a well-run banquet and catering operation can generate substantial profits for several reasons:

- **Banquets are predictable.** They have predetermined menus, hours, number of guests, and labor requirements.

- **Banquets and catered events allow flexibility in pricing**. Prime rib priced at $30 on the regular menu may bring $40 on the banquet menu due to the increased cost of banquet setup.

- **Food costs for banquets and catered events are lower.** This is due to the large volume and low food waste (because the number of guests is known).

- **Beverage costs are lower.** They can be controlled through pricing flexibility and volume purchasing.

- **Labor costs are lower.** Regular banquet/catering staff can be kept small and supplemented with part-time workers. Restaurants, on the other hand, must maintain a regular staff even during slow periods.

- **Additional income is generated from outside vendors**. Some banquet and catering operations work with preferred vendors (photographers, entertainers, bakeries, florists, and printers) who pay them a commission for business generated from banquet clients.

- **Banquets and catered events promote the rest of the operation and generate future business.** If guests enjoy their experience, they may return to the operation to book a function in the future.

Section 10.2

Booking and Planning Events

Function Book—a document that shows occupancies and vacancies of function and banquet rooms, used when planning events.

Contract—when booking events, the letter of agreement that lists every detail the two parties have discussed and agreed upon.

Function Sheet—lists all the details that apply to the catering function, including everything anyone at the food service operation might need to know to prepare for and provide service. Also called a Banquet Event Order (BEO).

Three documents play a primary role in booking and planning banquet and catering events:

- The **function book**, sometimes called the daily function room diary
- The **contract** or letter of agreement
- The **function sheet**, also called a banquet event order (BEO)

The Function Book

Managers and salespeople use the function book to determine if a certain room is available for a particular function at a particular time. The function book is also used to reserve a room after an event is sold so that no one else will commit the room for another function covering the same time period. The function book lists all of the operation's function space available for sale and has a daily time log for each space to facilitate the recording of sold blocks of time.

The function book's format depends on the size of the event planning operation and the number of function rooms. Some operations need less information than others, but entries typically include the group's name; the client's name, title, phone number, and e-mail address; the estimated number of guests; the name of the event; and the type of event (for example, lunch, meeting, expo). Using a function book to accurately keep track of sold and unsold space is very important to the operation as well as to clients. Function space that goes unsold represents lost income. That is why managers cannot afford to trust oral agreements with clients or make mistakes in making entries into the function book.

If negotiations are successful and a client decides to book with the operation, the salesperson will officially enter the event into the function book. A copy of the salesperson's proposal letter that the client has signed, a confirmation letter from the client, or a function room reservation form may serve as official authorization for the event.

Sample Function Book

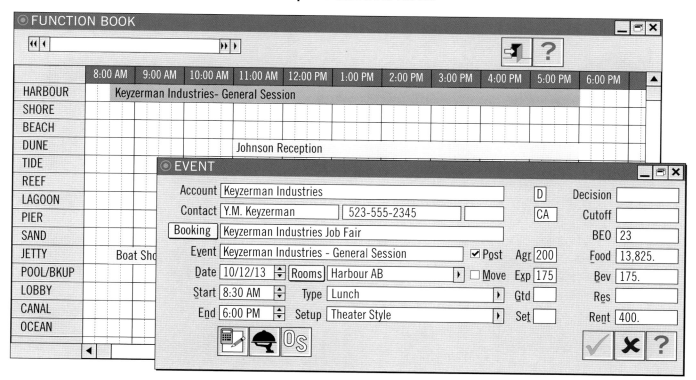

Guarantee—the figure given by the client to the property for the final number of attendees for an event.

Contracts or Letters of Agreement

Next, the salesperson draws up a contract or letter of agreement. Every detail that the two parties have discussed and agreed upon is covered in the contract. It is important to estimate attendance figures at the time the contract is signed. However, if the event itself will be held months or even years later, the operation might not require an attendance estimate on the signing date. In some cases (such as with conventions, which have optional attendance), ticket sales fluctuate so much from the original proposal that the group may need a larger or smaller room than was originally booked. On a date that is a certain number of days before the event, as specified in the contract, the client must state the final number of attendees who are expected. This number is the **guarantee**.

Tomas Hotel
Resort Lake Geneva

Event Contract

Keyzerman Industries
1234 Main St., Suite 21
Oviedo, FL 32721
1-523-555-2345

The contract typically requires the client to pay a specific portion of the estimated cost at least two weeks in advance of the event's date; clients usually pay any remaining balance within 30 days after the event. Food service operations generally reserve the right to cancel an event if the client has not made the required advance payment.

Typically, the following services are included in room rental rates:

- Setup labor for normal meetings (tables, chairs, tablecloths, ice water)
- Movement of large furniture in the room to other locations
- Removal of carpets
- Public address (PA) system and microphones
- Easels, chart boards, whiteboards, movie screens, and extension cords

The following services are often not included in room rental rates but are charged separately:

- Electrical layouts, plumbing, or other services for exhibits
- Computer equipment, interactive whiteboards, DVD players
- Table decorations
- A dance floor
- Service staff, including audiovisual, electrical, or other technicians

Function Sheets

Once the contract is signed, the salesperson must generate a function sheet, or BEO, to inform the rest of the banquet and catering staff about the event. A function sheet lists all the details that apply to the function. The salesperson who books the event completes the function sheet, then provides copies as necessary to the banquet/catering office, the manager who will schedule staff for the event, the beverage department, the accounting department, the convention service or floor manager, and the various kitchen departments. Software programs make it easier to generate function sheets.

Sample BEO

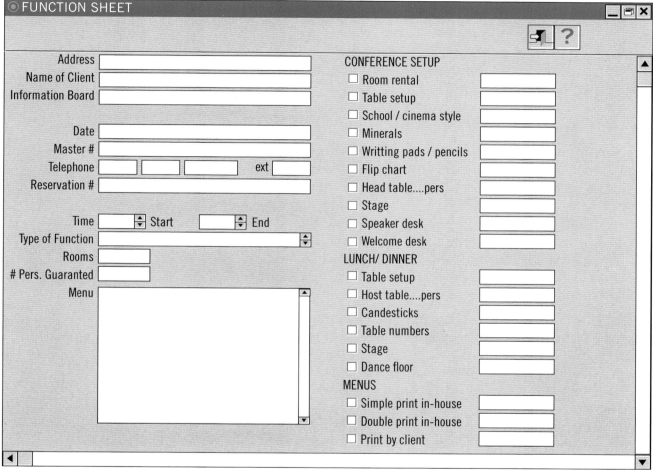

Section 10.3

Preparing for Service

Preparing for service for banquets and catered events can include creating menus and planning décor, setting up the function room or rooms; scheduling staff members; and preparing, plating, and storing banquet food. Sometimes, however, banquets and catered events are designed by outside design firms.

Setting up Function Rooms

The design and décor of function rooms, like the food and beverages that are served in them, can take many forms. A simple coffee break may be served in an undecorated, themeless room, while an elaborate reception featuring foods from around the world may be served in a function room that has complex decorations to fit the theme. The type of function room chosen and how it is decorated are largely dictated by the needs and expectations of the client, as well as the client's budget.

Managers should carefully plan the location of such room elements as bars, food buffet stations, ice carvings, garden and tree decorations, and stages for speakers or entertainers. The location of these elements affects the guests' experience in the room. Adequate space for display tables, guest tables, and other room elements (for example, stages and lecterns) is an important consideration for banquets and catered events. Crowded, hot rooms make for an unpleasant dining experience. Adequate space allows for more efficient movement of inventory and people. The client is usually responsible for reviewing any seating charts that the event may require. However, the manager can assist the client with that task and indicate the staff's preferences regarding seating arrangements.

Procedures for setting up function rooms vary according to the needs of the client and his or her group. The following is a partial list of placement activities required as elements of the function room:

- Runways, carpets, and pianos
- Dinner tables, meeting tables, head tables, chairs, sofas, and other seats
- Bars; buffets; and cake, registration, gift, and display tables
- Presentation and display equipment
- Linens, sugar bowls, salt and pepper shakers, and other tabletop items
- Cakes, candle holders, fountains, flowers, and decorations
- Numbers on each table or program booklets or other printed materials on each chair, if necessary

Because guests at banquets and catered events must be served quickly, service stations should be set up to allow for maximum staff efficiency. Function room service stations may have the following items:

- Microwave ovens
- Flatware
- Glassware
- Water, coffee, and tea
- Cream, sugar, stirrers, salt and pepper, and other condiments
- Placemats, linens, and napkins

Prior to opening the function room's doors and allowing guests to enter, the manager overseeing service for the event must ensure that the room setup is complete. The manager should walk through the function room (or assign someone else to do so) to make a safety check. No cords should be positioned where someone could trip over them; supports for tables, chairs, and stages should all be secure and not wobble; and doorways, hallways, and fire exits should not be obstructed.

Scheduling Staff Members

Managers must schedule the proper number of staff members and types of staff positions for each banquet and catered event. Based on the number of special functions scheduled each day, the banquet/catering director or manager must schedule staff to set up and break down function rooms, as well as staff to perform all the guest-contact service tasks involved in the events themselves. The number of servers and other personnel that are scheduled for an event varies by operation and the type of service being offered. Among top private clubs, for example, the ratio may be one server for every 10 to 15 guests.

Sample Staffing Ratio: Guests per Server

10-15 guests   1 Server

Training

Training staff members to be banquet servers requires that trainers have a fundamental knowledge of all service styles and skills that might be used at events the operation hosts. Rehearsals in which service actions are repeated a number of times are often the best way to help servers internalize service styles and skills. All of the details of the function sheet should be reviewed during practice sessions.

Banquet and catering personnel also must be trained to realize that, as guest-contact staff members, they give guests first and last impressions of the operation. Some guests at banquets and catered events may have unique service needs. For example, staff members who will serve international guests at functions should be trained to be sensitive to the guests' customs. Staff should also be trained in how to serve guests with disabilities.

Diversity

International customs that may impact banquet service include:

- Some international clients may present a small gift to the banquet or catering manager, who should be prepared to give a modest gift in return.
- Business banquets are popular in Chinese culture; they end promptly after the host rises and gives a toast.
- A Chinese guest named "Liang Cheng-wu" should be addressed as "Mr. Liang;" "Cheng-wu" is a compound of the man's first and middle names and it would be socially incorrect to use it.
- Children from Asian countries such as Thailand and India should never be patted on the head because the head is considered sacred in those cultures.

Preparing, Plating, and Storing Food

The input of the chef and other food production staff members should be used to develop menus for banquets and catered events. Some banquet and catering operations that handle events with large numbers of guests use an automated assembly line to portion meals. More commonly, however, operations use a manual plating process. The image below shows one arrangement of people, equipment, and supplies that can be used to plate and set up one kind of meal. As illustrated, one person carves and places slices of roast turkey on plates, then passes the plates along the table to a second staff member, who portions the fresh vegetables. A third staff member portions the mashed potatoes and slides the plates across the table to a fourth staff member, who places gravy on the meat. A fifth staff member cleans the plates of any spills, covers the plates, and loads them onto a mobile cart. Using this system, five staff members can plate food for 300 people in approximately 45 minutes.

Possible Setup for Plating

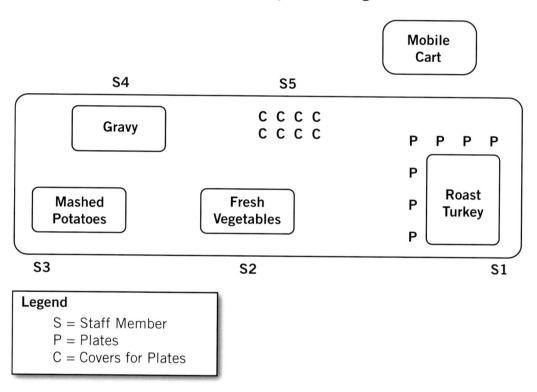

In banquet and catering service, time and temperature control for food is critical. It is virtually impossible to prepare hundreds of individual plates as service progresses. Therefore, foods are usually prepared for large banquets or catered events and then stored hot or cold in holding cabinets. Food must be kept out of the temperature danger zone (TDZ). Because the TDZ may be defined differently in various areas of the country, managers should check with local and state health authorities to make sure they are in compliance with safety codes.

Delivering Service

Because of all the planning and other preparatory work that goes into every banquet or catered event, you might think that a banquet or catering manager would only need to supervise staff from a distance during the event itself. In reality, last-minute issues and challenges often occupy the manager throughout an event. Challenges might include staff members calling in sick, extra guests, malfunctioning equipment, medical emergencies, inebriated guests, power failures, or entertainers who are late or fail to show up. The manager should either be present at the event or easy to reach, both by staff members and the client. Wise managers have contingency plans in place for the most common challenges.

Beverage Service

Managers must carefully plan procedures for providing beverage service to guests at banquets and catered events. Just as bars and lounges must do, banquets and catering operations must observe liquor laws, such as age limits and legal hours for beverage service. In some places, laws may require clients to obtain permits to serve alcoholic beverages to private groups in function rooms. Managers or salespeople are responsible for notifying clients about these requirements. The banquet and catering operation is also responsible for preventing underage drinking in its function rooms; the manager cannot delegate this responsibility to clients.

Many operations use one or a combination of the following beverage plans to provide beverage service at banquets or catered events:

Cash bar: Guests pay cash to the bartender or purchase tickets from a cashier to pay for drinks prepared by the bartender. The banquet/catering manager or salesperson generally specifies the drink prices in the contract; the prices can be the same or different from normal selling prices.

Host bar (charge by the drink): Charges the host by the drink using a system to keep track of the number of each type of drink served. Guests do not pay anything except tips. Managers will frequently reduce the prices of the drinks from normal prices.

Host bar (charge by the bottle): This plan involves charging for beverages consumed on the basis of bottles used or opened. An agreed-upon price for each bottle is assessed to the host.

Host bar (charge by the hour): This pricing plan charges hosts a fixed beverage fee per person per hour. It involves estimating the number of drinks guests will consume each hour and multiplying the number of drinks per person by an established drink charge to arrive at the hourly drink charge per person.

Wine service: Staff members circulate with bottles of several wines (red and white, dry and semi-dry) so that they can offer guests a choice. Alternately, operations may set up a portable bar so that bartenders can prepare the glasses to hand off to the servers.

Protocol for Special Banquets and Catered Events

Every banquet or catered event is special to the guests who attend it, and banquet and catering staff members must always be courteous and exercise common sense to make the guests' experiences as enjoyable as possible. However, there are some special banquets and catered events in which staff members must also understand **protocol**—the formal rules of etiquette used for ceremonies of state, military functions, and other special events.

There are rules that dictate the proper way to do things when very special guests are served. Managers and service personnel who will come in direct contact with special guests must understand and be able to practice protocol. The following examples illustrate the types of issues that can come up.

Green Practices

Green practices in the hospitality and tourism industry have also affected banquet and catered events service. Guest preferences have changed to reflect this greener approach. For example, many guests today are opting for healthier catered meals, including menus that feature local or organic foods. Banquet and catering operations are using sustainable supplies, replacing bottled water with water pitchers to reduce waste, and donating leftover food to charitable organizations.

At formal events, the seat of honor at the head table is to the right of the host. The second seat of honor is to the left of the host. If another seat of honor is required, it is the second seat on the right of the host. The rest of the seats at the head table should be allocated according to the rank or prominence of the guests. These guests should be assigned seats by alternating from the right to the left of the host out from the center of the head table.

Protocol for Seating Guests at the Head Table

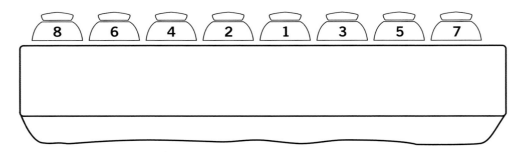

```
8    6    4    2    1    3    5    7
```

Legend

Seat 1	=	Host of Function
Seat 2	=	Guest of Honor
Seat 3	=	Next Highest Ranking Person
Seats 4-7	=	Next in Rank
Seat 8	=	Person with Least Prominence

Flag display is also important in protocol. In the United States, for example, at a cocktail party, a standing gathering, or an event with theater seating for which flags must be positioned before the guests arrive, the U.S. flag is placed on the left side of the front of the room, as viewed from the dining area. If multiple flags are displayed, the U.S. flag takes the center (highest) position. The second most important flag goes immediately to the left of the U.S. flag, from the audience's perspective, the third most important flag goes immediately to the right of the U.S. flag, and so on.

When flags are used behind a podium, the national colors are placed on the physical right of the speaker as he or she addresses the audience. When displayed behind the speaker's platform without a pole, the flag must be flat against its display surface and must have its longest dimension parallel to the floor, directly behind and slightly above the podium. Staff members should never use the flag of any country as a table cover, drape, or any other type of decoration. To decorate with bunting that has the national colors of the United States (red, white, and blue), staff members should place the color blue uppermost, then white, and finally red in the lowest place.

After Service

After the completion of food and beverage service at an event, the manager in charge must perform several after-service tasks. One such task is supervising staff members to ensure that they complete their breakdown and clean-up duties properly. Managers must evaluate how well the operation handled the event. The experience gained from each event can help with the planning of other events. Guest comments must also be sought to provide guest input into continuous quality improvement.

Checklist for Post-Event Duties

Banquet/Catered Event Staff
❑ Clear all tables of china, glass, and flatware.
❑ Remove all linens, flowers, and decorations.
❑ Straighten legs on all tables.
❑ Rearrange all chairs around tables neatly.
❑ Store salt and pepper shakers, sugar bowls, water pitchers, and other tabletop items.
❑ Clear all remaining carts and lock them.
❑ Remove candles and any melted wax from candelabras and return to storage.
❑ Check out with supervisor on duty.

Banquet/Catered Event Supervisor
❑ Supervise the banquet/catered event staff.
❑ Turn off public address system.
❑ Collect microphones and cords and return to proper storage area(s).
❑ Collect projectors and other audiovisual equipment and return to storage.
❑ Search area for valuable items left behind.
❑ Check cloakroom and restroom areas.
❑ Secure any items found and turn in to the Lost and Found no later than the following day.
❑ Inspect for fire hazards.
❑ Turn off lights.
❑ Lock all doors. (If band is moving out, remain until the move is completed.)
❑ Leave written information regarding any maintenance problems or items helpful to the supervisor who will open the room the next day.
❑ Leave written information on the manager's desk regarding any guest complaints or serious problems among staff members.
❑ Lock, secure, and turn off lights and air conditioning units in all other function rooms.

Controls

Managers must establish systems of control for the food and beverages served in banquets and catered events.

Food Controls

Payments may or may not be collected from clients at the time of the banquet or catered event; the contract for each event specifies the payment terms that the operation and the client agreed upon. However, when the banquet actually occurs, the operation must count the number of guests served to determine if payment is due for guests served in excess of the original estimate. The responsibility for determining the number of guests served rests with the manager in charge of the event. Performing more than one count is a good way to ensure accuracy. It is often a good idea to involve the client in the process. Managers try to avoid disagreements over counts, and when the client monitors or is otherwise involved in determining the count, he or she is less likely to dispute it later.

Beverage Controls

Managers can simplify the control procedures for beverages since fewer kinds of alcoholic beverages are generally available at banquets or catered events than there are in dining rooms or restaurants. For example, if only two types of wine are available, management can easily reconcile the amount of alcohol sold with the amount of income collected.

The amount of alcoholic beverages issued to a portable bar can be recorded on a form. Managers should remember to count partial bottles as whole bottles if the payment plan is "charge by the bottle." By conducting a beginning and an ending inventory, the amount of each product actually used can be determined. In a "by the drink" payment plan, the amount of income that the servers should have generated from a particular product can be determined by converting the amount of alcohol used into standard portion sizes and then converting that into the number of drinks sold.

Guest Comments

After major functions, the client may meet with the operation's managers to give feedback and to settle accounts. After small functions, the review process may be more modest: the manager in charge may ask the client to fill out an evaluation form. A telephone call to the client a day or two after the event provides the manager with an opportunity to thank the client and ask for additional feedback. This reinforces for the client the operation's commitment to guest service. It also helps communicate to clients that their future business is desired.

Using Feedback in Planning

Planning is a critical activity for banquets and catered events, and feedback about past events can help managers plan future events. Regardless of whether an operation holds a review meeting with the client after an event, managers should hold such a meeting with all staff members who were involved in providing service during the event. These meetings are particularly helpful when mistakes occurred. Such mistakes may happen again if managers do not take the time to review them and discuss possible solutions. Managers and staff should relay to each other any comments from guests or the client. This exchange should lead to action plans to correct problems that were mentioned by guests. Continuous quality improvement is the key to the development of a profitable and guest-pleasing banquet and catering operation.

Guest Feedback	Action Plan
Food was cold.	Check temperature of holding tables.
Long wait to be served.	Increase staffing ratio (fewer guests per server).
Cultural customs not observed.	Hold cultural sensitivity training for banquet staff.

Apply Your Learning

Section 10.1
1. Where can event planners work?
2. Provide an example of a cultural event.
3. Compare the return on sales for a banquet with the return on sales in a regular dining room. Which is more profitable? Explain your answer.
4. Why are food costs for banquets and catered events lower than for regular food and beverage operations?
5. Explain how additional income may be generated from outside vendors.

Section 10.2
1. What are the three documents that play a primary role in booking and planning banquets and catered events?
2. Managers and salespeople use the _____ to determine if a certain room is available for a particular function.
3. What document should list every detail that the salesperson and the client have discussed and agreed upon?
4. What is the function sheet, and who should have a copy of it?
5. List two examples of services that are typically included in room rental rates.

Section 10.3
1. Name some typical equipment or supplies found in function room service stations.
2. What must the managers overseeing service do prior to the event?
3. True or False? The temperature danger zone (TDZ) is the temperature at which the food is in danger of burning.
4. What is the best way to train banquet and catering service staff?
5. True or False? The automated assembly line style of portioning meals is the most common in today's banquet and catering operations.

Section 10.4

1. What are some challenges that managers and staff members may face just before or during an event? List three examples.
2. What kinds of liquor laws must banquet and catering operations observe?
3. How is a cash bar different from a host bar?
4. On which side of the host is the seat of honor? On which side is the second seat of honor?
5. True or False? An example of a decorative and creative table covering would be the guest of honor's national flag.

Section 10.5

1. What are the two types of controls managers must establish systems for?
2. Why is it important for managers to calculate the actual number of guests served?
3. Why is it a good idea to involve the client in the process of counting guests?
4. What are three ways to solicit guest comments about the event?
5. How is guest feedback used in planning future events?

Unit 5

Managing Business Operations

T wo back of the house divisions essential to a property's operation are human resources and accounting. The employees in these divisions do not interact with guests; however, the divisions provide important support for the property's revenue centers. The human resources department is responsible for employee interviewing and hiring, benefits, and compliance with labor laws. The accounting or finance department is responsible for budgeting, managing operational expenses, and revenue management.

This unit will explore how the functions of human resources and finance interface with the rest of the operation. It will focus on the role of management in these divisions and the specific job responsibilities of managers.

Chapter 11

Human Resources

COMPETENCIES

1. Identify the four basic rules in preparing for interviews, assess the strengths and weaknesses of different types of interview approaches, and differentiate between closed-ended and open-ended questions.

2. Identify the employment laws that impact the hospitality and tourism industry and the role of human resources managers in applying these laws.

3. Distinguish between direct and indirect compensation, and identify factors that influence pay.

4. Explain the concept of corporate social responsibility, and describe examples of how hospitality and tourism companies are including corporate social responsibility initiatives in their organizations.

Hospitality Profile

NewCastle Hotels & Resorts

Marian R. Barbieri
Vice President
of Human Resources
New Castle Hotels & Resorts

Marian R. Barbieri has been with New Castle in various capacities since its inception in 1980 and has led the company's human resources effort for the past 25 years. Her leadership in human resources provides proven policies and procedures that ensure compliance with all the legal aspects of the business, while at the same time delivering a positive work experience. New Castle prides itself on its diverse workplace, positive employee relations and staff recognition, competitive wages and benefits, high guest and employee engagement scores, and below industry staff turnover.

After graduating high school, Ms. Barbieri attended the Grace Institute and started working as a secretary in 1977. Soon after, she began working for David Buffam, who founded New Castle Investment Inc. with the goal of building a hotel ownership company. Ms. Barbieri wished to be more involved in company management and started taking college classes, eventually graduating with a degree in Hospitality Management from NYU in 1986. At that time, she was handling insurance, labor, bookkeeping, and renovations for New Castle but determined HR was her passion. In 1991, Ms. Barbieri received a certificate in Personnel Administration from Fairfield University. Since 1988, she has worked in HR with the company, becoming a director and then vice president overseeing all HR practices for New Castle in the U.S. and Canada. She is also a partner in the firm.

Ms. Barbieri currently sits on the AH&LA HR committee. She is a member of the Society for Human Resource Management (SHRM) and was nominated for HR Leader of the Year by the Southern Connecticut chapter of SHRM in 2007.

Introduction

The human resources division, sometimes called the personnel division, assists other divisions in recruiting and selecting the most qualified job applicants. It also administers insurance and other benefit programs, handles personnel-related complaints, ensures compliance with labor laws, is involved with labor union matters, and administers the company's wage and salary compensation programs. In operations that are not large enough to justify a separate human resources office or position, the general manager may handle the human resources functions.

Good managers see themselves as developers of people and as guardians of their company's most valuable asset—its employees. People who choose human resources as a career usually have a good deal of empathy and are excellent negotiators. Human resources managers are concerned with the whole equation of people and productivity. They are often tasked with developing and implementing programs to maintain and improve employee morale. In addition, their job description includes counseling employees, resolving disputes, disciplining, evaluating, motivating, developing, promoting, rewarding, and communicating with all the employees of the company. Human resources managers are responsible for ensuring that the organization is engaging in ethical practices with regard to the treatment of employees, guests, and the local community.

Pineapple Fun Fact

Many hospitality companies donate "leftovers" (unused, wholesome food) to charitable organizations to help feed the hungry. In the past, much of this food was sent to landfills because companies were worried about being held liable if any of the products caused harm to the recipients. However, in 1996, President Bill Clinton signed into law the Bill Emerson Good Samaritan Food Donation Act. This act protects good faith food donors by limiting liability for companies that donate food products for the benefit of the community.

Interview and Hiring Practices

Interviewing is the most common selection method used by companies to evaluate job applicants. Despite their popularity, many problems exist with the reliability of interviews, including a lack of objectivity, a lack of uniformity in the interview process, and a lack of training for the interviewer. Managers can improve the reliability of interviews through careful preparation and having a thorough knowledge of the various types of interviews.

Preparing for Interviews

The four basic rules of interviews are:

1. Do your homework before the interview. Lack of knowledge about the candidate sends signals that you either did not care enough to prepare in advance or that you are disorganized.

2. Establish the appropriate setting. Create an environment that focuses solely on the candidate. Interruptions are distracting and inappropriate during an interview.

3. Establish a rapport. Put the candidate at ease to get him or her talking.

4. Know the job. It is impossible to find the right candidate unless you fully understand the job requirements.

BE PREPARED!

Open-Ended Questions—
designed to elicit a full, meaningful answer using the subject's own knowledge or feelings.

Closed-Ended Questions—
require a short or single-word response, such as "yes" or "no."

Types of Interviews

Interviews generally fall into three categories: unstructured, semi-structured, and structured. In unstructured interviews, questions are not planned in advance. Instead, the interviewer directs the interview down whatever path seems appropriate at the time. This approach is best suited for experienced interviewers who have thoroughly prepared for the interview.

Semi-structured interviews involve preparing or planning the issues to be explored but also allowing for flexibility during the process. This approach uses **open-ended questions**, designed to elicit thorough responses from the candidate. **Closed-ended questions**, on the other hand, require only a "Yes" or "No" answer.

Closed-Ended Question	Open-Ended Question
Did you enjoy your previous job?	What aspects of your previous job did you like best?
Do you get along with your co-workers?	How have you resolved conflicts with co-workers in the past?
Do you prefer to work individually or on a team?	What is your preferred work style?

In structured interviews, questions are prepared in advance and are asked the same way and at the same time during an interview. This type of approach results in answers that are comparable between candidates. However, the information collected through a structured interview is narrower and may not reveal important strengths and weaknesses about a candidate.

Making the Right Impression

Interviewers are often an applicant's only source of contact with the company. Because the interviewer represents the company and the people who work there, a company should be careful to choose a good representative. It is important that the interviewer creates a realistic impression during the interview. Since interviews can actually be considered the initial stage of orientation for an applicant who comes on staff, it is critical to communicate what the job really entails. For example, telling an applicant for a management trainee position that she would make important decisions about room rates and property locations obviously does not establish a realistic perspective of the job.

It is unlawful to ask applicants certain questions, as they can lead to discriminatory practices. Interviewers should avoid inquiries about:

- An applicant's name that would indicate his or her lineage, ancestry, national origin, or descent

- Marital status or childcare arrangements

- An applicant's age, sex, disability, or race

- Whether the applicant rents or owns; the names and relationships of people with whom the applicant resides

- Birthplace of the applicant or the applicant's parents

- Applicant's religious denomination or affiliation

Employment Laws

Affirmative Action—an active effort to hire or promote members of a protected group to overcome past discriminatory practices.

Reverse Discrimination—discrimination against members of a majority group in favor of a minority or historically disadvantaged group.

As you learned in Section 2.5, the EEOC is the federal commission created by the Civil Rights Act of 1964 to establish and monitor employment standards in the United States. The EEOC is responsible for enforcing federal laws that make it illegal to discriminate against a job applicant or an employee because of a person's race, color, religion, sex (including pregnancy), national origin, age (40 or older), disability, or genetic information. It is also illegal to discriminate against a person because he or she complained about, filed a charge of, or participated in a discrimination investigation or lawsuit.

Most employers with at least 15 employees are covered by EEOC laws. Human resources managers are responsible for implementing and monitoring equal employment opportunity (EEO) policies in the workplace. The laws apply to all types of work situations, including hiring, firing, promotions, harassment, training, wages, and benefits.

Affirmative Action

In addition to EEO policies, many organizations have **affirmative action** programs. Although all employers are required to abide by EEO laws, only federal employers are required to have affirmative action programs. Affirmative action represents an obligation employers have to hire members of protected groups to overcome past discriminatory practices. An example of affirmative action would be a program designed to recruit, hire, or promote qualified members of a protected group, such as women, minorities, Vietnam-era veterans, or people with disabilities.

Affirmative action can be a controversial topic. Those who favor affirmative action believe that it is necessary in order to right wrongs suffered by minority groups who have been discriminated against in the past. Those who oppose it say that it leads to **reverse discrimination** against people who are not members of protected groups, which can foster resentment and perpetuate prejudice.

Executive Orders and Court Decisions

Not all legislation affecting employer-employee relations is included in the major federal employment acts. Executive orders, issued by the president of the United States, and rulings in court cases have also helped shape employment practices over the past 40 years.

Many states and municipalities have enacted laws that protect groups not included in the federal legislation. These laws prohibit discrimination based on sexual orientation, physical appearance, political affiliation, contagious diseases, and so on. Because these provisions can change so radically from state to state, human resources managers should conduct a careful review of state and local EEO laws to ensure their organizations are in compliance.

Special Issues in Hospitality and Tourism Operations

Hospitality and tourism human resources managers must be aware of the potential for EEO problems for several reasons:

- The hospitality and tourism industry is the largest employer of minimum-wage employees in the United States.

- Many hospitality and tourism companies have poor records of promoting women to top-level management positions.

- The large number of female employees working for male managers creates situations conducive to sexual harassment charges.

- In the past, some segments of the industry have emphasized appearance as a condition of employment—for example, hiring only pretty young employees as greeters in a restaurant.

- Historically, the hospitality and tourism industry has placed sex designations on some jobs, such as refusing to hire women as hotel stewards because it is presumed they cannot lift heavy objects.

- As the overall age of the workforce increases, companies must ensure that age discrimination does not occur (for example, not putting older workers in training programs, not promoting older workers, or forcing older employees to retire).

- Recruitment advertising that specifies age or sex is illegal. For example, sex discrimination occurs when advertisements use sex-specific terms such as "maid," "waiter," or "hostess." Ads that specify certain ages, such as "college student" or "retiree," may discourage people from other age groups from applying.

Diversity

The Lilly Ledbetter Fair Pay Act of 2009 extends the period of time that women are able to file a claim of wage discrimination. Lilly Ledbetter worked as a supervisor at a Goodyear plant for almost 20 years. After her retirement, she sued the company for paying her significantly less than her male counterparts. The lawsuit eventually reached the Supreme Court, which denied her claim because she did not file suit 180 days from her first pay check, even though she did not know about the wage gap at the time. This new legislation means that with each new paycheck affected by the discriminatory action, the six-month time frame for filing a lawsuit resets.

Managing Compensation and Benefits

Direct Compensation— payment of money to an employee.

Shift Differential—added pay for work performed at other than regular daytime hours, such as evening or night shifts.

Indirect Compensation— given as a condition of employment rather than in direct exchange for productive work.

Cost of Living—the real dollar value of a worker's purchasing power for ordinary necessities such as food and clothing.

W hen most people hear the word "compensation," they think about the wages or salaries that people earn in return for the work they do. However, wages and salaries are only part of the total compensation employees receive. An effective compensation program consists of both cash and non-cash rewards—salaries and wages as well as other benefits.

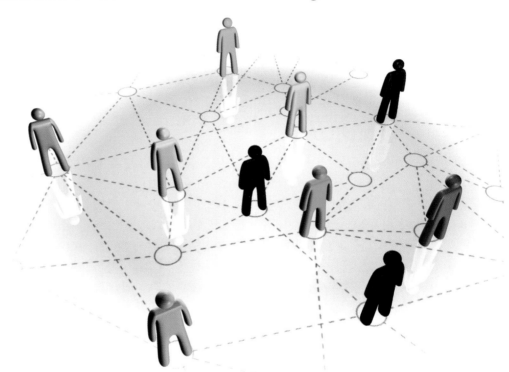

Compensation

Compensation types can be broken down into direct and indirect, as well as immediate and deferred. **Direct compensation** involves an employer's payment of money to an employee in exchange for that employee's productive work. Direct immediate compensation includes base pay, merit pay, bonuses, and **shift differentials**. Direct deferred compensation includes money earned in one period that is not paid until a later period, such as retention bonuses paid out after a certain number of years. **Indirect compensation** is given as a condition of employment rather than in direct exchange for productive work. Health insurance coverage, vacation, and retirement savings plans are examples of indirect compensation.

Types of Compensation

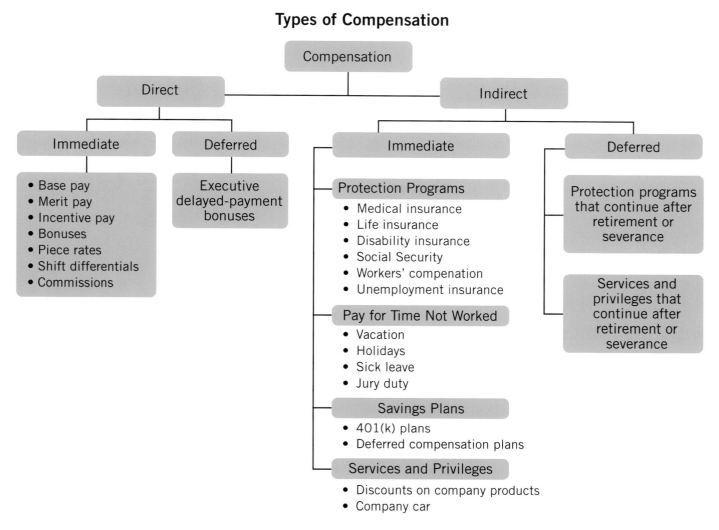

The following factors influence the amount and type of compensation employees may receive:

Cost of Living: The **cost of living** refers to the real dollar value of a worker's purchasing power. As the value or purchasing power of the dollar changes, companies must adjust their compensation rates to remain competitive. Geographic location also affects compensation. For example, a salary of $25,000 in Henderson, North Carolina, would have more purchasing power than that same salary in New York City.

Labor Market: The number of workers available in the market influences compensation. If there is a shortage of available workers, compensation rates would have to be higher in order to attract employees. If, however, unemployment is high and many people are looking for work, compensation rates will be lower.

Unions: Labor unions negotiate compensation and benefits for their members. Many union contracts contain a cost of living adjustment clause, which means employees receive increases in their compensation as cost of living increases.

Government: Laws that mandate minimum wage, overtime pay, and retirement benefits affect the rates at which companies compensate employees.

Benefits and Incentives

Most employers recognize that benefits and incentives lead to greater employee productivity and performance. They are a good way to retain employees and increase job satisfaction—offering a great benefit package is an indication of an organization's commitment to its employees. However, it can also become costly for the organization. The human resources team helps upper management to identify a benefit and incentive plan that fits with the organization's objectives.

The benefits offered by most organizations fall into four categories:

Mandatory Benefits: Social Security, unemployment compensation insurance, and workers' compensation

Voluntary Benefits: group life insurance, group health insurance, and alternative health plans

Pension and Retirement Benefits: Individual Retirement Accounts (IRAs) and Salary Reduction/401(k) Plans

Other Benefits: educational assistance, child and dependent care programs, flexible benefits plans, vacation pay, holiday pay, sick leave, jury duty pay, bereavement leave, flexible work schedules, and cap on work hours

Both individual and group incentives can play significant roles in improving productivity in hospitality and tourism organizations. Individual incentive programs include merit pay, bonus plans, and commission programs. These types of programs work well when the work is not too interdependent or when individual improvement most benefits the organization. However, they also require a great deal of administrative work. Group incentive programs, on the other hand, are most useful when cooperation and teamwork are the goals. Profit-sharing and stock ownership are common group incentive plans. These plans have the disadvantage of having a negative effect on employees when the company has a bad year. In addition, they may end up unfairly rewarding employees who do not perform well. Other types of incentives include company merchandise, trips, and creative rewards, such as "Take Your Pet to Work Day."

Corporate Social Responsibility

Corporate social responsibility (CSR) is the obligation of an organization's management to make decisions and take actions that enhance the welfare of society as a whole. In the early twentieth century, most business leaders felt that their only responsibility was to those who had a direct interest in the success of their organization. Wealthy business owners gave money to charity but paid their employees very low wages and broke labor strikes by force. Managers today realize that their businesses are an important part of society, and society plays a vital role in the success of their businesses. Being socially responsible is a big part of an organization's long-term success.

TERMS YOU SHOULD KNOW

Corporate Social Responsibility— the obligation of an organization's management to make decisions and take actions that enhance the welfare and interests of society as a whole.

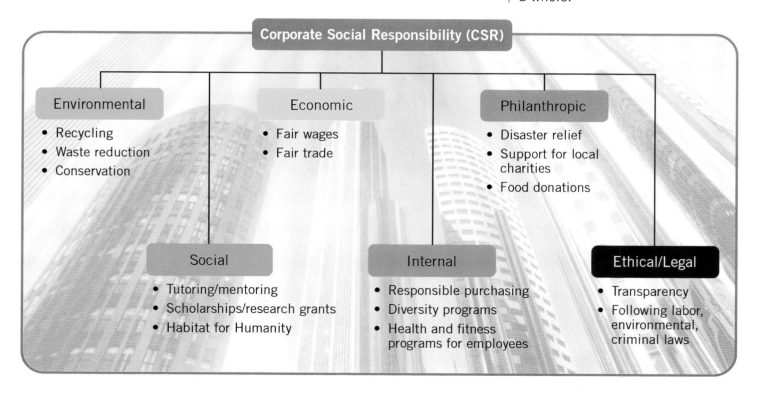

Corporate Social Responsibility (CSR)

Environmental
- Recycling
- Waste reduction
- Conservation

Economic
- Fair wages
- Fair trade

Philanthropic
- Disaster relief
- Support for local charities
- Food donations

Social
- Tutoring/mentoring
- Scholarships/research grants
- Habitat for Humanity

Internal
- Responsible purchasing
- Diversity programs
- Health and fitness programs for employees

Ethical/Legal
- Transparency
- Following labor, environmental, criminal laws

Stakeholder—someone who can affect or be affected by the actions of the business as a whole.

Whistleblower—a current or former employee or manager of an organization who reports unethical behavior on the part of the organization to people or entities that have the power to take corrective action.

CSR aims to embrace responsibility for the company's actions and encourage a positive impact on its **stakeholders** through its activities. A stakeholder is someone who can affect or be affected by the actions of the business as a whole. Typical corporate stakeholders include employees, customers, suppliers, creditors, owners, investors, unions, the government, and the community. Although many corporations today are participating in CSR initiatives, there is still an ongoing debate about their effectiveness. The following table lists some of the pros and cons of CSR:

Pros	Cons
Reduced operating costs	Financial benefits hard to measure
Enhanced image and reputation	High costs and administrative time of CSR programs
Greater customer loyalty	Choosing the "right" causes to support
Increased ability to attract and retain employees	Interferes with the nature of business (making profits)
Greater access to investment capital	Unethical motives
Potential avoidance of fines or lawsuits	Giving businesses too much power

Ethical Behavior and CSR

CSR and ethics go hand-in-hand. Organizations cannot develop social responsibility toward the community without first making a commitment to ethical business practices. Although the unethical conduct of companies often receives the most media attention, it is important to note that most businesses follow the rules. Developing a company code of ethics and emphasizing the importance of ethical behavior in the workplace is often the domain of the human resources department. Ethical issues can arise in hiring, firing, and promotion decisions, which is why it is essential to involve human resources managers in these processes. Sometimes when an organization acts in an unethical manner, people are motivated by their individual ethics to report these actions. These individuals are referred to as **whistleblowers**. They are protected by federal and state "whistleblower laws" that allow them to report misconduct without fear of retaliation from their companies.

CSR in the Hospitality and Tourism Industry

Many hospitality and tourism companies today have dedicated CSR departments and incorporate CSR strategy directly into the business strategy of their organizations. For example, a hotel chain may choose to purchase and serve only fair trade coffee and tea. Leading hospitality organizations such as Hilton, Starwood, Choice, Starbucks, and McDonald's are now providing yearly reports about their CSR efforts. The following are just a few examples of the programs and initiatives hospitality companies engage in regularly:

- Sol Meliá, a Spanish hotel and resort chain, donates one euro to the United Nations Children's Fund (UNICEF) for every hotel reservation made through its website.

- Kimpton Hotel & Restaurant Group hosts Kimpton Cares Month during which employees volunteer to make a positive social and environmental difference on a local level by donating blood, raising money for humane societies, planting trees, and collecting food for the hungry.

- Hilton allows guests to convert their guest reward points to contributions to charitable organizations such as the American Red Cross, the City of Hope Cancer Center, and the National Coalition for the Homeless.

- Berjaya Hotels & Resorts is involved in biodiversity conservation and is focusing on coral reefs around Malaysia.

- McDonald's in the United Arab Emirates has launched a biodiesel campaign in which used vegetable oil is collected from its restaurants and converted into biodiesel to fuel its fleet of trucks.

- Tourism Toronto provides parents of children with special needs with weekend tourism packages, giving them an opportunity to relax and recharge. The organization also awards scholarships to college students enrolled in hospitality and tourism programs.

Apply Your Learning

Section 11.1
1. What is another name for the human resources division?
2. Name three responsibilities of human resources.
3. Explain the differences between how human resources functions are handled in large operations vs. small operations.
4. Why do you think human resources managers need to have empathy?

Section 11.2
1. As an interviewer, why is it important to do your homework before the interview?
2. Explain the difference between open-ended and closed-ended questions.
3. In what type of interview are questions prepared in advance and asked the same way and at the same time during an interview?
4. Is it important that the interviewer creates a realistic impression of the position during the interview? Why or why not?
5. Name three types of questions interviewers should avoid.

Section 11.3
1. Compare and contrast EEO laws and affirmative action programs.
2. Define the term "reverse discrimination." What is the relationship between reverse discrimination and affirmative action?
3. True or False? It is acceptable to hire greeters in a restaurant based on their age and appearance. Explain your answer.
4. In what instances might recruitment advertising be illegal? Explain your answer.

Section 11.4

1. State whether the following are examples of direct or indirect compensation:
   A. Salary
   B. Vacation pay
   C. Shift differential pay
   D. Health insurance coverage
   E. Bonus pay
2. If there is a shortage of potential workers, what will likely happen to compensation rates?
3. Define the term "cost of living." How does location affect cost of living?
4. Group life insurance is an example of a _____ benefit.
5. True or False? Benefits and incentives lead to greater employee productivity and performance. Explain your answer.
6. What is a disadvantage of individual incentive programs?

Section 11.5

1. How are CSR programs today different from charitable contributions in the past?
2. Who are a company's stakeholders?
3. List two pros and two cons of CSR programs.
4. Why do you think it is important to have laws that protect whistleblowers from retaliation?
5. What is the role of the human resources department in business ethics?

Chapter 12

Managing Operational Finance

COMPETENCIES

1. Discuss how revenue centers and cost centers are managed to ensure a property's profitability.

2. Identify the components of income statements and balance sheets.

3. Distinguish between operations and capital budgets and explain how to use each appropriately.

4. Explain the purpose of revenue management in the hospitality and tourism industry.

5. Use productivity standards and staffing guides to manage labor costs.

6. Identify the tax responsibilities a hospitality and tourism leader must manage.

HVS

Victoria S. Richman
Chief Financial Officer
HVS Hotel Management
HVS Asset Management

Victoria (Vicki) S. Richman is chief financial officer of HVS Hotel Management and HVS Asset Management (Newport). She oversees all of the financial and accounting operations of the companies and their hotels, as well as being responsible for asset management, litigation support assignments, and human resources. Ms. Richman serves as a trusted advisor to hotel investors and lenders by providing the understanding of a hotel's investment potential, detailed financial analysis, strategic planning, and an unparalleled eye for quality. Her work as an expert witness is relied upon by attorneys across the country seeking credible and unassailable hotel industry expert testimony.

Previous to her current position, Ms. Richman's background includes systems analyst for Hibernia National Bank, a large regional bank based in New Orleans; director of consulting for Stephen W. Brener Associates, a premier hotel consulting firm based in New York; and director of a hotel development consulting firm based in Minneapolis.

Ms. Richman is a member of the Financial Management Committee of the AH&LA. This committee is responsible for administering and writing the *Uniform System of Accounts for the Lodging Industry*, the definitive standard presentation of hotel financial statements.

Ms. Richman holds a BA in Political Science from Brown University and an MBA from the Wharton School at University of Pennsylvania. She was profiled in *Who's Who of American Women* (16th Edition). Ms. Richman was also featured on National Public Radio and *The Wall Street Journal* for being the first person to sell a hotel via eBay in the early days of the Internet.

Section 12.1

Introduction

TERMS YOU SHOULD KNOW

Financial Reporting Center—an area of responsibility for which separate revenue and cost information must be collected.

Just as every operational area of a business has expenses, such as labor costs and supplies, so does the business as a whole. Most hospitality and tourism businesses can be organized into expense, or cost, centers and revenue centers. Revenue centers generate income for the business through the sale of products or services to guests. For example, the rooms division and the food and beverage division are the main revenue centers for hotels. Cost centers, on the other hand, do not generate revenue directly but act as support centers for the areas producing revenue. Departments such as marketing, security, and accounting are cost centers.

The key to managing revenue and cost centers to ensure a property's profitability is to generate as much revenue as possible while keeping expenses as minimal as possible. However, managers who focus only on revenue centers are missing a crucial piece of the puzzle. Cost centers also contribute to revenue and profit by increasing guest satisfaction. A parking garage operated by a hotel is a revenue center, while the hotel's security department is a cost center. Even though security is an expense, it makes guests feel safe, thus increasing customer satisfaction and contributing to higher levels of repeat business.

Each revenue or cost center is a separate **financial reporting center**. A financial reporting center is an area of responsibility for which revenue and cost information must be collected. This information is then used to prepare financial reports, which you will learn about in the next section. Certain departments may not be large enough to warrant a separate financial reporting center. For example, information systems and human resource functions may be combined with other hotel functions to form the financial reporting center called administrative and general.

Pineapple Fun Fact

Modern electronic systems allow managers to easily track time and attendance. Instead of traditional "punch in" systems, these trackers require employees to swipe an ID card and enter a code. Even more innovative systems use fingerprint or eye retina identification. This helps ensure that only the employee himself or herself can clock in and out. Using such systems can help cut down on administrative time and decrease human errors associated with manual time entry. Managers can use the data from time and attendance systems to track overtime, absences, and scheduled time off, as well as to develop employee schedules.

U.S. Lodging Industry

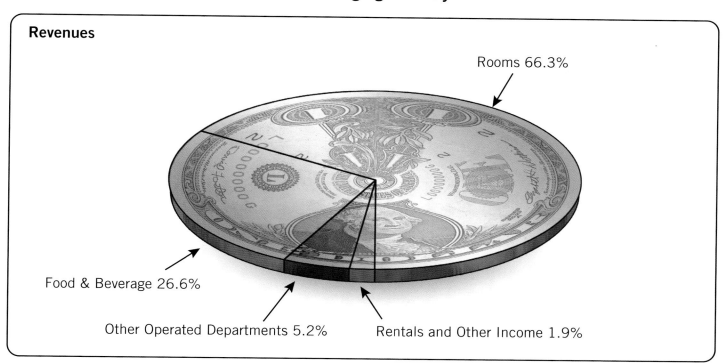

Revenues

Rooms 66.3%

Food & Beverage 26.6%

Other Operated Departments 5.2%

Rentals and Other Income 1.9%

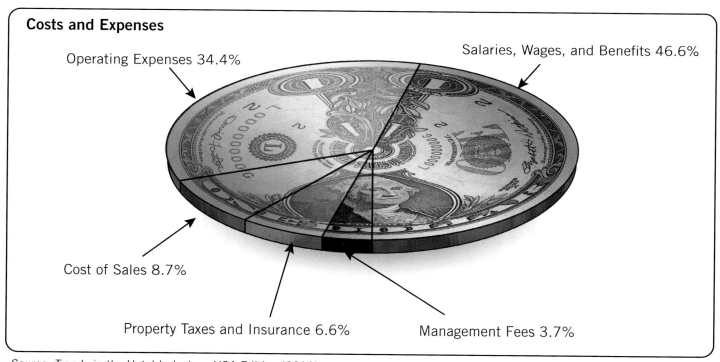

Costs and Expenses

Operating Expenses 34.4%

Salaries, Wages, and Benefits 46.6%

Cost of Sales 8.7%

Property Taxes and Insurance 6.6%

Management Fees 3.7%

Source: Trends in the Hotel Industry—USA Edition (2011)
(San Francisco: PKF Consulting, 2011)

Financial Statements

Income Statement—provides important information regarding the results of operations for a stated period of time.

Balance Sheet—reports the financial position of an operation on a specific date by showing its assets, liabilities, and equity.

In today's fast-paced world of business, hospitality and tourism managers need to know as much as possible about the financial aspects of their operations. Knowledge of accounting principles and basic financial statements, such as **income statements** and **balance sheets**, helps managers gauge the soundness of their accountants' analysis and advice.

Income Statement

An operation's income statement provides important information regarding the results of operations for a stated period of time, usually one month. The income statement can have many names. One term that is often used is profit and loss statement (P&L statement) because the statement shows whether the property achieved a profit or loss for a specified time period.

Information reported on income statements is developed through a bookkeeping process. As transactions occur, bookkeeping entries are made in the appropriate accounts. At the end of the month, trial balances and various adjustments are made to ensure that account balances accurately reflect the month's activity. Since the income statement reveals operating results, it is an important measure of the effectiveness of management. An income statement generally shows revenue, cost of sales, gross profit, and expenses.

A critical part of a manager's job is controlling expenses, which can be done by comparing the budget and the income statement to see if actual operating costs exceeded the budget. For example, a restaurant manager may want to compare actual food costs to budgeted costs. The technical term for "food cost" is "cost of sales": the cost of the food used to generate the food revenue produced during the accounting period.

$$\{ \text{Cost of Sales} = \text{Beginning Inventory} + \textbf{Purchases} - \textbf{Ending Inventory} \}$$

The food cost percentage is calculated by dividing the cost of sales by the food revenue and multiplying by 100:

$$\left\{ \frac{\text{Food Cost of Sales}}{\text{Food Revenue}} \times \textbf{100} = \text{Food Cost Percentage} \right\}$$

Sample Income Statement—Restaurant

BRANDYWINE RESTAURANT
INCOME STATEMENT
MONTH ENDING JANUARY 31, 20XX

Sales	Amount ($)	Percent
Food	533,250	71.9
Beverages	208,500	28.1
Total Sales	741,750	100.0
Cost of Sales		
Food	217,033	40.7
Beverages	58,172	27.9
Total Cost of Sales	275,205	37.1
Gross Profit		
Food	316,217	59.3
Beverages	150,328	72.1
Total Gross Profit	466,545	62.9
Other Revenue	8,250	1.1
Total Revenue	474,795	64.0
Controllable Expenses		
Salaries and Wages	203,981	27.5
Employee Benefits	35,604	4.8
Direct Operating Expenses	48,214	6.5
Music and Entertainment	6,676	0.9
Marketing	14,093	1.9
Utility Service	18,544	2.5
General and Administrative Expenses	40,055	5.4
Repairs and Maintenance	12,610	1.7
Total Controllable Expenses	379,777	51.2
Profit Before Occupation Costs	95,018	12.8
Occupation Costs		
Rent, Property Taxes, and Insurance	35,604	4.8
Interest	6,676	0.9
Depreciation	17,060	2.3
Other Additions and Deductions	(2,967)	(0.4)
	56,373	7.6
Net Income Before Income Tax	38,645	5.2

Balance Sheet

A balance sheet reports the financial position of an operation on a specific date by showing its assets, liabilities, and equity.

Assets: anything a business owns that has commercial or exchange value, such as cash, land, buildings, furniture, equipment, and supplies.

Liabilities: claims by others, such as creditors, to property assets.

Current liabilities: obligations that will require an outlay of cash within 12 months of the balance sheet date.

Noncurrent liabilities: long-term debt.

Equity: claims by the owner to assets.

On every balance sheet, the total assets must balance with the total of the liabilities and equity sections:

$$\{ \text{Assets} = \textbf{Liabilities} + \text{Equity} \}$$

Comparative Balance Sheets
TOMAS HOTEL 7 RESORT

	December 31 20X2	December 31 20X1	Change from 20X1 to 20X2 Amount ($)	Change from 20X1 to 20X2 Percent
ASSETS				
Current Assets:				
Cash	$104,625	$85,600	$19,025	22.2%
Marketable Securities	784,687	155,465	629,222	404.7
Accounts Receivable (net)	1,615,488	1,336,750	278,738	29.9
Inventories	98,350	92,540	5,810	6.3
Other	12,475	11,300	1,175	10.4
Total	2,615,625	1,681,655	933,970	55.5
Property and Equipment				
Land	905,700	905,700	0	0
Buildings	5,434,200	5,434,200	0	0
Furnishings and Equipment	2,617,125	2,650,500	(33,375)	(1.3)
Less: Accumulated Depreciation	1,221,490	749,915	471,575	62.9
Total	7,735,535	8,240,485	(504,950)	(6.1)
Other Assets	58,350	65,360	(7,010)	(10.7)
Total Assets	10,409,510	9,987,500	422,010	4.2%
LIABILITIES				
Current Liabilities				
Accounts Payable	$1,145,000	$838,000	$307,000	36.6%
Current Maturities of Long-Term Debt	275,000	275,000	0	0
Income Taxes Payable	273,750	356,000	(82,250)	(23.1)
Total	1,693,750	1,469,000	224,750	15.3
Long-Term Debt				
Notes Payable	50,000	0	50,000	N.M.
Mortgage Payable	1,500,000	1,775,000	(275,000)	(15.5)
Less: Current Maturities	275,000	275,000	0	0
Total	1,275,000	1,500,000	(225,000)	(15.0)
Total Liabilities	2,968,750	2,969,000	(250)	0
OWNERS' EQUITY				
Common Stock	1,750,000	1,750,000	0	0
Additional Pad-In Capital	250,000	250,000	0	0
Retained Earnings	5,440,760	5,018,500	422,260	8.4
Total	7,440,760	7,018,500	422,260	6.0
Total Liabilities and Owners' Equity	$10,409,510	$9,987,500	$422,010	4.2%

N.M. = not meaningful

Operational Expenses and the Capital Budget

Capital Budget—a plan for the purchase of major assets.

Operations Budget—a plan for recurring expenses that must be paid on a periodic basis.

What causes one business to prosper and another one to fail? As discussed in chapters 3 and 4, guest service is an important factor in the success or failure of a business. Poor guest service will hurt a company's bottom line because unhappy guests will not return or recommend the company to others. A company that provides outstanding guest service, on the other hand, will see a positive impact on its financials. However, guest service is not the only contributing factor. Often, the difference between successful and unsuccessful hospitality and tourism operations is that the successful ones are organized. Managers of well-organized businesses are able to budget and control expenses to maximize profits.

Every successful hospitality business has a master plan integrating the activities of all the revenue centers, cost centers, and other departments. This master plan outlines objectives, human resources policies, steps stating how to achieve goals, and a way to monitor the progress of the organization. Master plans take many forms, but they all include one common element: budgets.

Managers at all levels must participate in the preparation and planning of budgets. A large company may have a budget committee composed of top executives who provide guidance and coordination of the budgeting phase. A budget director, usually an upper-level accountant, supervises the process. The accounting department provides historical and other financial data to departmental managers and executives for the forecasting of revenue and expenses. The expertise of departmental managers also contributes greatly to successful budget planning and preparation.

A hospitality business uses many types of budgets. It uses a **capital budget** to plan and control the purchase of major assets. It uses an **operations budget** to budget sales and expenses in order to achieve a desired profit.

Capital Budget

Capital budgets reflect an organization's long-term plan for purchasing major assets. They require executive planning and approval because of the assets' significant costs. Organizations often take out loans to pay for capital expenditures. In the capital budgeting process, managers are asked to submit a list of their present and future asset requirements. For example, the front office manager's list might include tablet computers to be used by front desk staff or new reservations software. The chief engineer might request a new boiler or updated guestroom bathroom fixtures. Top-level executives then perform long-range planning for:

- Replacing present assets
- Adding new assets
- Expanding present facilities
- Purchasing land for development
- Acquiring other operating businesses

TERMS YOU SHOULD KNOW

Variable Expenses— expenses that have a direct relationship with sales volume.

Fixed Expenses—expenses that stay the same regardless of sales volume.

Management decides on the priorities of asset purchases. Those purchases that will have the best return on investment for the company will generally get higher priority. Capital expenses are reflected on the balance sheet.

Operations Budget

The operations budget is a profit plan that incorporates all revenue and expenses of the business. It is forecasted for the year and then divided into monthly plans. Operational expenses include items such as payroll, supplies, rental costs, contracted services, and other resources required for the daily operation of the business.

Preparing the operations budget first requires that departmental sales and expenses be forecasted and approved by the budget committee. The accounting department then reviews these preliminary departmental plans and merges them into a combined budget. In its final format, the operations budget is identical to an income statement, except that the amounts are estimates and not actual.

Types of Expenses

Expenses include all the costs involved in providing the goods and services a business offers to guests. They can be categorized as variable or fixed, depending on how they react to changes in sales volume. Sales volume is measured using the number of meal covers, room nights, guest occupancy, and sales of other goods. A useful equation that can be used to determine cost is as follows:

$$\{ \text{Total Cost} = \textbf{Variable Cost} + \text{Fixed Cost} \}$$

Variable expenses have a direct relationship with sales volume. If sales go up, variable expenses also go up. Managers can control variable expenses by using forecasts to predict labor costs or costs of materials/supplies, such as how many housekeepers to schedule or how much food to order. **Fixed expenses**, on the other hand, are not affected by sales volume. They stay the same whether the property has one or 100 guests on any given day. Examples of fixed expenses for hospitality and tourism businesses are rent, property taxes, insurance, and interest.

Revenue Management

Revenue Management—a technique used to predict consumer demand and optimize product availability and price to maximize revenue.

Revenue management, sometimes called yield management, means selling the right product to the right consumer at the right time for the right price. The practice started in the airline industry, but today, many industries use revenue management, including:

- Car rental and train travel companies
- Theaters and ticket agents
- Hotels
- Restaurants

For many years, airlines have used sophisticated revenue management pricing systems. These automated marketing programs allow airlines to control the inventory and pricing of airplane seats by forecasting the demand for seats on a given flight or route and then adjusting prices to maximize revenue. For hotels, revenue management means not selling a room today at a low price to sell it tomorrow at a higher price or selling a room at low price today if you do not expect higher demand. While at first this may seem counterintuitive, saying "no" to some business can actually increase long-term profits. Hotels use revenue management to carry out practices such as:

- Setting the most effective pricing structure for guestrooms
- Limiting the number of reservations accepted for any given night, room type, or length of stay, based on the expected profitability of a reservation
- Reviewing reservation activity to determine whether actions, such as lowering rates, should be taken
- Negotiating volume discounts with wholesalers and groups
- Enabling reservation agents to be effective sales agents rather than merely order takers

Revenue management requires the use of complex computer programs to:

1. Forecast the number of reservations, cancellations, and no-shows a hotel can expect on a given day.

2. Track the availability of guestrooms.

3. Compute the maximum rates that those rooms can be sold for, based on demand, availability, and other fluctuating factors.

As revenue management systems become more sophisticated, their scope is expanding. For example, today many hotels use them to manage their meeting space as well as their guestroom space. By tracking demand for meeting space, they can maximize the revenue stream from it. Some business owners feel that revenue management systems sometimes encourage discounting; others think that frequently-changing prices can confuse guests. But, if used properly, revenue management can be an effective tool.

Responsibilities of the Revenue Manager

The revenue manager is responsible for ensuring that the hotel is maximizing its revenue by balancing the room rates guests pay with hotel occupancy. The challenge the manager faces is to secure the highest possible rate for each potential guest, while not turning away any potential guests simply because room rates are too high. The revenue manager works cooperatively with the sales department, the reservations department, and often other departments to determine which room rate strategies should be applied to ensure the hotel achieves its room revenue goals. Hotel sales team members often check with the revenue manager before quoting room rates for groups or local business associates. The revenue manager also establishes room rates for the reservation office and works with the hotel's many intermediaries, including the hotel's website, corporate Internet sites, third-party websites, airline reservation systems, visitors bureaus, and others.

Creating a Culture of Revenue Management

Revenue management is more than just a technique to yield higher revenues. It is a philosophy and culture that has to be implemented throughout the organization. A manager's job is to develop a culture of revenue management where all employees understand the reasons for rejecting some business and everyone sells not only a price but also a value. The following steps can help put revenue management into practice:

• Hold a meeting with the sales and reservations departments to agree on a shared vision and objectives. Set short- and long-term strategy together.

• Train your team to record reservation information. Keep consistent records of data such as reservations on the books, waitlist, denials, walk-outs, cancellations, and no-shows.

• Familiarize yourself and your team with all the options and reports available in your PMS.

• Make decisions based on knowledge and data, not on feelings.

Managing Labor Costs

The hospitality and tourism industry is labor intensive. It takes a lot of people, not machines or computers, to produce top-quality guest service. Hospitality and tourism companies typically spend 30 percent or more of their revenue to meet payroll costs. This is a high percentage considering many hospitality and tourism positions are minimum wage or entry level. Controlling labor costs can be achieved through employee training and careful scheduling, a combination that produces higher productivity and better service. No hospitality and tourism operation can afford unproductive employees and wasted labor hours.

Every operation must provide good, if not superior, service within its own economic limitations. Any business could schedule more than enough employees to give good service all the time, but that would not be profitable. Overstaffing can produce unnecessary labor costs, which must come out of the operation's profits. But understaffing can be just as disastrous. While having too few employees to serve guests might decrease labor costs in the short term, over time it will likely increase turnover and decrease profits. The stress of constantly working short-handed will cause employees to quit. In addition, if guest expectations are not met, revenues will decrease due to guest dissatisfaction and lost business.

Using the right number of employees at the right time helps ensure that guests remain satisfied and employees work at a pace that is neither too fast (quality standards are not met) nor too slow (productivity standards are not met). However, it's important to note that if the volume of business increases by 50 percent, a manager may not have to increase the staff by 50 percent to meet production requirements. This is known as economy of scale—the amount of time required to complete a task does not increase at the same rate as the increase in business volume. For example, the time required to set up the serving station or to ice the salad bar will be the same no matter how many guests arrive to dine at a restaurant.

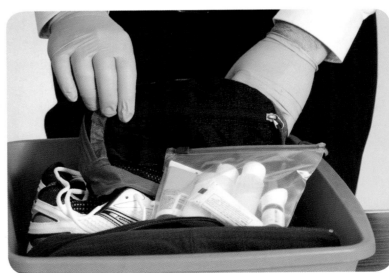

Productivity Standards

The first step in managing labor costs is developing productivity standards. Productivity standards define the acceptable amount of work that must be done within a specific time frame according to a specific performance standard. Performance standards explain the quality of the work that must be done. For example, a productivity standard for housekeepers establishes the time it should take one trained housekeeper to clean one guestroom according to the department's performance standards. The following example presents a sample worksheet that a housekeeping manager can use to determine the productivity standard for full-time housekeepers.

Step 1—Determine how long it should take, on average, to clean one guestroom according to the department's performance standards.

      Approximately 30 minutes

Step 2—Determine the total shift time in minutes.

      8.5 hours × 60 minutes = 510 minutes

Step 3—Determine the time available for guestroom cleaning.

Total shift time...510 minutes
Minus:
    Beginning-of-shift duties ....15 minutes
    Morning break (paid)..15 minutes
    Lunch break (unpaid) ....30 minutes
    Afternoon break (paid)...15 minutes
    End-of-shift duties ....15 minutes
Time available for guestroom cleaning ....420 minutes

Step 4—Determine the productivity standard by dividing the result of Step 3 by the result of Step 1.

$$\frac{420 \text{ minutes}}{30 \text{ minutes}} = 14 \text{ guestrooms per 8-hour (paid time) shift}$$

Staffing

Once the manager has determined the productivity standard, he or she can use it to develop a staffing guide. Using the forecast of expected business, the manager can properly schedule the right number of employees to work each day. If a hotel has 250 guestrooms, it will take a total of 125 labor hours to clean them at 30 minutes (.5 hours) per room.

250 (total number of rooms) × 0.5 (number of hours per room) = 125 (total labor hours)

If the hotel is forecasted to be at 90 percent occupancy, that means there will be 225 rooms to clean the next day.

250 (total number of rooms) × 0.9 (occupancy percentage) = 225 (rooms to clean)

Therefore, it will take about 113 labor hours to clean 225 rooms.

225 (rooms to clean) × 0.5 (number of hours per room) = 112.5 (rounded to 113 hours)

Sample Staffing Guide for Housekeepers

Productivity Standard = 30 minutes/room											
Occupancy %	100%	95%	90%	85%	80%	75%	70%	65%	60%	55%	50%
Rooms Occupied	250	238	225	213	200	188	175	163	150	138	125
Housekeepers' Labor Hours (rooms only)	125	119	113	107	100	94	88	87	75	69	63

The staffing guide helps the manager determine how many employees to schedule for any given day. For example, when the hotel is at 90 percent occupancy, dividing 225 guestrooms by the 14 per shift standard indicates that it will take 16 full-time housekeepers to clean those rooms.

225 (rooms to clean) ÷ 14 (rooms per 8-hour shift) = 16.07 (rounded to 16 housekeepers)

The actual number of housekeepers scheduled will depend on how many of the employees are full-time and how many are part-time. The manager might schedule 12 full-time employees who clean 14 guestrooms each in an 8-hour shift and 8 part-time employees who clean about 7 rooms each in 4-hour shifts.

Using the staffing guide, the manager can determine the labor costs for each day by multiplying the total number of hours worked by the hourly rate. So, if housekeepers earn $13 per hour and work a total of 113 hours, their total wages for that day will equal $1,469. This information can be used in the budgeting process to determine the operational costs for the housekeeping department.

Work Schedules

Whenever possible, work schedules should be developed to meet the day-to-day, and even hour-by-hour, demands of business volume. For example, if a large convention group is expected to check in between 2 p.m. and 4 p.m., additional front desk agents might be needed during those hours. If a restaurant's busiest time is during happy hour, more servers and bartenders might be scheduled during the rush time than are scheduled for other hours of the evening shift. Alternative scheduling techniques can help managers meet business demands, as well as the needs of employees by increasing morale and job satisfaction. Some examples of alternative scheduling include:

Staggered work shifts. By staggering and overlapping work shifts, the manager can ensure that the greatest number of employees is working during peak business hours.

Compressed work weeks. Full-time employees can work a 40-hour week in four 10-hour days.

Split shifts. A split shift schedules an employee to work during two separate time periods on the same day, such as during breakfast 8-10 a.m. and during lunch 12-3 p.m.

Part-time employees. Employing a large number of part-time workers can give the manager greater scheduling flexibility. Part-time employees can easily be scheduled to match peak business hours. Also, employing part-time workers can reduce labor costs because the costs of benefits and overtime pay generally decrease.

Temporary or seasonal employees. Temporary employees typically are not seeking full-time employment because of personal circumstances, such as being a student, having young children at home, or having another full-time job. They can fill in at a large banquet, during employee illnesses, or in other similar circumstances.

Managers may find the following tips helpful when developing and distributing work schedules:

- A schedule should cover a full workweek.
- Workweeks are often scheduled from Saturday to Friday because weekend leisure business is difficult to predict beyond a three-day forecast.
- The work schedule should be approved by appropriate managers before it is posted.
- Schedules should be posted in the same location and at the same time each week, at least three days before the beginning of the time period for which they apply.
- Days off and vacation time should be planned as far in advance as possible.
- The work schedule for the current week should be revised based on updated forecasts if necessary. Any changes should be communicated to affected employees.

Green Practices

Compressed work weeks and carpooling can benefit the environment by removing congestion from the roads and helping keep the air clean. The average car with a single driver emits 1.10 lbs of carbon dioxide per mile, but a carpool with three people decreases that number by two-thirds. Whenever possible, managers should encourage employees to carpool or to take public transportation to work. Companies can even offer incentives for those who choose to carpool, such as preferred parking, rideshare matches, or financial rewards. Managers should take the needs of carpoolers into account when scheduling, because a lack of matching work hours among employees can be a major barrier to carpooling.

Taxes: Reporting and Remitting

Hospitality and tourism industry managers must be aware of their reporting and **remitting** requirements in regard to taxes. Tax responsibilities vary by state and local municipality. Managers must ensure that tax **withholdings** are being handled correctly through payroll.

Employee Withholdings

The federal government requires that employers withhold taxes from the wages and salaries of all employees and pay these amounts directly to the federal government. Taxes are paid to the Internal Revenue Service (IRS). Some states also require employers to withhold state tax. Wages include all payments an employer pays to an employee, whether in cash or goods. Lodging or meals provided to an employee are also counted as income and are subject to taxes unless the meals and lodging are given "for the convenience of the employer." For example, employees on a cruise ship are provided accommodations and food because it is convenient for the cruise ship company. Wages also include any tips that employees earn, unless the total amount of the tips is less than $20 per month.

Employers must annually provide each employee with two or more copies of the Wage and Tax Statement, or Form W-2. This IRS form lists the total wages the employee was paid and the amount of tax withheld. Employees then use this information to file their federal tax returns.

a Employee's social security number **033-00-0002**	OMB No. 1545-0008		
b Employer identification number (EIN) **17-0000000**		1 Wages, tips, other compensation **24000**	2 Federal income tax withheld **1,500**
c Employer's name, address, and ZIP code **TOMAS HOTEL AND SPA** **123 N GENEVA PARKWAY** **LAKE GENEVA, FL 32223-9322**		3 Social security wages	4 Social security tax withheld **340**
		5 Medicare wages and tips	6 Medicare tax withheld **156**
		7 Social security tips	8 Allocated tips
d Control number **5454562**		9	10 Dependent care benefits
e Employee's first name and initial Last name Suff. **CHRIS H JONES** **7575 E REST HEAVEN RD** **OVIEDO, FL 32224**		11 Nonqualified plans	12a
		13 Statutory employee ☐ Retirement plan ☐ Third-party sick pay ☐	12b
		14 Other	12c
			12d
f Employee's address and ZIP code			

15 State	Employer's state ID number	16 State wages, tips, etc.	17 State income tax	18 Local wages, tips, etc.	19 Local income tax	20 Locality name
FL	17-0000000	24000.00	1350.00			

Form **W-2** Wage and Tax Statement   **2012**   Department of the Treasury—Internal Revenue Service
Copy 2—To Be Filed With Employee's State, City, or Local Income Tax Return.

SAMPLE

Sales Tax Collection

Hospitality and tourism businesses often charge their customers tax in addition to the room rate or rate for services rendered. Restaurants and other tourism-related businesses charge a sales tax. In addition, they may charge a hospitality tax on all prepared foods and beverages. These funds are used for tourism-related activities and improvements. Hotels charge an **occupancy tax**, sometimes called a lodging or accommodations tax. This money is paid to state or local governments. The tax is a percentage of the total sale price, but the amount of the tax and specific laws pertaining to it vary by location.

Online Sales Tax Issues

Due to the growing popularity of booking through online travel agents (OTAs), disputes over taxes have arisen between local governments and websites such as Travelocity, Expedia, Orbitz, Hotwire, Priceline, and Hotels.com. Normally, state and local tax authorities collect their taxes directly from hotels. However, some municipalities believe that they are not receiving the full sales or occupancy taxes they are due on rooms sold through OTAs. For example, if the occupancy tax is 11 percent, and you stay in a $100-a-night room, your tax would be $11. An OTA might buy that room from the hotel for $80 and sell it to you for $100. Thus, the hotel would only receive and remit tax on the $80 rate, which is $8.80, or $2.20 less. Many municipalities have filed lawsuits to try to pursue the balance, but OTAs have argued that the taxes do not apply to their businesses because they are not hotels.

Apply Your Learning

Section 12.1
1. What are the main revenue centers for hotels?
2. List two examples of cost centers.
3. How can cost centers contribute to revenue and profit?
4. What is a financial reporting center?

Section 12.2
1. How are income statements used as control measures by management?
2. What does "cost of sales" mean? Write the formula for cost of sales.
3. What three categories appear on a balance sheet?
4. Compare and contrast current liabilities and noncurrent liabilities.
5. True or False? On every balance sheet, the total assets must balance with the total of the liabilities and equity sections.

Section 12.3
1. What must managers of well-organized businesses do in order to maximize profits?
2. What is the purpose of a capital budget?
3. How do departmental managers assist in creating a capital budget?
4. What are some examples of operational expenses?
5. Which type of expenses stay the same whether the property has one or 100 guests?
6. How can forecasts be used to manage variable expenses?

Section 12.4
1. List three types of businesses that use revenue management.
2. Why might a reservation agent decide not to sell a room on a particular day?
3. Which departments must cooperate with the revenue manager to ensure the hotel achieves its room revenue goals?
4. What might happen if the revenue manager sets rates too high?
5. What is the first step a manager might take when trying to create a culture of revenue management at his or her company?

Section 12.5

1. What is the relationship between productivity and labor costs?
2. Explain the dangers of overstaffing and understaffing.
3. The productivity standard at the Red Cedar Hotel is 15 guestrooms during an 8-hour shift. If the hotel has 400 guestrooms and is expected to be at 80 percent occupancy, how many housekeepers will be needed to clean on that day?
4. What are staggered work shifts? How can they help manage labor costs?
5. Why are hospitality and tourism business workweeks often scheduled from Saturday to Friday?

Section 12.6

1. What does the term "remitting" mean?
2. Which of the following is never considered wages for tax purposes: cash or goods, discounts on merchandise or services, tips, or meals and lodging?
3. What is the purpose of the W-2? What kinds of information does this form show?
4. Is the occupancy tax the same in every hotel in every state? Explain your answer.

Unit 6

Sales and Marketing

Today's hospitality and tourism organizations have shifted their focus from strictly sales to using combined sales and marketing strategies. While marketing and sales are not the same, they are interrelated, and both are needed to maximize revenue. A hospitality and tourism organization can have the greatest marketing plan in the world, but it will be wasted if the company does not have an effective, customer-oriented sales staff. Conversely, a company can employ a great salesperson, but he or she will waste time and money if target markets and goals are not clearly defined in the marketing plan.

Both marketing and sales are, first and foremost, customer oriented. Every action is aimed at the ultimate goal of serving customers. Marketing focuses on trend research and the development of successful sales techniques, while sales consists of direct efforts to sell the property through personal sales calls, telecommunications, and mailings. The success of today's—and tomorrow's—hospitality and tourism products will be a direct result of the combined efforts of highly trained, competent, and innovative sales and marketing professionals who are dedicated to making an impact on the ever-changing hospitality industry.

Chapter 13

Marketing

COMPETENCIES

1. Describe the organization of marketing departments, and explain management's role in marketing.

2. Summarize the marketing mix: the four Ps and the four Cs.

3. Identify the steps of a marketing plan.

4. Describe the channels of distribution within the hospitality and tourism industry.

5. Explain how to prepare a marketing budget.

6. Identify trends that affect marketing in the hospitality and tourism industry.

CARLSON REZIDOR
HOTEL GROUP

Aurora Toth
Vice President of Marketing
Carlson Rezidor Hotel Group

Aurora Toth is vice president of marketing for Carlson Rezidor Hotel Group. She is responsible for managing agency relationships, brand advertising, promotions, social media content strategy, and interactive marketing planning for Country Inns & Suites by Carlson and Park Inn by Radisson Hotels. Ms. Toth has 28 years of marketing experience, including several corporate leadership roles as well as consultant work on customer insight and marketing strategies for startup companies.

Prior to working for Carlson, Ms. Toth served as vice president of marketing for Christopher & Banks Corp., where she was responsible for developing brand strategy for three brands. She served as vice president of Corporate Development/ Innovation and vice president of marketing at The Musicland/ Best Buy, where she was responsible for all brand strategy, consumer research, interactive and marketing/advertising efforts for Sam Goody, Suncoast, and Media Play brands. She has worked in various marketing roles for Supervalu, Inc. and the Toro Company. Ms. Toth began her career in consumer packaged goods marketing at Procter & Gamble working with the Pringles, Duncan Hines, and Orange Crush brands.

Ms. Toth serves as a mentor in the Menttium 100® program, where she provides coaching and guidance to women to help them grow and develop in their careers. She holds a master's degree in Business Administration from the Carlson School of Management at the University of Minnesota and a bachelor's degree from Miami University in Oxford, Ohio.

Introduction

Marketing departments vary with the size, type, and budget of the hospitality and tourism firm. At small properties, a salesperson usually handles all types of business. He or she may manage the property's marketing initiatives and call on meeting planners, travel agents, tour operators, and other sources of potential business. Still smaller hotels and restaurants may have to combine sales and marketing under another department or have the general manager direct marketing and sales efforts. Large operations generally have separate marketing and sales departments that work together to promote the business and bring in revenue. Although the responsibilities of the marketing management team vary depending on the company, a brief description of typical duties and responsibilities is outlined below:

General Manager: The success or failure of an operation's marketing and sales program starts with top management, and a marketing-oriented general manager is the key to a firm's sales efforts. In smaller firms, the general manager may take on the responsibilities of advertising and public relations. He or she might also make personal sales calls outside of the office on high-priority business.

Director of Marketing: The director of marketing is considered the head of the sales effort in large operations. Some directors of marketing are actively involved in sales, while others just focus on leading the division. The director of marketing must be able to perform a variety of management tasks, such as setting objectives and policies, making decisions, and selecting and supervising the sales and marketing staff. The five main supervisory tasks of the marketing director are:

- Planning: determining what needs to be done and deciding how to meet goals and objectives
- Organizing: creating a structured approach to using staff to their fullest advantage
- Staffing: training employees and helping them develop new skills
- Directing: overseeing programs and motivating and guiding staff to do their best
- Controlling: setting standards, measuring performance, and taking corrective action

Market Research Coordinator: The main responsibilities of the market research coordinator include researching current market trends, marketing and sales strategies used by competing companies, and general consumer trends. The organization uses this research to develop sales strategies.

Director of Advertising and Public Relations: This position involves coordinating all promotional materials, establishing a good public image for the company, and helping select advertising media.

Director of Revenue Management: In the past, many companies relied on the director of marketing to maximize profits. However, increasingly, they are creating a specific position dedicated to forecasting supply and demand and researching the potential profitability of groups.

Director of Convention Service: Hotels that have significant convention and meeting business will generally employ someone responsible for overseeing the servicing of group business. This person must work closely with all departments, coordinating with sales, food and beverage, the front office, and the banquet setup crew.

Organizational Chart of a Marketing and Sales Division for a Large Hotel

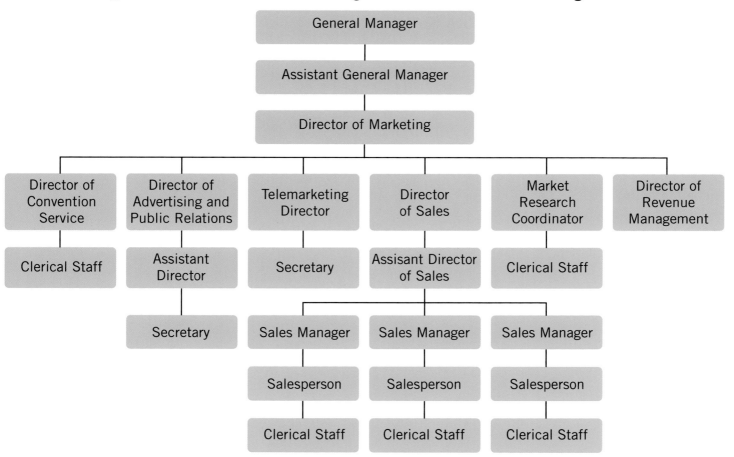

Pineapple Fun Fact

In 2009, a small tourism board in Australia created an innovative marketing campaign to promote a little-known island off the Great Barrier Reef. The "Best Job in the World" campaign was a job search conducted through social media for a new "caretaker" for Hamilton Island. The six-month post involved exploring tropical islands off the coast of Queensland and writing a blog with photos and videos to attract visitors to the area. The campaign elicited more than 34,000 YouTube entries from applicants in 200 countries, upwards of 7 million visitors to the site, and nearly 500,000 votes. As a result of the campaign, Amway Australia chose the island as the site of its annual conference, and the airline Virgin Blue started a direct flight from Sydney due to the rise in demand from travelers. In 2013, the "Best Job in the World" was expanded to six positions: Chief Funster, Outback Adventurer, Park Ranger, Wildlife Caretaker, Lifestyle Photographer, and Taste Master. Each comes with a salary package worth $100,000 Australian dollars.

The Marketing Mix

Marketing Mix—a planned mix of the controllable elements of a marketing plan: product, price, place, and promotion.

Niche Marketing— concentrating marketing efforts on a small but specific segment of the population.

The term **marketing mix** is used to explain how several variables work together to satisfy specific consumer needs. The task of the marketing manager is to form these variables into a marketing mix to meet the needs of each consumer group or market segment targeted by the company. As you learned in Year 1 of this program, the marketing mix is made up of the four Ps: product, price, place, and promotion.

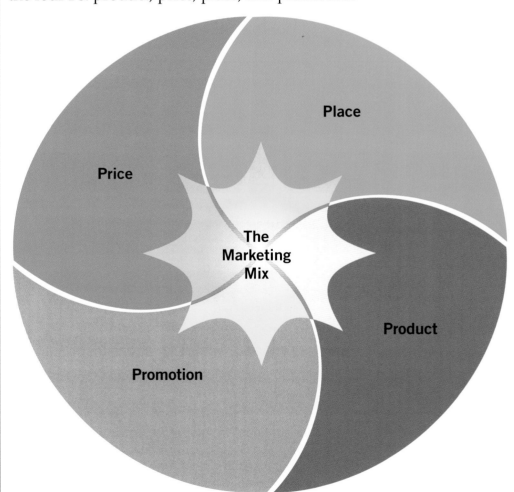

In recent times, the concept of the four Cs has been introduced as a more consumer-driven version of the four Ps. This model attempts to change the focus from mass marketing to **niche marketing**.

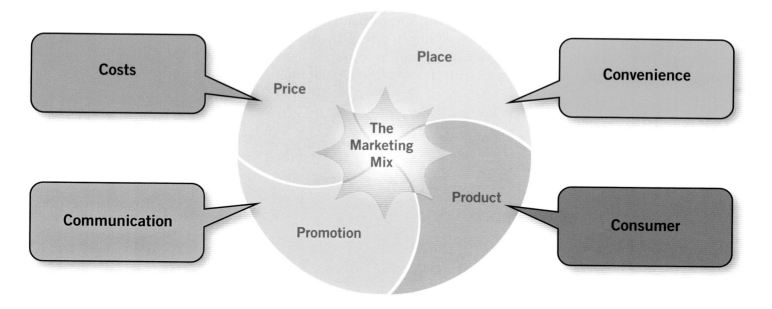

Consumer: Instead of creating a product and trying to sell it to a mass market, the marketing team should study what the consumer wants and needs and then create a custom solution.

Cost: The price of an item is only one part of the total cost. For example, a fast-food restaurant has to consider not just the price of its hamburgers but also many other factors affecting total cost, including the customer's cost for not selecting a competitor's hamburger, the cost of driving to the restaurant, and the health costs of eating meat. A business that relies strictly on offering the lowest price is going to be vulnerable to competition in the long term.

Convenience: The marketing team must consider how each subset of the market prefers to buy — online, on the phone, or from a catalogue. Convenience takes into account the ease of finding the product, finding information about the product, and buying the product, .

Communication: While promotion is a message from the seller to the consumer, communication is more of a two-way street. Communication can include traditional advertising, public relations, social media, viral marketing, customer service, and any other form of communication between the organization and the consumer.

Marketing Mix Decisions

One element may be stressed over another when appealing to a specific target market, but the elements of the marketing mix are interrelated. A decision about one variable usually affects the other variables in the mix. In addition to managing the four main variables, marketing managers must be aware of other, uncontrollable variables that might affect the marketing mix. For example, an economic recession cannot be controlled by marketing staff, nor can an energy crisis, natural disasters such as earthquakes and floods, or weather conditions. Other external factors might include:

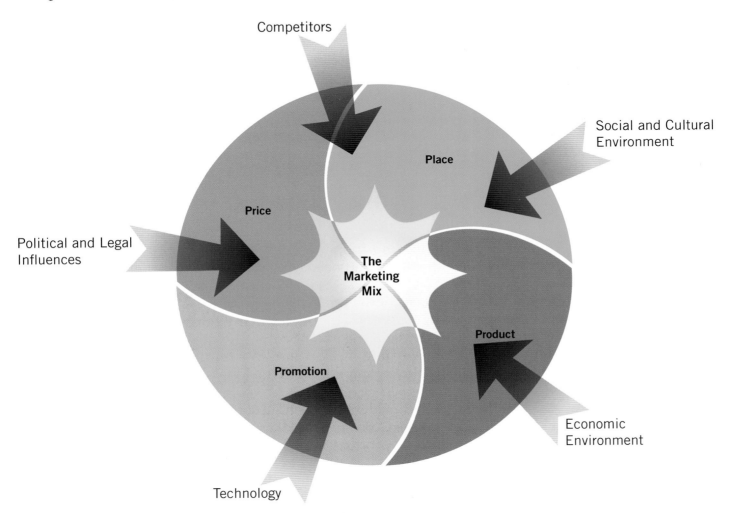

Successful marketing efforts must take both controllable and uncontrollable variables into account to create the perfect marketing mix. A carefully researched, planned, and managed sales and marketing effort must be developed to ensure that the organization attracts guests and keeps them.

Steps of a Marketing Plan

O nce the proper marketing mix has been determined, the marketing director must create a marketing plan to communicate throughout the organization. A good marketing plan forces managers to think ahead and make better use of the operation's resources. The plan creates an awareness of any problems and obstacles the marketing team might face and clearly defines the responsibilities of various departments and individuals to make sure efforts are not duplicated.

The marketing plan may take many forms but should include these five key steps:

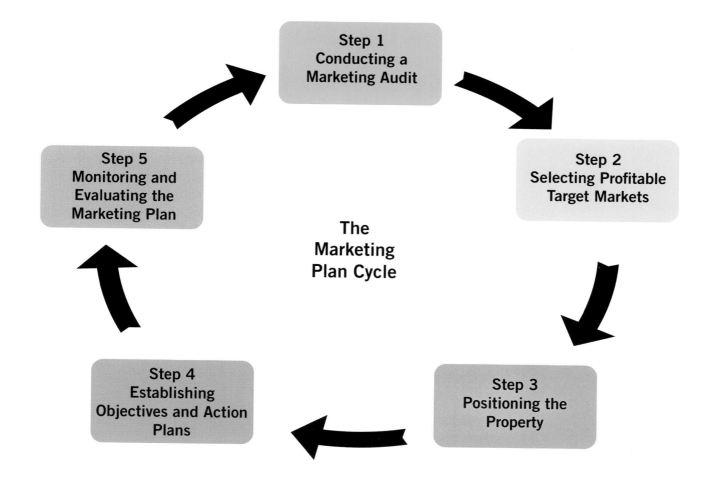

The Marketing Plan Cycle

Step 1
Conducting a Marketing Audit

Step 2
Selecting Profitable Target Markets

Step 3
Positioning the Property

Step 4
Establishing Objectives and Action Plans

Step 5
Monitoring and Evaluating the Marketing Plan

Step 1: Conducting a Marketing Audit

The **marketing audit** is the research step in the planning process. It involves gathering, recording, and analyzing information about your company, the competition, and the marketplace to assist in decision-making. There are several ways of gathering this information. The easiest place to start is by looking at your own operation. Internal information gathering can include looking at guest histories and sales data, which can quickly be obtained from the guest registration system and an analysis of point-of-sale data. Information can also be collected from guest comment cards and from the company's employees and managers. Another way to collect data is from external sources. Consumer surveys can provide information about shopping behavior, attitudes, and responses to advertising. Marketing information can also be obtained from trade associations and journals, government sources, and travel and visitors bureaus.

A complete marketing audit consists of three parts:

- **Property Analysis:** an unbiased self-appraisal used to assess the strengths and weaknesses of your business. Suggestions for improving weaknesses should be included.

- **Competition Analysis:** looks at profitable guest groups the competition is targeting; a competitive advantage your company has that the competition does not; and weaknesses in the competition's marketing strategies on which your company can capitalize.

- **Marketplace Analysis:** researches the company's positions in the marketplace and environmental issues that can affect business to help reveal additional opportunities to promote the company.

Step 2: Selecting Profitable Target Markets

A key step in creating the marketing plan is analyzing the target market and identifying the most profitable market segments. Two important factors to consider when selecting a target market segment are the attractiveness of the segment and how well it fits with the company's objectives, resources, and capabilities. For example, the event and meeting segment can be very profitable, but it may not make sense for a small B&B to add meeting room space to go after this market segment because it does not fit with the property's overall goals.

The following are some aspects that should be considered when evaluating the attractiveness of a market segment:

- Size of the segment (number of guests)
- Growth rate of the segment
- Competition in the segment; brand loyalty of existing customers in the segment
- Sales potential; return on investment

Market segments should also be evaluated in terms of how well they fit with the company:

- Whether the company can offer superior value to guests in this segment
- The impact of serving the segment on the company's image
- Whether the company has the resources or wants to make the investment required to serve the segment

Step 3: Positioning the Property

Every organization projects a certain image in the minds of the public. This perception is known as the market position. The following questions can help the marketing team develop a positioning strategy:

- Who are we? What do we stand for?
- How does our company differ from the competition? Are there areas in which we can set ourselves apart?
- What areas of the company are not producing the desired revenue or response? How can we expand opportunities to attract business?
- Which market segments are most beneficial to us? What are their needs and wants?

Step 4: Establishing Objectives and Action Plans

Marketing objectives should be set for each market segment and revenue center. To be effective, the objectives should be realistic, specific, and measurable. Once the objectives are set, action plans can be created. Action plans can be as simple or as complicated as necessary, but they need to be very specific, incorporating:

- Description of the types of business and the market segments to be solicited
- Definition of the target customers
- Rates/packages/promotions/special plans
- Objectives (increase meeting room business by 20 percent over weekend periods May-August)
- Action steps and budgets

Step 5: Monitoring and Evaluating the Marketing Plan

As with other business objectives, it is important to periodically evaluate how well the plan is working and make changes if necessary. The more carefully the marketing effort is measured, the easier it will be to plan future marketing activities.

Section 13.4

Channels of Distribution

Channel of Distribution—an entity through which the consumer may purchase all or parts of a travel product or service.

Travel Intermediary—an entity that makes travel arrangements for others.

Since the hospitality and tourism industry serves so many consumer segments, it has established **channels of distribution** through which it markets its products and services. A channel of distribution is an entity through which the consumer may purchase all or parts of a travel product or service. Advances in technology have created a dynamic environment within the distribution channels, and hospitality marketing managers must know how to use these systems to the organization's advantage.

Although consumers are able to purchase travel products or services directly, many choose to use the services of **travel intermediaries**, such as travel agents, tour operators, and travel websites. A captive intermediary is someone who does not receive a commission for handling travel arrangements for others. Examples include administrative assistants and office managers. A commercial intermediary, on the other hand, works for a commission for handling individual or group travel arrangements.

In addition to travel intermediaries, Global Distribution Systems (GDSs), ground operators, and air carriers are popular channels of distribution used in the hospitality industry. GDSs are commonly used by travel agents, business travelers, and corporate travel departments. These central reservation systems were initially developed by the airline industry but now also offer hotel, car rental, and other travel reservations and services. Ground operators are those businesses that provide ground services related to a tour at destinations, such as accommodations, meals, sightseeing, or local transportation. Travel bookings are the largest component of online commerce today, according to a study commissioned by the International Air Transport Association. Airline ticket sales account for the largest portion of travel bookings with more than $85 billion annually.

Travel Agents
Retail travel agents
Travel management companies
Tour operators
Charter travel companies

Travel Websites
TripAdvisor
Urbanspoon
Lonely Planet
Virtual Tourist

Metasearch Engines/ Fare Aggregators
Kayak
Travelzoo
Cheapflights
Skyscanner

OTAs
Expedia
Priceline
Orbitz
Travelocity

The Marketing Budget

The marketing budget shows the costs of the marketing department's plans for the fiscal year. It should help everyone understand the overall marketing strategy and the role of each marketing tool in the plan. There are a number of methods marketing managers can use to prepare the budget. It can be beneficial to prepare the budget using several different methods to provide a reality check on the budgeting process.

One method of budget preparation involves using the percentage of sales—industry average method. For example, most companies in the industry spend on average 15 percent on marketing, with 5 percent on advertising, 7 percent on sales, and so on. You can compare these averages with your own budget. If you are higher overall or in one category, you must examine the reasons for the differences. Similarly, using the competitive method, you select your closest leading competitors and compare your marketing budget to theirs.

Another method of creating a budget, the task method, begins by looking at the objectives (such as revenue increase desired) and the tasks needed to accomplish them (marketing tools such as advertising). The sum required to accomplish all the tasks is the overall marketing budget. The task method often uses a **zero-base budget**. In traditional budgeting, departmental managers justify only variances from past years, based on the assumption that the "baseline" is automatically approved. By contrast, in zero-base budgeting, every line item of the budget must be approved, rather than only changes. Each expense is analyzed and justified each year to determine if it will yield better results than spending the same amount in another way. The budget is established after each detailed action plan is prepared and the amount required to complete each task estimated, rather than determining the marketing budget as a fixed percentage of the overall budget and then deciding how to spend it.

A marketing budget generally contains the following components:

Marketing Objectives: short- and long-term objectives

Budget Overview: one-page summary of the major expenditure categories and marketing mix

Marketing Calendar: visual summary of how and when media expenditures will be made

Program Plan Summaries: summaries of the major program plans or marketing tools (such as new image/branding campaign, website, or advertising creation)

TERMS YOU SHOULD KNOW

Zero-Base Budget—a budget built from the ground up, starting from zero, requiring that every expenditure be reanalyzed and justified annually.

Industry Trends and Marketing

TERMS YOU SHOULD KNOW

Environmental Scanning— the study of marketing trends.

Successful marketing management requires keeping current on industry trends and acting on them before your competition does. The study of trends is referred to as **environmental scanning** in marketing circles and is an essential part of hospitality sales and marketing. Major trends affecting marketing efforts in the hospitality and tourism industry include:

Globalization: U.S. restaurant and hotel chains continue to establish an international presence to serve U.S. travelers and to meet the demand for U.S. products abroad. At the same time, international brands are building outlets in the United States. McDonald's now has franchises in more than 119 countries, and other chains, including Burger King, Wendy's, Pizza Hut, KFC, and T.G.I. Friday's, are following this trend. The global marketplace offers both opportunities and challenges. Marketing efforts have to be sensitive to cultural differences.

Partnership Marketing: This trend allows hospitality and tourism companies to enter new markets, expand products and services, enhance their image, and better serve customers, all without increasing marketing budgets. It involves forming alliances with other companies who are not direct competitors but serve similar markets. The partnerships can be between different hospitality companies, such as Pizza Hut Express outlets in Holiday Inns or Starbucks in hotel lobbies. They can also be between hospitality products and consumer goods, such as Bath and Body Works toiletries in Renaissance Hotels or Disney toys and books in McDonald's Happy Meals.

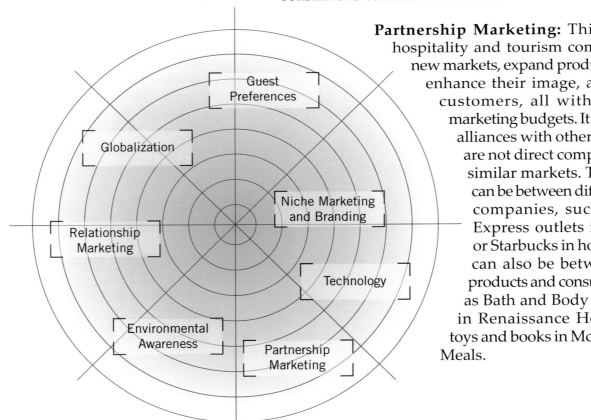

Guest Preferences

Globalization

Niche Marketing and Branding

Relationship Marketing

Technology

Environmental Awareness

Partnership Marketing

Niche Marketing and Branding: This strategy is often used by hotels and restaurants to meet the needs of various segments and to create customer loyalty. Aside from the three broad categories of luxury, midscale, and economy, hotels and restaurants are creating a number of brand names and images within these segments. Ramada Worldwide, for example, offers Ramada Plaza Hotels (luxury), Ramada Inns (mid-priced), and Ramada Limited (economy) properties. Wolfgang Puck, a fine dining restaurant, expanded its brand with Wolfgang Puck Express, a casual dining venture. P.F. Chang's China Bistro also owns a fast-casual restaurant called Pei Wei.

Technology: New technology has affected the way hospitality companies approach sales and marketing efforts. Yield and revenue management and other research software, computerized forms and reports, and time management systems have helped sales and marketing staff to maximize revenue. Companies are using technology to build loyalty and sales. For example, promoting a property's technology upgrades may bring in more business. Disney has introduced an electronic wristband that allows guests to pay for merchandise and dining, reserve character meetings, secure a place to watch the parades, access their resort rooms, and much more. Access to such detailed guest data will help Disney refine its offerings and customize its marketing messages.

Environmental Awareness: Hospitality and tourism operations all over the United States and the world are going green and letting their guests know about it. In addition, ecotourism has created an opportunity for some companies to target new market segments.

Guest Preferences: Hospitality and tourism operations must keep abreast of guests' changing preferences and the latest demographic trends. Marketing and sales efforts must cater to guests who are tech-savvy, time-conscious, and health-conscious. They are used to self-service and prefer to do things themselves to save time. Instead of taking extended family vacations, they are increasingly opting for multiple shorter vacations throughout the year. When they do take a longer trip, they usually choose adventure or fantasy vacations.

Relationship Marketing: Because of the wide range of hospitality choices available, it is essential for hospitality companies to build a repeat customer base. Marketing is shifting its focus away from maximizing profits on individual transactions toward making sure that every guest is a repeat guest. This means taking the time to develop relationships with guests and making sure their expectations are met and their needs anticipated for their next visit. Marketing staff should encourage collection of internal data about guests to help them refine their target markets and marketing strategies.

Apply Your Learning

Section 13.1
1. How would a marketing department at a large company differ from one at a small property?
2. Why is it important to have a marketing-oriented general manager?
3. Which marketing position is responsible for researching current market trends, the marketing and sales strategies used by competing companies, and general consumer trends?
4. Why is the director of convention service part of the marketing department?
5. What are the duties of the director of advertising and public relations?

Section 13.2
1. What are the four controllable variables that make up the marketing mix?
2. Why must the marketing mix variables be researched and planned to ensure a successful marketing effort?
3. List the four Cs of marketing, and explain how they differ from the four Ps.
4. Explain the relationship between price and cost.
5. What kinds of external factors can impact the marketing mix?

Section 13.3
1. True or False? A marketing audit is concentrating marketing efforts on a small but specific segment of the population.
2. What are some aspects that should be considered when evaluating the attractiveness of a market segment?
3. Why is it important that a target market segment fit with the organization's overall goals, resources, and capabilities?
4. Why is positioning important?
5. What should action plans include?

Section 13.4

1. An entity through which the consumer may purchase all or parts of a travel product or service is called a _____.
2. Which type of travel intermediary works for a commission for handling individual or group travel arrangements?
3. Who most often acts as a captive intermediary?
4. What are GDSs, and who uses them?
5. List two examples of group operators, and describe the types of services they provide.

Section 13.5

1. Describe how to use the percentage of sales—industry averages method to create a marketing budget.
2. Why might it be beneficial to prepare a marketing budget using several different methods?
3. How does a zero-base budget differ from a traditional budget?
4. True or False? A marketing calendar is a visual summary of how and when media expenditures will be made.

Section 13.6

1. Why do hospitality marketing departments engage in environmental scanning?
2. Provide an example of partnership marketing in the hospitality industry.
3. What impact has technology had on the hospitality and tourism industry in recent years?
4. What is relationship marketing, and why is it so important in today's hospitality market?

Chapter 14

Sales

COMPETENCIES

1. Describe training techniques managers can use to build an effective sales team.

2. Identify the methods used to manage an effective sales team.

3. List the tools and processes used to sell to global audiences.

4. Outline the needs of special market segments and the sales strategies used to reach those segments.

5. Summarize strategies for selling to the digital traveler.

**Leslie Menichini
Vice President of
Sales and Marketing
Rosen Hotels & Resorts**

From Orlando to Las Vegas to California, Leslie Menichini has worked in some of the finest properties that this country's entertainment capitals have to offer. Over a more than 30-year career in the industry, she has held various sales and marketing and service positions. In her current role, Ms. Menichini is the vice president of sales and marketing for Rosen Hotels & Resorts. She joined the Rosen team in May 2001 to build and lead the pre-opening sales efforts for Rosen Shingle Creek, where she was responsible for pre-marketing and sales for the 1,500-room hotel. Her role has since expanded to overseeing the centralization and synergy efforts of sales and marketing, in addition to staff development and revenue management, of the Rosen Centre, Rosen Plaza, and Rosen Shingle Creek.

Previously, Ms. Menichini was in Las Vegas, where she was executive director for Park Place Entertainment and also director of sales for Bally's/Paris Las Vegas and was instrumental in the opening of Paris Las Vegas. Prior to Las Vegas, she was on the sales team at the Walt Disney World Swan and Dolphin Resort as an assistant director of sales and various other sales positions. Ms. Menichini arrived in Florida from California, where she was on the opening team as director of sales at the Westin Mission Hills Resort in Rancho Mirage.

Ms. Menichini is serving on the board for the Orange County Convention & Visitors Bureau Sales Convention Committee. She is also a Meeting Professionals International (MPI) U.S. Council co-chair, Society of Incentive Travel Executives (SITE) board member, and sits on the events management board at the Rosen College of Hospitality Management at the University of Central Florida.

Introduction

Large hospitality and tourism companies generally have a specialized sales staff, including full-time specialists for group and individual sales. In the largest organizations, the degree of specialization can be carried even further, with salespeople assigned to specific market segments: one salesperson may be assigned to corporate meetings business, another to tour business, still another to association business, and so on. This level of specialization is usually only practical for chain operations. Small organizations may add sales to the general manager's job description, only employ one or two salespeople, or combine sales into another department's responsibilities. Sales management positions in an organization may differ but can include the director of sales, the assistant director of sales, and the sales manager.

The Sales Area

Whether the organization is large or small, the sales office may be one of the first areas a potential client sees, and first impressions are just as important with clients as they are with guests. Potential clients should be properly greeted by the sales receptionist or administrative assistant. The sales area should be accessible but private. The furniture should be tasteful, the offices well lit and properly ventilated, and the design uncluttered and professional.

Property information sheets and brochures, sample menus, and news clippings about the organization make good pre-sale tools. The décor should include photographs of events, guestrooms, meeting rooms, and the organization's staff; any awards received by the organization; and travel/trade association plaques or certificates. Above all, every member of the sales office—from the manager to the clerks—should be knowledgeable about the property and ready to share information about the property's attributes.

Building an Effective Sales Team

Since effective sales people are so important to an organization's sales efforts, it is essential that a good sales staff be hired. Retaining good salespeople also makes good business sense since replacement costs can be extremely high, both in terms of training a replacement and in business lost over the hiring and training period. In addition, when salespeople change jobs, loyal clients may follow them, resulting in lost business for the organization.

To build an effective sales team, the sales manager should be aware of a number of characteristics common to successful salespeople:

1. Professionalism

2. Communication

3. Intelligence

4. Analysis

5. Motivation

6. Efficiency

7. Persistence

8. Empathy

9. Curiosity

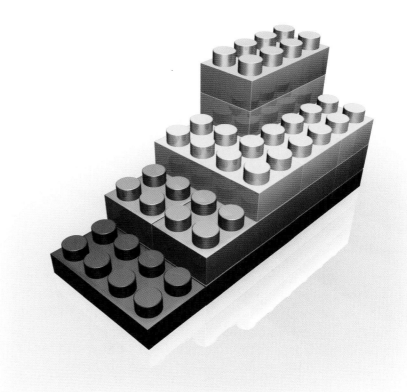

Most people are not "born salespeople," but with the right training, almost anyone can become an asset to an organization's sales staff.

Pineapple Fun Fact

Many hospitality and tourism businesses are using flash sales on daily coupon websites like Groupon and LivingSocial to help drum up business. Restaurants, museums, bowling alleys, tour companies, indoor skydiving adventure centers, ski resorts, and small B&B properties are offering discounts of up to 50%, and budget-minded consumers are enthusiastically buying them. LivingSocial estimates that about 70% of bookings on flash-sale sites are made by people who had not planned to take a trip before being presented with the offer. Flash sales can help lure new customers who will return to buy regular-priced goods and services in the future. Flash sale websites give businesses with small marketing budgets more visibility.

Training for Sales Success

Once hired, salespeople must be trained. Even experienced salespeople can benefit from training, as they will learn more about the specifics of the organization and what is expected of them. Effective training allows salespeople to sell more productively. After the initial training, salespeople should be provided with opportunities for continuing education, such as seminars or sales skills workshops. Job coaching along the way can provide support and increase sales success.

Building Blocks

Each salesperson should have a firm foundation in the following key areas:

- Knowledge about the company
- Office procedures
- Performance standards
- Salesmanship

Thoroughly knowing about the company gives salespeople confidence when making sales calls. Each new salesperson should be given a complete tour of the operation (hotel, restaurant, resort, cruise ship, theme park) to become familiar with the its staff; the facilities, services, and products offered; and the strengths and weaknesses of the operation. Salespeople should know about the rates and booking policies, hours of operation, seating capacities, meeting and banquet facilities, audiovisual equipment available, recreational facilities, menus, and information about the local area. They should take the time to visit or experience local attractions in order to be able to recommend them to clients.

Each salesperson should know the sales office routine. A supervisor should explain the sales office hours; the office computer system; booking policies; the function books; sales forms and reports; and past, present, and future promotional material. Salespeople should know to whom they report and also how to delegate work to administrative or clerical staff. Equally important is knowledge of the office's standard operating procedures (SOPs). SOPs are written instructions explaining how business activities (such as expense reports, VIP room policies, and booking procedures) should always be handled.

Every salesperson should know exactly what is expected of him or her in terms of deadlines, sales quotas, numbers and types of sales calls, and internal communication. New salespeople should receive a detailed, written job description; specific long-term and short-term goals; and a territory, specialization, or number of accounts. Salespeople are required to understand the market segments they are expected to target.

Also, salespeople should take the time to study the psychology of selling. Recognizing the motivations for buying decisions and the different personality types of buyers can help salespeople become more successful at their craft.

Training Techniques

Although methods of training vary from company to company, there are several common techniques that hospitality organizations use:

1. **Simulated sales calls:** These are sales calls acted out by the sales staff. A new salesperson can make a sales presentation and be critiqued by other staff members. If the session is recorded, the new salesperson can watch the video to see where he or she can make improvements.

Double Calling—calls on which a new salesperson is accompanied by the director of sales or a senior salesperson.

2. **Double calling:** There are three types of **double calling**—calls on which a new salesperson is accompanied by the director of sales or a senior salesperson. On joint calls, supervisors are there as equal team members to help sell. On coaching calls, supervisors observe but do not take part. On model calls, supervisors conduct the sales to demonstrate selling skills.

3. **Market segmentation drills:** Since all selling is based on satisfying customer needs, salespeople must understand the needs, characteristics, and requirements of each market segment. New and experienced salespeople can meet to discuss market segment characteristics and the sales tactics that work best with each segment.

4. **Case study exercises:** In this training exercise, the sales staff is challenged to create a sales action plan for another company. It may be a competitor or an imaginary company. This helps salespeople hone their skills and learn strategies they can apply to their own sales efforts.

5. **In-basket drills:** The trainee is given a stack of written communications (e-mails, letters, messages, memos, and directives) to act on within a limited period of time. This exercise provides insights into how well the salesperson judges priorities and uses time.

Managing a Sales Team

Managing hospitality and tourism salespeople is different from managing other positions. First, in today's highly competitive market, it is often necessary for salespeople to be away from home and family for extended periods of time. Salespeople are also away from the office, making it difficult for them to have close ties with the rest of the sales and marketing team and to keep abreast of what is going on in the company. In addition, it can be discouraging for salespeople to put a lot of effort into a presentation and not make a sale.

A sales manager must become involved in a number of areas to ensure that sales volume goals are met or exceeded and that costly employee turnover is kept to a minimum. Sales management involves:

- Training and motivating
- Scheduling and assigning accounts
- Supervising

You learned about the importance of training in the previous sections. Motivating salespeople is also a key element of meeting sales goals. One of the most effective methods of motivation is simply providing personal encouragement or recognition for a job well done. Monetary rewards can also provide motivation. In addition to salaries and regular commission, sales incentive programs offer rewards that build team spirit, give extra recognition to good performers, and help reduce sales staff turnover. Incentive programs may include cash bonuses, merchandise, or vacation trips. They should be developed to give individuals or departments a specific reward for meeting specific objectives.

Scheduling salespeople involves analyzing the needs of the company and the strengths and weaknesses of individual salespeople. It is important to choose salespeople who can relate to the market segments they are selling to. If travel is required for a particular account, the manager may need to consider whether his or her staff's family situations prohibit extended periods away from home.

Diversity

Does diversity pay? According to a study published in the American Sociological Review, a workforce made up of employees of both genders and varying racial backgrounds results in more positive business outcomes. The study found that companies reporting the highest levels of racial diversity brought in, on average, nearly 15 times more sales revenue than those with the lowest levels of racial diversity. Companies with a more diverse workforce consistently reported higher customer numbers than those organizations with less diversity among staff. For instance, those companies with the highest levels of gender diversity accounted for an average of 15,000 more customers than organizations with the lowest levels of gender diversity. In addition, as racial and gender diversity levels increased in a company's workforce, its profits relative to those of its competitors also increased.

One of the key elements of sales management is assigning accounts. When assigning account responsibility, several factors must be considered. These include the number of accounts, the geographical area (territory), and the market segments that will be covered by each salesperson. The manager must decide whether it makes more sense to break accounts down by market segment or to assign one salesperson to an account as the contact for all types of business.

Managers employ different approaches to supervising the efforts of the sales staff. Some review weekly activity reports, while others supervise staff more closely by periodically testing them on their knowledge and skills. Managers should also review sales staff's personal quotas on a regular basis to make sure that they are performing to the best of their ability.

Sales Office Communication System

For a sales office to operate at maximum efficiency, clear lines of communication must be established both within the sales office and with other areas of the company. Good communication ensures that all team members have the same information. Regularly scheduled meetings are a good way to make sure everyone is on the same page:

- Managers can hold brief daily meetings with salespeople to discuss the day's sales and the next day's schedule. Weekly staff meetings can cover new business prospects, new bookings, conventions, promotions, publicity, and lost business.

- Monthly sales meetings are held to discuss tentative and definite bookings for the next month, review progress made in achieving sales goals, and discuss new marketing promotions.

- Annual or semi-annual sales meetings should include all of the company's employees. These meetings are an opportunity to discuss the marketing plan with the entire staff and obtain ideas and suggestions from all employees. Sales and advertising programs should also be discussed.

Selling to Global Audiences

Specialty sales are a major source of revenue for the hospitality and tourism industry, and one of the most profitable specialty segments is the international travel market. In fact, travel and tourism is one of the United States' top exports. When foreign tourists come to the U.S. and buy services, it counts as exports because they are spending foreign money on something produced in the U.S.

International Travelers

Most travelers to the U.S. fall into three categories: North American travelers, European travelers, and other international travelers (Asian, Australian, African, etc.). It is difficult to compile a general profile of the international traveler because visitors from different countries are interested in different attractions and have varying needs. But it is possible to define several patterns in this market:

Point of origin: While more than half of the international travelers currently visiting the United States come from Canada or Mexico, the number of North American travelers is declining. More and more travelers are coming from countries such as Japan, Brazil, Argentina, Korea, and China.

Reasons for travel: International travelers from Europe and Japan cite the lower costs of goods and services as an important factor in choosing travel to the U.S.

Destinations: International travelers often visit large cities, such as New York, San Francisco, and New Orleans, that offer cultural events and nightlife. Some opt for seeing natural wonders like the Grand Canyon or Niagara Falls, while others do adventure trips, such as whitewater rafting.

Length of stay: Europeans typically receive four to six weeks of vacation and average 20 nights for trips overseas. The Japanese stay an average of nine nights in the U.S. on leisure trips. International business travelers normally stay for a shorter length of time, but some choose to take vacation time at the conclusion of their business trips and extend their stay.

Selling Effectively to a Global Market

Sales personnel in charge of selling to global audiences face a different set of challenges. The following tips can help salespeople make their international pitch more effective:

- **Do your research.** The more you know about the target country's lifestyle, slang, favorite foods, and cultural elements, the easier it will be to make your presentation a natural fit for the market.

- **Visit the place you are marketing to.** Nothing will help you sell to Brazilians like a trip to Brazil. The goal of the visit should be understanding the market and how to position your product.

- **Learn what is offensive.** Different cultures find different things offensive. Learn what images, expressions, styles of dress, or behaviors your clients might be offended by.

- **Learn the language.** Consider hiring salespeople who are fluent or have a basic understanding of the language or employing a translator to make it easier to communicate with prospective clients.

- **Find people to trust.** Take the time to network and build relationships with local professionals to help you break into the new market.

- **Partner with convention or visitors bureaus.** Salespeople specializing in the international market can assist in promoting your product by conducting sales missions to foreign countries, provide sales leads, conduct familiarization tours for qualified buyers, and offer advertising partnerships that target potential international guests. They usually also speak the local language.

- **Check out the competition.** See what their weaknesses are and what markets they are not serving.

- **Develop a master plan.** Planning in advance will help prevent overextending your resources.

- **Stay ahead of global trends.** Read industry publications to stay aware of the changing marketplace so you can adjust your sales techniques and presentations as necessary.

Online Presence

Since online sales make up a majority of bookings, optimizing your organization's online presence is an effective way to reach out to an international audience. Reaching an international audience entails understanding a region's cultures, laws, and online behaviors.

Having the company website translated into other languages is going to make it easier for international travelers to get information about the services and amenities your property provides. When selling to a global audience, your company should be aware of regional regulations on products, advertising, and sales tactics. For example, in some countries, certain types of advertising are subject to approval by governing bodies. Various sales promotion tactics—such as contests, sweepstakes, and buy one, get one free offers—are usually regulated differently across borders.

Using Search Engine Optimization (SEO), you can customize your searches based on the target location. English-language search engines like Google, Yahoo, and Bing are not necessarily the ones your international guests use in their home countries. Do the research and choose a local search engine. Work with native speakers to figure out native keywords that would best be associated with the content of your website.

In addition to translating your website, include a currency conversion feature so that guests in other countries can convert purchase amounts into their own currency. Colors and symbols have different meanings for different cultures, and you should adapt your website design to your target audience. Lastly, you can adapt your social media presence for various languages by creating multiple Facebook and Twitter accounts for various regions or adding subtitles to YouTube videos.

Section 14.5

Selling to Special Segments

While business and leisure travelers still make up the majority of sales in the hospitality industry, many lodging properties are targeting specialized market segments to ensure consistent occupancy. Reunion groups (family, class, or military), juries, out-of-town wedding or funeral guests, truckers, train crews, sports teams, and movie crews are just a few examples of the small or special market segments that many properties are now targeting. A property's ability to appeal to these segments will vary depending on its products, services, and location. However, these segments can provide a major source of revenue for companies willing to spend the time and money to research them and to modify their products and services to meet the market's needs.

Reunion Groups

Needs

- Affordability
- Accessibility, including shuttle services
- Hospitality suite
- Recreational amenities and activities for all ages

Sales Strategies

- Focus on value and professional expertise
- Advertise in specialty publications
- Contact national reunion organizations (National Association of Reunion Planners)

Destination Weddings

Needs

- Recreational activities (swimming, shopping, golf, spa)
- Facilities for rehearsal dinner, ceremony, reception, and post-wedding brunch
- Honeymoon suites

Sales Strategies

- Participate in or stage a bridal fair
- Create unique package deals
- Invite couples for a personal tour

Sports Teams

Needs
- Location no more than 30 minutes from stadium or field
- Efficient registration
- Meeting rooms
- Food services able to meet special dietary needs

Sales Strategies
- Solicit league offices of professional and independent teams
- Contact college or high school athletic offices/programs
- Offer special rates to teams and fans
- Attend annual "teams" trade show

Truck Drivers and Train Crews

Needs
- Low prices
- Ability to check in and out at odd hours
- Truck parking with electrical outlets

Sales Strategies
- Create a trucker-specific frequent-stay program
- Drop off sales info at truck stops, weigh stations, and warehouses
- Contact the train line's main office

Movie Crews

Needs
- Food and beverage services
- Block of guestrooms and office facilities
- Crew entertainment
- Special requests from stars

Sales Strategies
- Contact the state's movie commission
- Make personal contact with movie production offices
- Reach out to local destination marketing organizations

Sequestered Juries

Needs

- House all members on one floor
- Rooms must open to interior corridor
- Telephones, televisions, and radios must be removed from guestrooms
- No contact with hotel employees
- Newspaper reporters and television crews must be kept away

Sales Strategies

- Contact local courthouse or attorney general

Government Travelers

Needs

- Staying within **per diem** allowances
- Location near government offices or military bases

Sales Strategies

- Offer government rates based on per diem allowances for your city
- Direct sales
- Join government meeting organizations

Construction Crews

Needs

- Rooms during the week with four- to seven-night rates
- Free coffee and/or breakfast
- Early-morning wake-up calls
- Extended-stay properties

Sales Strategies

- Visit construction sites and leave property information with project superintendent
- Advertise in trade publications

Per Diem—a dollar figure allocated to cover lodging, meals, transportation, and gratuities for government employees traveling on official business.

Selling to the Digital Traveler

A majority of travel bookings are completed digitally, whether through a company's website, an OTA, or a mobile device. While searches for travel information have been relatively stable on desktops, they have grown by 68 percent on mobile devices and by 180 percent on tablets. Nearly 38 million people use their smartphones to research travel. And people are not just doing their research digitally—an estimated 16 million Americans book travel from their mobile devices. Hospitality and tourism organizations must make their digital presence and their ability to sell their products and services digitally a priority.

Customers today have access to an unprecedented amount of information to use when making purchasing decisions. They consult an average of 10 sources of information online before booking travel. In addition, they are highly influenced by the opinions of others. Seventy percent of people who look at online travel reviews end up changing their minds about where they will go or stay. However, when deciding between two hotels, 65 percent of people say that seeing a management response would sway them to book with the responding hotel. This is good news for hospitality and tourism companies. It means that if they join in the conversation, they have an opportunity to personify and shape their brand and influence sales. The following are some things to consider when selling to the digital traveler:

Search engines: 86 percent of people start with a simple web search. Being on page one of search results is critical, especially because few people go to page two. Companies can also use pay-per-click (PPC) advertising, a model in which the company pays the publisher each time the ad is clicked.

Responsive web design: a website that provides an optimal viewing experience—with a minimum of resizing, panning, and scrolling—across a wide range of devices (desktop, tablet, and smartphone).

Ease of booking: the booking link is clearly visible, and the booking process has no more than three to five steps.

Rate and image parity: rates and images of the property are consistent across distribution channels. It often benefits the company to have the cheapest rates on its own website.

Reservation recovery: 80 percent of travelers begin but do not complete a reservation. Companies can create an automated way of reaching out to those consumers to remind them to complete the booking.

Web statistics: many websites, such as Google Analytics, offer a way to track which users go to a website and what they do once they are there. This can help a company adjust its target market and website design to generate more bookings.

Hypertargeting: sending highly targeted advertising messages to very specific groups of people. For example, if a snowstorm is about to hit the Midwest, a resort in a sunny location might consider placing an advertisement on the Weather Channel website to try to attract customers who want to escape the dreary winter weather.

Social media: companies can set up a social engagement desk to monitor what is being said about the company on social media outlets. This allows them to interact and get personally involved with customers instead of waiting until customers come to them.

Quick Response (QR) Codes: barcodes that have become common in consumer advertising. Smartphone users can install an app with a QR code scanner that can read the code and convert it to a URL, directing the smartphone's browser to the company's website. QR codes can be placed in ads in airline magazines, roadside traveler guides, and tradeshow displays to be scanned by mobile devices.

Customer relationship management (CRM): a model for managing a company's interactions with current and future customers. Personalized marketing can increase sales, and personalized service can increase brand loyalty.

Balanced approach to OTAs: while a property does not want the majority of bookings to come from OTAs due to the commission costs, it is important to have an OTA presence because it can help drive traffic back to the company's website. Seventy percent of direct bookers visit an OTA first.

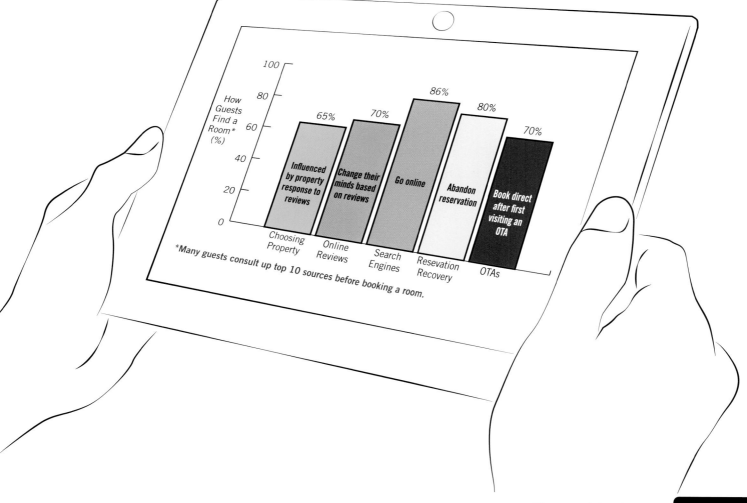

Apply Your Learning

Section 14.1
1. Why is it important that the sales area make a good first impression?
2. Would it be a good idea to locate the sales office in the basement of a hotel? Why or why not?
3. Which of the following is not an appropriate form or décor for the sales area: photographs of events, guestrooms, meeting rooms, the organization's staff, staff members' personal vacation photos, or awards received by the organization? Explain your answer.
4. What two things make up the replacement costs for a salesperson who leaves an organization?
5. List three characteristics of successful salespeople.

Section 14.2
1. What can be done after the initial training to increase the chances of a salesperson's success?
2. Define SOPs. Explain why they are important for sales staff to know.
3. What is double calling?
4. Name and describe the three types of double calling.
5. If a sales manager asks sales staff to create a sales action plan for another company, which training technique is he or she using?

Section 14.3
1. What is the purpose of sales incentive programs?
2. What factors must be considered when assigning account responsibility?
3. True or False? It is important to choose salespeople who can relate to the market segments they are selling to.
4. Why should the sales office establish a communication system?
5. What generally happens during annual or semi-annual sales meetings?

Section 14.4

1. True or False? Europeans generally take shorter vacations than the Japanese.
2. How might visiting the country you are targeting help you be a more effective salesperson?
3. Explain the importance of staying ahead of global trends.
4. Why is it important to be aware of a country's laws regarding sales tactics and advertising?
5. List three ways to make a company website global-friendly.

Section 14.5

1. Why are many lodging properties targeting specialized market segments?
2. What kinds of needs do destination wedding travelers have?
3. What sales strategies can be used to sell to movie crews?
4. Define the term "per diem."
5. Why do you think sports teams are a profitable specialty market?

Section 14.6

1. Where have searches for travel information shown the most growth?
2. Why should companies aim to be on the first page of search results?
3. True or False? Responsive web design means that a company responds to requests for information from customers.
4. Why do you think a customer might begin but not complete a travel booking? How can reservation recovery help with this phenomenon?
5. When might hypertargeting work better than other kinds of marketing?

Unit 7

Safety and Security

T ravelers expect and demand safe and secure experiences at the hospitality and tourism businesses they choose to visit. Owners and investors expect and demand that a property will be operated as efficiently and profitably as possible. Employees expect their workplace to be healthy and safe. A hospitality and tourism business that implements safety and security programs that fulfill the wishes of these groups begins each day with a competitive edge.

Safety and security go hand in hand in the hospitality and tourism industry. The professionals who hold these positions in the industry are responsible for both the safety and security of guests and employees. Chapter 15 will focus on managing workplace safety, including risk management and following Occupational Safety and Health Administration (OSHA) requirements. Chapter 16 will cover managing security operations, including guestroom security, emergency response planning, and operational emergencies.

Chapter 15

Safety

▶ **Section 15.1**
Introduction

▶ **Section 15.2**
Managing Workplace Safety

▶ **Section 15.3**
Risk Management and Insurance

▶ **Section 15.4**
OSHA: Following the Requirements

COMPETENCIES

1. Describe why workplace safety is a significant responsibility of the hospitality and tourism manager.

2. Explain the benefits of a workplace safety committee, its goals, and its communication processes.

3. Define risk management, and identify the steps of the risk management process.

4. Identify ways to follow OSHA requirements.

starwood
Hotels and Resorts

David Kimmins
Senior Director, Global Safety,
Security & Asset Protection
Starwood Hotels & Resorts
Worldwide, Inc.

As Starwood's chief security officer, David Kimmins is responsible for Starwood's risk control activities worldwide including safety, security, and fire protection. He is a founding member of the Hotel Security Working Group (HSWG), a partnership between the Department of State and major U.S. and international hotel chains. The HSWG was established to promote the safety and security of hotel guests and employees by creating a forum for members to openly share security information, best practices, and educational initiatives.

As a member of the Department of Homeland Security, Commercial Facilities Sector Coordinating Council, Mr. Kimmins played a leading role in developing a protective security measures guide for the lodging industry. He has also worked with the Department of Homeland Security and the Los Alamos and Argonne National Laboratories on a number of initiatives to improve the means used by federal, state, and local government authorities to assess risks and threats to commercial facilities and develop appropriate coordinated response measures and protocols for managing potential terrorist threats or incidents.

Prior to joining Starwood in 2006, Mr. Kimmins was the international risk control director for Wal-Mart Stores, Inc., with responsibility for all their international business operations. His educational background includes a B.S. in Environmental Management & Technology from the University of Sunderland and an M.S. in Process Manufacturing Management (Chemical Engineering) from Teesside University. He is an active member of AH&LA's Safety & Security Committee and started his term as the chair in 2013. He is also a member of the Real Estate Roundtable's Homeland Security Task Force.

Introduction

TERMS YOU SHOULD KNOW

Workers' Compensation—a form of insurance providing wage replacement and medical benefits to employees injured on the job in exchange for the employee giving up the right to sue the company for negligence.

The safety of guests and employees is a primary concern of hospitality and tourism managers. It is their responsibility to review safety risks, create safety programs, and train all employees in following proper safety procedures. Guest illnesses and injuries can create negative publicity, which can result in lost business. They can also lead to lawsuits, costing the company millions of dollars in legal fees.

Employee illnesses and injuries can also have negative effects. In addition to calling in sick and not being able to work, sick employees could infect guests. Workplace injuries could lead to **workers' compensation** claims. Workers' compensation is a form of insurance that provides compensation, often in the form of wage replacement and medical benefits, to employees who are injured on the job. In general, an employee with a work-related illness or injury can get workers' compensation benefits regardless of who was at fault—the employee, the employer, a co-worker, a customer, or some other third party. In exchange for these guaranteed benefits, employees usually do not have the right to sue the employer in court for damages for those injuries. Each state has its own laws for workers' compensation that employers must follow.

Pineapple Fun Fact

OSHA aims to ensure worker safety and health by working with employers and employees to create better working environments. OSHA's mission is to reduce on-the-job injuries, illnesses, and deaths. Before 1970, the American workplace was much more dangerous than it is today—an estimated 14,000 workers died every year from workplace accidents. Since its inception in 1971, OSHA has helped to cut workplace fatalities by more than 60 percent and occupational injury and illness rates by 40 percent. At the same time, U.S. employment has doubled from 58 million workers at 3.5 million worksites to more than 115 million workers at 7.2 million sites.

Hospitality and tourism businesses have many areas of concern in regard to safety. Restaurants and other food service establishments must concern themselves with food safety and the safety of employees around kitchen equipment. Lodging properties must focus on pools, hot tubs, gyms, and other recreational areas. Theme parks must establish safety controls and procedures for rides. Transportation services should train employees in defensive driving and remind guests to take precautions, including buckling up and storing their personal belongings properly.

Global travel has also increased safety concerns in hospitality and tourism. Guests traveling overseas may need to take health precautions, depending on the country they are visiting, such as avoiding certain local foods, updating their vaccinations, and bringing enough prescription medications for the duration of the trip. Other international travel concerns include infectious diseases, such as cholera and malaria, and chemical/biological terrorism incidents. Cruise ship passengers must be particularly aware of the Norovirus. The U.S. Department of State and the Centers for Disease Control and Prevention (CDC) offer tips and information to travelers about these topics on their websites. Many tour operators pass on the recommendations of these government agencies to their guests.

Managing Workplace Safety

While safety is everyone's responsibility, it is a good idea for hospitality and tourism managers to create a safety committee to help ensure the effectiveness of their safety programs. In addition, safety committee involvement is a valuable means for creating company-wide acceptance of safety programs. Employees can assist in establishing safety policies, reviewing accidents, recommending corrective action, and participating in safety inspections.

The Value of Communication

One of the purposes of the safety committee is to bring management and staff together in a cooperative effort to improve the safety and health of workers. Therefore, it makes good business sense to include representatives from management to line-level employees. A safety committee will succeed only if it requires management's participation. Managers should not make the mistake of thinking that just because the committee exists, they do not have to do anything else. At the same time, managers should not dominate committee meetings; they should allow all participants to contribute. Communication between the safety committee and the rest of the staff should occur in both directions. In addition, staff should share safety information with guests as dictated by company policy.

Many companies establish a written operating policy before creating a safety committee. Such policy establishes the committee's mission, guidelines for membership, member duties, and general procedures for handling a variety of safety issues.

The Role of the Safety Committee

The safety committee should be an open forum for management and staff to communicate safety-related concerns. The benefits of such communications may be substantial. Every hazard the committee identifies and helps eliminate means significant potential savings in accident costs. The safety committee can serve as a valuable problem-solving group that addresses workplace conditions, morale, and quality. By developing solutions, the safety committee improves the company's competitive advantage. The committee also provides an excellent arena for employees to improve their skills in communication, problem solving, meeting management, and analysis. In fact, some companies make safety or other committee involvement a prerequisite for managerial advancement.

Safety Committee Meeting Agenda

1. Call meeting to order/roll call.

2. Review minutes of last committee meeting.

3. Review results of periodic workplace safety inspections.

4. Review accident investigations. When appropriate, submit suggestions to management for the prevention of future incidents.

5. Review reports of alleged hazardous conditions.

6. Review and evaluate employee suggestions. Submit recommendations when appropriate.

7. Agree on a time and place for the next committee meeting.

Risk Management and Insurance

Risk Management—the protection of corporate assets through the identification, determination, and management of the risks a corporation faces.

The goal of the **risk management** process is to reduce the company's exposure to risk to "acceptable levels." This does not mean that these are the lowest levels possible or that they are economically the least expensive; it does mean that the survival of the company is not threatened as a result. With the logical approach of risk management, businesses can avoid potentially catastrophic levels of loss and keep the overall cost of risk at reasonable economic levels.

The four steps in the risk management process are:

1. Identification of Risk

2. Assessment of Potenial Losses

3. Selection of Proper Risk Management Instruments

4. Studying the Plan and Implementing Decisions

Identification of Risk: The first step in identifying risk is to take an inventory of the company's assets and establish their value. These include physical assets, such as buildings, vehicles, and equipment, and people assets, such as employees. Businesses also need to recognize the potential risk to income and profits. For example, a hotel that has a fire may not only lose physical assets and have physical injuries to employees, it is also likely to experience a loss in income and profits while it is closed for rebuilding and renovation. The next step is to identify potential perils and hazards, or things that can cause a loss. These might include everything from fire to a failure to regularly clean the grease traps in the kitchen.

Assessment of Potential Losses: The management must then assess the maximum potential losses, or costs, to the business. Once those numbers have been determined, the manager (or owner) must decide his or her risk comfort levels. These will vary based on the individual.

Selection of Proper Risk Management Instruments: The manager or owner must now determine how to handle those risks. One important way to deal with risks is through **loss control**. Loss control involves taking actions to reduce the frequency or severity of losses, such as installing sprinklers for fire safety or training employees to report theft. Risks can also be avoided completely in some instances through preventive actions. However, even when actions are taken to control losses, the risk is not completely eliminated; there needs to be some means of paying for the loss. For this reason, businesses obtain insurance. Loss can also sometimes be shifted onto another party. For example, if a security company is contracted by a business and a loss occurs, the security company, and not the business that employed it, would be held responsible.

Studying the Plan and Implementing Decisions: Each of the risk management practices discussed should be added to a comprehensive risk management plan for the company. Before it is implemented, the plan should be studied by management and legal consultants. In large companies, a separate risk management department may be tasked with implementing the plan. In smaller companies, some of this responsibility may fall to the insurance agents. It is important to review the plan periodically and make changes as necessary.

TERMS YOU SHOULD KNOW

Loss Control—actions to reduce the frequency and/ or the severity of the various losses that can occur.

Purchasing Insurance

Just as you purchase insurance for your car in case of an accident, businesses must purchase insurance to cover the costs of various risks. Purchasing insurance can help minimize financial expenses due to losses. In addition, state and federal laws dictate that companies purchase certain types of insurance and have minimum amounts of coverage. Commercial insurance typically includes:

- Commercial property coverage (buildings and personal property)
- Commercial crime coverage (cash and property in safe-deposit boxes)
- Boiler and machinery coverage (boilers, refrigeration systems, engines, generators)
- Inland marine coverage (for goods shipped to the property over land)
- Commercial general liability coverage
- Commercial automotive coverage

Depending on their location and other circumstances, companies may decide to purchase additional insurance, including flood insurance or marine coverage (for goods shipped over water). In addition, all companies must have coverage legally mandated by the government, such as workers' compensation and employers' liability insurance.

Section 15.4

OSHA: Following the Requirements

The federal government regulates work areas and businesses with respect to safety through OSHA. OSHA requirements are extensive and mandate safety regulations and practices for many industries, including hospitality. Regulations focus on the areas where employees work, materials used on the job, and other safety issues. OSHA standards are primarily designed to protect the employee—not the guest. In lodging properties, the housekeeping and facilities managers will have to deal with OSHA regulations most often. But almost every hospitality and tourism business, from spas to restaurants to cruise ships to theme parks, should be aware of OSHA requirements.

Work Areas

OSHA standards cover such areas as hallways, storerooms, and service areas. These standards require that work areas be kept clean, neat, and sanitary. Hallways, passageways, and stairways should have railings. Any stairway with four or more steps must have at least one railing.

Exits

OSHA standards require that exits be clearly marked and that they not be blocked. Exit doors should never be locked from the inside. The routes to exits should also be marked so that an escape path can be easily followed. All properties must have written emergency escape plans. The plans should specify where employees are to go in case of emergency and have procedures to account for all employees during and after the emergency. Plans should also establish rescue and medical duties for employees or local services.

The standards dictate the maximum occupancy level of individual rooms and the building, based on the number of exits, available fire protection, and building construction.

Sanitation

OSHA specifies that all waste containers be leakproof and have a tight-fitting cover. Waste must be removed on a timely basis without creating a hazard to public health.

Bathrooms must be equipped with hot and cold water and soap. Hand towels, paper towels, or air dryers should be provided. The number of toilets is recommended based on the number of employees of each sex. If employees are required to shower, the employer must provide the same items as in the bathrooms, including individual towels. Properties should have one shower for every ten employees of the same sex.

Food and beverages must not be consumed in washrooms or storage areas that may contain hazardous chemicals. If an employer provides meals, the food must be wholesome and not spoiled. It must be prepared, served, and stored in a sanitary way to avoid contamination.

Signs and Tags

 Danger signs warn of immediate hazards, such as a chemical spill or dangerous equipment. Danger signs are red, black, and white.

 Caution signs are used to warn about a potential hazard, such as a wet floor. Caution signs are yellow and black.

 Safety instruction signs are used to give general safety instructions. For example, these signs may be used to instruct employees not to eat, drink, or smoke in a certain area. They are usually green and white or black and white.

 Accident prevention tags are temporary means of letting employees know about hazards or defective equipment, such as when a vacuum cleaner is out of order. They should be red with white or grey letters.

First Aid

First aid supplies should be stocked and readily available. Stations for flushing eyes or other body parts should be located near work areas. Employees who are injured should have access to an in-house doctor or nurse's station or should be sent to a medical facility nearby.

OSHA Inspections

Managers should be aware that OSHA compliance officers have the authority to inspect a property. These inspections are often done without notice. Compliance officers may wish to inspect the property, equipment, and records. They want to see that the OSHA poster, which informs workers of their rights under OSHA, is prominently displayed. The inspection can also include safety committee records, environmental sampling, and private discussions with employees. A management representative should accompany the inspector. Failure to be in compliance with OSHA regulations can result in fines or the business being forced to close until the issues are resolved.

Apply Your Learning

Section 15.1

1. What are the potential negative effects of guest injuries and illnesses on a hospitality and tourism business?
2. Why might a company have to pay workers' compensation benefits?
3. What are some safety concerns in theme parks?
4. What unique safety concerns do global travelers face?
5. True or False? It is recommended that guests traveling overseas wait to fill their prescriptions until they arrive at their destination.

Section 15.2

1. How does having a safety committee help hospitality and tourism businesses avoid potential safety risks?
2. How does serving on the safety committee benefit employees?
3. True or False? Managers should not dominate safety committee meetings.
4. Who should be part of the safety committee?
5. What are some tasks a safety committee member might be asked to participate in?

Section 15.3

1. Define risk management.
2. Taking an inventory of the company's assets and establishing their value is part of which step of the risk management process?
3. Give an example of a loss control action.
4. Provide an example of an instance where a loss might be shifted onto another party.
5. Why must companies purchase insurance?
6. Why might a hospitality and tourism business choose to purchase marine coverage?
7. What types of coverage are legally mandated?

Section 15.4

1. What OSHA regulations must be followed in regard to exits?
2. What feature do stairways need for safety?
3. List the items that must be provided in washrooms.
4. What color should a caution sign be?
5. Do OSHA compliance officers need to provide notice of an inspection? Why do you think that is?

Chapter 16

Security

COMPETENCIES

1. Describe how security should be used as a management tool.

2. Explain how surveillance, safe deposit boxes, and access control measures are used to protect guests and assets.

3. Summarize the nature of employee security issues, and identify the role of human resources in dealing with them.

4. Identify what should be considered in an emergency preparedness plan, and detail the role of the media relations spokesperson.

Hospitality Profile

Mark A. Sanna
Vice President,
Corporate Security
Hyatt Hotels, Inc.

As vice president and chief security officer for Hyatt Hotels Inc., Mark A. Sanna is responsible for the strategic management of Hyatt's security programs and initiatives, designed to protect guests, employees, and operations at the company's hotels around the world. He works with all levels and functions within the company to continually assess the security and business risks to the enterprise, changes in global conditions, company growth, and industry developments. He is charged with developing strategies and tactics for dealing with such risks through the development, implementation, and administration of Hyatt's security program.

Mr. Sanna began his career in security as a Foreign Service Officer with the Department of State. He has more than 20 years of extensive international security and law enforcement experience. Before coming to Hyatt, Mr. Sanna served as the senior director of Global Security at Kraft Foods, Inc., where he was responsible for the security operations of the largest food company in the United States, with more than 100,000 company employees working at 3,800 facilities in 148 countries around the world. He was responsible for managing global travel security, crisis management, security assurance, and employee security awareness programs.

As a member of the AH&LA's Safety & Security Committee, Mr. Sanna was part of a team that, in conjunction with the U.S. Department of Homeland Security, developed the *Eye on Awareness®—Hotel Security Training*. This training program is designed to help front-line staff recognize, report, and react to suspicious situations at their property. Hyatt Hotels was among the first to pilot the program.

Introduction

P roviding security in any hospitality and tourism operation is the broad task of protecting people—guests, employees, and others—and assets. Crimes involving the theft of assets usually result in greater losses than crimes against persons, but crimes against persons have a greater effect on public relations. They may affect occupancy and cause high legal expenses.

Providing appropriate security for any hospitality and tourism operation is a never-ending activity. Without continuous awareness at the management level, an operation's security may suffer. All members of the management team should be involved in developing security guidelines. The special needs and circumstances of the particular operation must be incorporated in the procedures. For example, is the property located in a high-crime area? Does the operation need procedures for dealing with natural disasters common to the local area? Do children frequently get separated from their parents on the property? Is there a lot of petty theft from both guests and employees?

The security guidelines should be reviewed by legal representatives while in draft form. Upon approval, the information should be provided to all employees. Employees will be more likely to review the material if they are given specific assignments than if the report details the entire security operation. Turnover and changes in job assignments necessitate a regular review of the program to keep all employees aware of their security responsibilities.

While recognizing the need for protection of guests, employees, and the assets of each, management must also recognize that guests and employees may themselves create security problems by stealing property and services from the company. Guests may become intoxicated and cause damage to property, or disgruntled employees may pose a security issue. Hotel managers have the right to evict guests with due cause.

Security should be recognized and used as a management tool. Whether the size of the property requires a large security staff or allows for the security function to be assigned to one or several on-premises security staff, the security role should be clearly defined and implemented. The protection of guests, employees, and assets requires managers and all other employees to be constantly alert to possible security breaches.

Pineapple Fun Fact

Boston's Nine Zero Hotel was the first hotel in the world to use iris recognition technology. The system is installed in the hotel's $3,000-a-night Cloud Nine penthouse suite. Guests have images of their irises recorded at the hotel concierge's desk, and the images are stored in a database. When guests access the suite, a video camera-like device takes a picture of their iris and matches it to the database record. The images expire upon check-out. VIP guests appreciate the high level of security the system provides. The system also identifies employees accessing the premises through the employee/vendor entrance. It can grant and deny access based on time and days, for flexible work schedules.

Hotel Security: Access Control and Guestroom Security

Hotel guests want to feel secure in their guestrooms, and they want to know that their belongings and personal assets are secure when they leave for the day. The main ways to accomplish this are through the use of surveillance equipment, safe deposit boxes, and access control.

Employees play a central role in watching for trouble and protecting guests and property from loss and unauthorized access. All employees should be trained to watch for suspicious persons or situations. They should understand how to operate surveillance equipment and how to use it most effectively to control access to a property. Effective access control develops procedures for responding to the information gained through surveillance equipment and observations of employees.

Surveillance

Surveillance plays a major role in guest and property security. It can take different forms, including patrols or using equipment, such as **closed-circuit television (CCTV)**. CCTV uses video cameras to record what is going on in various areas of the property and sends the signal back to a central location of monitors where security personnel can monitor it. Enough personnel must be available to monitor and respond to situations that may develop.

In addition to CCTV monitoring, security personnel should patrol the premises. Patrols should follow a varied pattern, in terms of both timing and area, to avoid setting a consistent pattern that criminals can observe and work around. Employees from other departments can also help in the surveillance of the property. For example, front desk employees should be able to observe the lobby, the entrance, and the elevators. Housekeepers can alert security to anything suspicious in the guestrooms. Security officers and other hotel employees should be trained in what to look for. In general, hotel employees should be on the lookout for any unauthorized persons, potential drug dealers, or smugglers. Incidents should be reported to the appropriate authorities.

TERMS YOU SHOULD KNOW

Closed-Circuit Television (CCTV)—the use of video cameras to transmit a signal to a specific place.

Safe Deposit Boxes

By law, a property must notify guests if a safe deposit box is available on premises. Normally, these notices take the form of a posting in the guestrooms. Management is responsible for developing and monitoring safe deposit procedures for each property. All employees with safe deposit responsibilities should be trained in these procedures and be aware of the reasons for the various rules. Supervisors should stress the importance and seriousness of safe deposit responsibilities, ask for an immediate report of any unusual incidents, and require accurate, up-to-date records and complete compliance with procedures. Some general safe deposit box procedures to follow include:

- Safe deposit boxes should be located in an area to which there is limited access.
- Unauthorized persons, whether guests or employees, should not be allowed in the area.
- Two keys should be required to open any safe deposit box: the guest key and the control or guard key.
- Only people authorized to grant access to boxes should ever have the guard key.
- Only one guest key should be issued for each safe deposit box.
- If the guest key is lost, the box should be drilled open in the presence of a witness, the guest, and someone from the property.

Access Control

Access control is the most vital of all safe deposit responsibilities. Management should establish access procedures and make sure that employees are following them for every access, regardless of how often it is or how well the employee knows the guest.

1. Require the guest to sign his or her name on a form requesting access.

2. Compare it to the signature on the agreement signed when the box was issued.

3. Accompany the guest to the safe deposit area.

4. Use the guest key and control key to open the box.

5. Give the box to the guest and give him or her some privacy.

6. Never handle or be alone with the guest's valuables.

7. When the guest is finished, re-lock the box and return the guest's key.

In-Room Safe

In-room safes are another way for guests to protect their valuables while staying at a property. Such units can have key, keycard, digital keypad, or credit card reader opening systems. Postings in the guestrooms should be made to make it clear to the guests that safe deposit boxes or a safe is provided in the offices for the storage of guest valuables, and that management is not responsible for any valuables not placed there.

Lost and Found

Clear procedures should be developed to deal with lost and found items. The way the items are treated will depend on state law. The responsibility for the lost and found items should be assigned to one department, such as the front desk or housekeeping. All found items should be turned over to the lost and found department and be entered in a log that lists where the item was found, its description, the date, and the name of the employee who found it. Lost and found personnel should bag, tag, and store the item. If the item is valuable (wallet, jewelry, money, credit cards), it can be placed in a safe deposit box. When the article is claimed, it should be recorded in the log. If it is mailed to the owner, the date it was mailed should be logged. All calls to the property regarding lost items should be routed to the department handling the items to avoid giving the wrong information to the caller.

Section 16.3

Employee Security Issues

There is a tendency in many properties to concentrate on security incidents involving guests. However, internal security problems, like theft by employees, can erode profits. The restaurant and lodging industries are particularly susceptible to internal theft since their materials can be easily exchanged for cash or used directly by the thief. High employee turnover and the large size of many properties limit their ability to effectively secure their operations against internal theft. The management team must involve the security staff in controlling internal theft on a department-by-department basis.

The following examples represent some potential internal theft opportunities and possible solutions.

Internal Thefts	Monitoring Strategies
Employees cheating on their time sheets	Department managers review time sheets; a time-keeping system that verifies employee identity
Employees who no longer work at the hotel remaining "on the books" and receiving pay	Verify that checks issued by the property are received by the individuals to whom they are addressed
Managers and supervisors using gardeners, painters, and maintenance personnel for personal services on company time	Make sure employees know that these services are not acceptable and how to report such incidents
Employees placing long-distance phone calls	When reviewing bills, look for 900 numbers (costly per-minute charges) or off-hour calls made from executive and administrative offices
Unauthorized employees taking meals	Spot-check of food facilities by security personnel at off-peak hours
Employees taking home property or guest assets	Designate a separate employee entrance that is monitored by security staff or surveillance equipment; restrict employee parking to an area away from the building

The Human Resources Department

The human resources department faces security considerations even before an employee is hired. Since a property is responsible for the acts of its employees, care should be taken to hire only the best people. Potential new hires should be screened. The following types of screening may be considered:

- Criminal conviction check
- Background check through professional investigators
- Fingerprinting and submitting to local law enforcement
- "Honesty exams"
- Credit check (especially for employees handling cash)
- Department of Motor Vehicles check (for employees involved in valet parking or other vehicle operation)

Every application form should include a statement warning that any false information provided may result in immediate discharge. Orientation materials and the employee handbook should state that theft will also be considered grounds for dismissal.

HR should maintain records on any instances of employee discipline, including the reasons for the actions. It is also HR's responsibility to perform **exit interviews**. The exit interview should be an informal session conducted on the employee's last day of work. Departing employees sometimes have interesting things to say. They might offer suggestions about how to improve their department or provide information about illegal activities on the property.

Violence and Drug Abuse

Unfortunately, there has been an increase of violence in the workplace in recent years. A serious effort must be made during the initial interview stage to screen out individuals with violent inclinations. In addition, there should be specific policies in place for dealing with violence. Management should be aware of risk factors in certain positions that might lead to violence, such as access to weapons or other dangerous items. They should never ignore an employee's history of confrontations, threats, or violence.

Drug and alcohol abuse can lead to theft, violence, and other inappropriate behavior. Management should have specific policies to follow when it finds that an employee is using or dealing drugs on the premises. To help reduce the problems related to drugs and violence, some companies choose to offer employee assistance programs, which provide employees with help in dealing with drug and alcohol dependence or anger management. They can also provide stress management training.

Emergency Management and Media Relations

E ach property should have a written emergency preparedness plan on which every employee has been trained. A good plan can mitigate losses and minimize loss of repeat business because it can allow the organization to get back to normal operations faster. A written plan also demonstrates that a company has taken "reasonable care" to protect guests and their assets, which can protect the company from liability.

Emergency Management Plan

There are five factors that can influence an emergency management plan:

1. Location of the property

2. Personnel

3. History of previous emergencies

4. Types of emergencies

5. Local resources and disaster relief agencies

The parts of an emergency management plan should include:

- **Staffing:** identify employees trained in first aid or those who have skills that might be useful, such as carpentry or cooking, and assign emergency responsibilities
- **Evacuation:** establish primary and secondary evacuation routes and meeting places, and determine whose responsibility it is to activate the plan
- **Equipment:** regularly inspect safety equipment and emergency supplies (fire alarms, phones, exits, lighting, sprinklers, generators, first aid, blankets and cots, food and water)
- **Communication:** determine how the property will communicate in case of an emergency with employees, employees' families, guests (including those with disabilities and those who do not speak English), the corporate office, and the media
- **Property Protection:** shut down, cover, or move equipment to a safe area; store computer files; lock pantries and freezers; shut off energy sources; cover windows with plywood and lay out sandbags
- **Documents:** gather building and site maps, insurance papers, emergency call lists, and resource lists

Once all employees have been trained in emergency procedures, management should schedule live and functional drills and periodically do pop quizzes to make sure employees know what to do. If possible, live training drills should take place in cooperation with local community resources, such as the fire department.

Media Relations

Emergencies and bad news involving a hospitality and tourism business may negatively affect the public's perceptions of the property. While good news is often forgotten, bad news may create a lasting memory, and its effects on the business may be devastating. Effective media relations can help to minimize these effects.

Both management and employees should know how to address the media before an emergency occurs. The property should designate a spokesperson to whom all media inquiries should be referred. The following steps of a crisis communication plan will show management to be responsible, competent, and cooperative in a time of emergency:

1. All facts and statements should be released through a designated spokesperson.
2. Information should be shared as soon as it becomes available and can be confirmed.
3. The media should be allowed access to the property except for areas that are unsafe or have been declared off-limits by investigators.
4. Whatever the nature of the crisis, the management should publicly express concern for the victims of any harm, loss, or inconvenience caused by the crisis.
5. Management should publicly pledge to cooperate with all investigating authorities and, if necessary, conduct its own study of the incident.

Apply Your Learning

Section 16.1

1. What should a hospitality and tourism security program protect?
2. Who should be involved in creating security guidelines?
3. How does it help the overall security goals for employees to be given specific emergency responsibilities?
4. What should management do in the event of employee turnover or changing job assignments?
5. How might a guest be the cause of a security issue?

Section 16.2

1. How can CCTV be used to do surveillance on the property?
2. Why do security patrols need to follow a varied pattern and be done at different times of the day?
3. How many keys are needed to open safe deposit boxes? Why?
4. Why is it important that employees follow the same access procedures for safe deposit boxes every time?
5. True or False? The housekeeping department should always be responsible for the lost and found function.

Section 16.3

1. What is internal theft? Provide three examples.
2. What makes the restaurant and lodging industries particularly susceptible to internal theft?
3. True or False? Only line-level employees engage in internal theft.
4. How can the human resources department help prevent employee security issues during the hiring process?
5. How might employee exit interviews be helpful to management?
6. What is the purpose of employee assistance programs in the workplace?

Section 16.4

1. Why is it important for a lodging property to demonstrate that it has taken "reasonable care" to protect guests and their assets?
2. How can knowing the history of previous emergencies at a property help management when creating an emergency management plan?
3. What does the property protection part of the emergency management plan include?
4. Which documents should be part of an emergency management plan?
5. How can the media spokesperson appear concerned and cooperative during an emergency?

A

Active Listening—requires the listener to be an active participant in the communication process. p. 86

Affirmative Action—an active effort to hire or promote members of a protected group to overcome past discriminatory practices. p. 216

À la Carte Menu—offers and prices each food item on an individual basis. p. 170

Area Inventory List—all items within each area of a hotel that are the responsibility of housekeeping. p. 126

Autocratic Manager—stresses immediate, short-term results over concerns about people; expects to be obeyed without question and makes decisions without staff input. p. 16

B

Balance Sheet—reports the financial position of an operation on a specific date by showing its assets, liabilities, and equity. p. 230

Biodegradable—objects made from organic material, such as plant and animal matter, that are capable of being broken down into harmless products by microorganisms. p. 119

Brand Execution—fulfilling a promise an organization makes to its customers. p. 92

Bureaucratic Manager—makes decisions by enforcing rules, regulations, policies, and procedures that are already in place; resists change. p. 16

C

Call Accounting—an application that captures, records, and costs out telephone usage. p. 93

Capital Budget—a plan for the purchase of major assets. p. 234

Capital Expenditures (CapEx)—the money used by a company to improve long-term physical assets such as property, buildings, or equipment. These are expenditures over a minimum dollar amount for the purchase of items and equipment expected to last more than one year. p. 148

Carbon Footprint—the total greenhouse gas emissions caused by an organization. p. 72

Carbon Offset—a reduction in emissions of carbon dioxide or greenhouse gases made in order to compensate for, or to offset, an emission made elsewhere. p. 118

Cashier Banking System—guests pay the cashier. p. 183

Centralized Organization—an organization in which most decision-making authority is at top management levels. p. 30

Channel of Distribution—an entity through which the consumer may purchase all or parts of a travel product or service. p. 258

Closed-Circuit Television (CCTV)—the use of video cameras to transmit a signal to a specific place. p. 299

Closed-Ended Questions—require a short or single-word response, such as "yes" or "no." p. 214

Contract—when booking events, the letter of agreement that lists every detail the two parties have discussed and agreed upon. p. 192

Corporate Social Responsibility—the obligation of an organization's management to make decisions and take actions that enhance the welfare and interests of society as a whole. p. 221

Cost of Living—the real dollar value of a worker's purchasing power for ordinary necessities such as food and clothing. p. 218

Cost per Occupied Room—the expenses required to operate each occupied room in the hotel, which include salaries and wages and the usage rates for recycled and non-recycled inventory items. p. 130

Cross-Train—to train an employee to do different jobs within an organization. p. 112

Custom-Made Items—made to individual specifications; more difficult to replace. p. 173

Cyclical Menu—changes daily for a certain number of days until the menu cycle repeats itself. p. 170

D

Daily Operations Report—summarizes the day's business and provides insight into revenues, receivables, operating statistics, and cash transactions related to the front office. p. 110

Daily Summary—also called the flash report, provides a snapshot of important operating statistics for the previous day, as well as month-to-date totals. p. 110

Daily Transcript—shows guest accounts that had transactional activity on that particular day. p. 110

Decentralized Organization—an organization where decision-making authority is distributed. p. 30

Deep Cleaning—the process of taking a room out of inventory and cleaning it more thoroughly than during regular daily maintenance. p. 126

Democratic Manager—focuses more on participative process than on short-term results; shares decision-making and problem-solving responsibilities with staff and is open to new ideas. p. 16

Demographics—the statistical data of a population, showing breakdowns of age, race, income, education, etc. p. 32

Direct Compensation—payment of money to an employee. p. 218

Diversity—the human quality of being different or varied. p. 32

Double Calling—calls on which a new salesperson is accompanied by the director of sales or a senior salesperson. p. 269

Empowerment—the practice of enhancing guest service and increasing profits by passing decision-making responsibility, authority, and accountability to every level within the organization. p. 31

Energy Management—measures taken to achieve the minimum possible energy use and cost while maintaining comfort levels. p. 151

Environmental Scanning—the study of marketing trends. p. 260

Exit Interview—conducted on a departing employee's last day of work for the purpose of obtaining feedback about the company. p. 303

Final Departmental Detail and Summary Report—prepared and filed for accounting division review to prove that all transactions were properly posted and accounted for. p. 110

Financial Reporting Center—an area of responsibility for which separate revenue and cost information must be collected. p. 228

Fiscal Year—a 12-month period, which may not necessarily coincide with the calendar year, over which a company budgets its spending. Also known as the financial year or budget year. p. 130

Fixed Expenses—expenses that stay the same regardless of sales volume. p. 235

Fixed Menu—does not change from day to day but may feature daily specials. p. 170

Fixed Staff Positions—must be filled regardless of the volume of business. p. 132

Forecasting—the process of analyzing current and historical data to determine future trends. p. 108

Frequency Schedule—indicates how often items on area inventory lists are to be cleaned or maintained. p. 126

Function Book—a document that shows occupancies and vacancies of function and banquet rooms, used when planning events. p. 192

Function Sheet—lists all the details that apply to the catering function, including everything anyone at the food service operation might need to know to prepare for and provide service. Also called a Banquet Event Order (BEO). p. 192

G

Gastropub—a bar and restaurant that serves high-end beer and food in a casual atmosphere. p. 13

Guarantee—the figure given by the client to the property for the final number of attendees for an event. p. 194

Guest Comment Cards—a method for guests to provide feedback to businesses about the guest experience. p. 68

Guest Experience—the observations, encounters, activities, or events a guest undergoes during a stay at a property. p. 48

Guest Loyalty—the faithfulness guests feel to a property based on a positive guest experience; choosing to stay at the same property repeatedly. p. 49

Guest Recovery—resolving complaints to the guest's satisfaction. p. 53

Guest Service Measurement (GSM)—a process used to measure guest satisfaction. p. 68

H

High-Balance Report—lists guest and non-guest accounts that have reached or exceeded assigned credit limits. p. 110

Housekeeping Status Report—shows the current housekeeping status of each room. p. 128

I

Inclusive—not excluding any particular group of people. p. 36

Income Statement—provides important information regarding the results of operations for a stated period of time. p. 230

Indirect Compensation—given as a condition of employment rather than in direct exchange for productive work. p. 218

Industry Segment—a grouping of similar types of businesses or products under one heading. p. 8

Issuing—the process of transferring supplies from storage areas to kitchen and dining areas. p. 174

J

Job Analysis—determining what knowledge an employee must have, what tasks each employee needs to perform, and the standards at which he or she must perform them. p. 135

Job Description—a summary of the duties, responsibilities, working conditions, and activities of a specific job. p. 113

Job Specification—a summary of the personal qualities, skills, and traits an employee needs to successfully perform the tasks outlined in the job description. p. 114

Just-in-Time Buying—the practice of buying products just before they are needed. p. 138

K

Key Control—procedures that control access to property keys in order to increase guest security and privacy and to reduce the possibility of theft. p. 107

L

Labor Costs—the sum of all wages paid to employees, as well as the cost of employee benefits and taxes paid by an employer. p. 111

Labor Union—an organization of workers formed for the purposes of protecting employee rights and for dealing collectively with employers about wages, hours, benefits, and working conditions. p. 111

Laissez-faire Manager—provides little or no direction and gives employees as much freedom as possible. p. 16

Leadership—the ability to lead a group of people by creating a vision and inspiring others to follow. p. 25

Loss Control—actions to reduce the frequency and/or the severity of the various losses that can occur. p. 291

M

Management—the organization and coordination of the activities of a business in order to achieve objectives. p. 25

Marketing Audit—gathering, recording, and analyzing information about a company, its competition, and the marketplace as the first step in creating a marketing plan. p. 256

Marketing Mix—a planned mix of the controllable elements of a marketing plan: product, price, place, and promotion. p. 252

Menu Engineering—evaluating the menu by studying the popularity and profitability of menu items. p. 170

Mission Statement—a broad description of an organization's reason to exist. p. 79

N

Niche Marketing—concentrating marketing efforts on a small but specific segment of the population. p. 252

Nonverbal Communication—use of visual cues, such as facial expression and eye contact. p. 40

O

Occupancy Report—lists rooms occupied that night and indicates guests who are expected to check out the next day. p. 127

Occupancy Tax—a tax imposed on a person who pays for a room or space in a hotel, motel, bed and breakfast, apartment hotel, or similar accommodation. p. 243

Open-Ended Questions—designed to elicit a full, meaningful answer using the subject's own knowledge or feelings. p. 214

Open-Stock Items—merchandise kept in stock that enables operators to replace or supplement articles, such as dishes, purchased in sets. p. 173

Operations Budget—a plan for recurring expenses that must be paid on a periodic basis. p. 234

Organic Foods—plants or animals raised without the use of chemicals. p. 185

Orientation—the process of introducing new employees to the company and their jobs. p. 81

P

Per Diem—a dollar figure allocated to cover lodging, meals, transportation, and gratuities for government employees traveling on official business. p. 277

Performance Evaluation—a periodic review that evaluates how well employees are meeting performance standards. p. 85

Power—the ability to influence others' behavior. p. 30

Private Branch Exchange (PBX)—a telephone exchange that serves a particular business or office. p. 93

Prix Fixe Menu—offers a complete meal with several courses for one price. p. 170

Professional Development—the process of continuing education by which an employee becomes proficient in his or her job. p. 28

Property Standards—basic requirements set to ensure safety, cleanliness, and good repair that all employees are expected to meet. p. 65

Protocol—the formal rules of etiquette used for ceremonies of state, military functions, and other special events. p. 201

Publicity—the media's gratuitous mention of an organization. p. 95

Public Relations—the process of communicating favorable information about an organization to the public. p. 94

Purchase Record—record of the brand, purchase price, and quantity of an item ordered. p. 174

R

Reclaimed—returned to a suitable condition for reuse. p. 156

Remitting—transmitting or sending money in payment. p. 242

Revenue Management—a technique used to predict consumer demand and optimize product availability and price to maximize revenue. p. 236

Reverse Discrimination—discrimination against members of a majority group in favor of a minority or historically disadvantaged group. p. 216

Risk Management—the protection of corporate assets through the identification, determination, and management of the risks a corporation faces. p. 290

Room Status Discrepancy—a situation in which the housekeeping department's description of a room's status differs from the room status information being used by the front desk to assign guestrooms. p. 128

S

Server Banking System—servers and bartenders use their own banks of money to collect payments from guests and retain the collected revenue until they check out at the end of their shifts. p. 183

Shift Differential—added pay for work performed at other than regular daytime hours, such as evening or night shifts. p. 218

Staffing Guide—a worksheet showing the number of labor hours that must be worked as the volume of expected business changes. p. 180

Stakeholder—someone who can affect or be affected by the actions of the business as a whole. p. 222

Submetering—monitoring the energy consumption of individual equipment or operational areas. p. 151

Supplemental Transcript—tracks the day's transactional activity for non-guest accounts. p. 110

Sustainability—the responsible, long-term use of Earth's resources that meets the needs of the present without compromising the needs of future generations. p. 73

T

Travel Intermediary—an entity that makes travel arrangements for others. p. 258

U

Urban Heat Island—a metropolitan area that is significantly warmer than the surrounding rural areas. p. 156

V

Values Statement—a description of the core values that should shape the culture of the organization and guide the behavior of individuals. p. 80

Variable Expenses—expenses that have a direct relationship with sales volume. p. 235

Variable Staff Positions—filled in relation to changes in hotel occupancy. p. 132

Verbal Communication—use of words. p. 40

Vision Statement—a description of the future of the organization. p. 80

Waste Energy—the energy, such as heat, produced as a by-product of energy consumption. p. 152

Whistleblower—a current or former employee or manager of an organization who reports unethical behavior on the part of the organization to people or entities that have the power to take corrective action. p. 222

Withholdings—deductions from income for tax or benefit purposes. p. 242

Workers' Compensation—a form of insurance providing wage replacement and medical benefits to employees injured on the job in exchange for the employee giving up the right to sue the company for negligence. p. 286

Zero-Base Budget—a budget built from the ground up, starting from zero, requiring that every expenditure be reanalyzed and justified annually. p. 259

Guest cycle, 45, 48–50, 101
Guest experience, 48
Guest loyalty, 49
Guest recovery, 53
Guest reviews, 51
Guest Service GOLD®, 70–71
Guest Service Measurement (GSM), 68

H

HACCP principles, 178
High-balance report, 110
Host bar, 201
Housekeeping status report, 128
Human resources, 11–12, 212–223, 303

I

Incentives, 41, 68, 168, 241
Inclusive, 36
Income statement, 230
Indirect compensation, 218
Industry segment, 8
Insurance, 147, 218–220, 286, 291
International travelers, 25, 39–41, 272–273
Internet, 93
Interviewing, 78, 146
Interviews, 89, 213–215
Issuing, 174

J

Job analysis, 135
Job breakdown, 83, 135–137
Job description, 113
Job specifications, 114
Just-in-tme buying, 138

K

Key control, 107

L

Labor costs, 111, 132, 180, 191, 238–241
Labor union, 111
Laissez-faire managers, 17
Leadership, 25
Leadership styles, 25
Leadership traits, 14
Letter of agreement, 192, 194
Liabilities, 232
Linen, 125, 130–131, 133, 139–140, 172, 173, 203
Listening, 78, 86, 92, 114
Loss control, 291
Lost and found, 301

M

Management, 25
Management styles, 16–17
Marketing audit, 256
Marketing mix, 252
Marketing plan, 255–257
Market segments, 33
Media relations, 96, 305
Menu engineering, 171
Menus
    Design, 164, 169, 171, 176
    Items, 69, 169, 170, 184
    Planning, 11, 191, 199
    Types of, 41, 112, 170
Mission statement, 79
Mobile devices, 93, 104, 278–279
Motivation, 26, 55, 84

N

Negotiation, 91, 193
Niche marketing, 253
Night audit, 109–113
Nonverbal communication, 40
Nutrition, 184

O

Occupancy, 50, 92, 110, 126, 129–132, 148, 240
Occupancy report, 127
Occupancy tax, 243
Open-ended questions, 214
Open-stock items, 173
Operations budget, 234
Organic foods, 185
Organizational charts, 125, 167, 251
Orientation, 81–83
OSHA, 286, 293
OTAs, 243, 279

P

Par levels, 133, 173
Payment, 109, 112, 147, 165, 170, 183, 194, 204, 242
Payroll, 238
Per diem, 277
Performance evaluation, 85, 113–115
Performance standards, 85, 134, 239
Plating, 199
Power, 30
Pre-arrival, 49
Pre-shift meetings, 71
Private Branch Exchange (PBX), 93
Prix fixe menu, 170
Problem solving, 31, 55–57, 90, 115

Productivity, 238
Professional development, 28
Promotions, 12, 113, 116
Property standards, 45, 65, 66, 67, 114
Protocol, 201
Publicity, 95
Public relations, 94, 96
Purchase record, 174

Q

Quality standards, 169, 178

R

Receiving, 53, 62, 86, 95, 104, 130, 174, 178
Reclaimed, 156
Recruitment, 168
Remitting, 242
Reservations, 12, 93, 132
Retention, 168, 218
Revenue management, 236–237, 251
Reverse discrimination, 216
Risk management, 290–291
Room status discrepancy, 128

S

Safe deposit boxes, 300
Safety, 55, 65, 82, 146, 153, 175–179, 187, , 197, 199
Safety committee, 288–289
Sanitation, 146, 161, 175, 177–179
Scheduling, 78, 93, 111, 180, 196, 198, 238, 241
Search Engine Optimization (SEO), 273
Seating, 53, 196, 202
Separation of duties, 112, 183
Server banking system, 183
Speaking, 78, 86–87
Special segments, 274–277
Staffing, 113, 130–131, 146, 161, 166, 180–181, 198, 205, 240–241
Staffing guide, 180–181, 240–241
Stakeholder, 222
Storing, 174, 178, 196, 199
Submetering, 151
Suggestive selling, 116
Supplemental transcript, 110
Supplies, 55, 84, 130–131, 135, 138, 172–175, 179, 199
Surveillance, 299
Sustainability, 73
Sustainable
    Building Materials, 72, 155–156
    Foods, 117, 178, 184–185

T

Taxes, 231, 242–243
Temperature Danger Zone (TDZ), 199
Training, 7, 11–12, 24, 29, 36, 38, 52, 55,
        63, 67, 70–71, 78, 81, 87, 89, 94,
        96, 113, 116, 126, 135–137, 168,
        178–179, 198, 205, 268–269, 305
Transportation, 48, 79, 161, 190, 241
Travel intermediary, 258
Travel Promotion Act of 2009, 25
TripAdvisor, 51
Twitter, 92, 165, 273

U

Urban Heat Island (UHI), 156

V

Values statement, 80
Variable expenses, 235
Variable staff positions, 132
Verbal communication, 40
Violence, 303
Vision statement, 80

W

Waste energy, 152
Whistleblower, 222
Wine service, 201
Withholdings, 242
Workers' compensation, 286
Writing, 12, 78, 86–87, 96, 168, 174

Y

Yield management, 236
YouTube, 92, 251, 273

Z

Zero-base budget, 259

Photo Credits
Year 2

Comstock: 240

Educational Institute: 45, 48, 53, 64, 102, 124, 132, 142, 144, 145, 147, 148, 149, 151, 152, 153, 154, 155, 165, 178, 288, 300, 303

Getty Images, Inc.: 48, 308, 322

iStock: cover, 3, 4, 6, 8, 9, 10, 16, 17, 18, 22, 24, 25, 32, 33, 37, 38, 39, 40, 46, 50, 52, 57, 60, 62, 63, 67, 68, 71, 76, 81, 82, 83, 85, 89, 94, 96, 97, 101, 104, 118, 122, 124, 134, 145, 161, 162, 165, 166, 168, 172, 175, 176, 177, 179, 184, 185, 188, 190, 191, 197, 200, 202, 204, 205, 209, 210, 212, 213, 214, 215, 217, 220, 226, 228, 232, 238, 239, 243, 247, 248, 251, 264, 266, 267, 269, 271, 272, 274, 275, 276, 284, 286, 287, 289, 291, 296, 298, 299, 301

ShutterStock: 33, 39, 63, 66, 172, 196, 204, 221

The American Hotel & Lodging Educational Institute (EI) would like to thank the following, which were gracious in permitting EI to photograph their properties:

Courtyard by Marriott® Orlando Downtown – 730 North Magnolia Avenue, Orlando, FL 32803

Rosen Shingle Creek – 9939 Universal Blvd., Orlando, Florida 32819